HATCHING CHARLIE

A Psychotherapist's Tale

Charles Creath McCormack

ISBN: 0692813438
ISBN 13: 9780692813430
Library of Congress Control Number: 2016919933
CreateSpace Independent Publishing Platform
North Charleston, South Carolina

Charles C. Mc Lonnell, MPH, MSW, LCSW-C
17/12/2017

To Ron Zuskin: An old friend from the moment we met. He always answers the 3 am call.

TABLE OF CONTENTS

Acknowledgements   vii
Prologue   xi

PART I: A GATHERING DARKNESS   1
    Chapter 1   Violence and Belittling—The Family   3
    Chapter 2   Violence and Racism—The World   23
    Chapter 3   Road Warriors   32
    Chapter 4   Chaos—Within and Without   37
    Chapter 5   Abysmal   42
    Chapter 6   Un-Civilization   54

PART II: PUSH BACK—HATCHING 101   63
    Chapter 7   Mad Pecking Adolescence   65
    Chapter 8   Risk Taking   77
    Chapter 9   Something Called Thinking   86
    Chapter 10   Lottery   99
    Chapter 11   Stumbling into the World   104
    Chapter 12   Escaping   113
    Chapter 13   Waylaid   126
    Chapter 14   Childbirth   133
    Chapter 15   Getting Schooled   139

PART III: If Only I Had Ears to Listen—Hatching 102   143
    Chapter 16 Asylum   145
    Chapter 17 Inpatient to Outpatient   150
    Chapter 18 Rule 1—Shit Happens   159
    Chapter 19 Power?   165
    Chapter 20 Out-Patient to In-Patient to Im-Patient   171
    Chapter 21 Psycho-Analysis   182

PART IV: Focused Pecking—Hatching 103   191
    Chapter 22 "Why just a Master Sergeant?"   193
    Chapter 23 Anguish and Joy of a Psychotherapist   198
    Chapter 24 Suicide   215
    Chapter 25 The Goths Are at The Gates   234
    Chapter 26 Coming Home, Again   242

PART V: Swallow the Shadow—Breaking Out   253
    Chapter 27 Love Stories   255
    Chapter 28 Meeting Myself   280
    Chapter 29 Writing Myself   291
    Chapter 30 The Only Dance There Is   296

PART VI: Reconciliation—Hatching Things In   317
    Chapter 31 Grand Fatherhood—The Children as the
              Father of the Man   319
    Chapter 32 Father-Out-Law   333
    Chapter 33 Grandfather Hood—Playtime   341
    Chapter 34 Boring and I Love it that Way   352
    Chapter 35 As Happy as I Can Stand   370
    Chapter 36 Why Change is Difficult   377

PART VII: Full Fillment – Sorta, Kinda   387
    Chapter 37 The Cliff   389
    Chapter 38 Au Revoir   397

ACKNOWLEDGEMENTS

W ow. What a journey this has been. Far different from the one traveled between 1993 and 2000 when writing my first book. That was truly a lonely endeavor, given its technical nature. But this book, *Hatching Charlie*, has been a community effort. Not only have I tried to steer clear of technical jargon, but it's also more engaging in that it's simply a book about the human condition, the pursuit of happiness, and the struggle to create a personally meaningful life, at least one man's attempt to do so. So more, although not all, have been attracted to the effort. Some people read part of the early manuscript, some read the whole of it but didn't offer much response. Others were helpful in providing data. I thank you all.

Then there were The Golden Few. Individuals that resonated with the work, who rose to meet it like butterflies seeking sunlight. My first responder, my daughter Keeley, read it within days and was genuinely enthusiastic, affirming the importance of the project and giving me the encouragement to continue. Daughter Caitlin offered invaluable criticisms in service of making the manuscript more readable and enjoyable. Caitlin was my *everyday reader*, unabashedly uninterested in psychological teachings and representing those who simply wanted a good read: priceless. If it didn't pass muster with Cait, it didn't pass.

Then there were Mark and Carol Ann, my younger brother and sister-in-law, who bubbled with excitement from the beginning, even forwarding a copy to their daughter Katherine. At one point, Mark, sensing I was becoming discouraged with the tepid feedback I was receiving from family and friends wrote, "Don't let the bastards get you down. It's good. I never lost interest."

In truth, there were no bastards; people were giving me what I wanted: their honest responses, even if unspoken. The other truth was that the earliest version wasn't good, more of a vomit draft rather than a finished product. But, importantly, Mark was affirming what I was trying to do at a time when I most definitely needed such affirmation.

Then there was my sister, Michelle, who wrote that she read the manuscript and would get back to me later and never did. Then, near the end of my writing, she wrote me an amazing letter that made me realize how the memories I was bringing up were rekindling her mourning. It made me wonder if the arousal of such uncomfortable feelings might partially explain the lack of response I gathered from the relative silence of others. Michelle recounted her time with Mom and Dad when Mom had her first episode with cancer and was given little chance to live. Michelle, age fifteen and living alone with the parents, tells a story that provides a glimpse of the human underbelly of each of my parents in a way that only a fifteen-year-old girl can. I borrowed from it liberally as I rewrote several chapters.

Then there was Patricia Alfin, a longtime supporter. She was the person responsible for moving my life in a different direction by bringing my first published work to the attention of the Washington School of Psychiatry. I hadn't seen her in several years when I unexpectedly ran into to her. She agreed to read the manuscript and quickly got back to me, seeing where the book was going even though it had not yet arrived, offering words of encouragement and valuable suggestions.

Jason "J-dawg" Thomas, my son-in-law, helped bring a greater racial sensitivity to my writing, working with me in particular on a chapter detailing my nighttime moped rides through the inner-city of Baltimore." Funny guy.

Then, there was Wayne "Killer" Kirgel, who I hadn't seen in years, living as we do on opposite coasts. I emailed him the manuscript because he is a major character in the book. He was enthusiastic, diving into the manuscript and editing an early version on his initiative.

During the writing of my first book, I had leaned heavily on the stout presence of my friend Ron Zuskin (The Z-Man), who had helped propel me through that journey by responding quickly and enthusiastically to each chapter, with concise and to-the-point commentary. With Ron, a synergy formed that became a perpetual motion machine powering me through that arduous process. But this time, Ron was very ill and not available. I marveled at how when I lost one support, another arose. Wayne was fantastic.

And then, miracle of all miracles, Ron rises from his bed, not only fully recovered but feeling better than he had in years. With his usual generosity of time, talent and mindless grace, he edited a later version of the manuscript, bringing it to a new level. Like a symphony conductor, he humored, cajoled, harangued, bitterly criticized and challenged me to make the book more immediate and more alive. It is he that came up with the title: Hatching Charlie.

Then there's Jane, my first wife, who, with profound trepidation, I asked to vet the chapter I had written on our relationship, giving her complete veto power over any words within it. I feared it might upset her—the last thing in the world I would want to do. My fears were totally unfounded. Jane not only approved the chapter wholeheartedly but didn't want to change a word. She felt it captured my care for her. An outcome I never anticipated and one that, given the tears it evoked from me, reminded that healing never stops. Jane also provided additional memories that made the book more accurate and more compelling.

Then there is my wife, Janet, who provided the time and space for me to pursue my writing—lots of time and lots of space — without guilt. She willingly read chapters upon request and became my go to person in that she was ever ready to read a chapter on the spot and give me her reactions right away.

Finally, there's my editor, Margaret K. Diehl, who is an incredible writer with three books to her name, each earning *New York Times* honorable mentions. She generously lent her time and expertise to teach me a little bit more about writing and to pinpoint what was missing and where. She gave in ways far beyond any remuneration I provided, becoming invested in the project and unstinting in her gentle but firm criticisms. Her literary ear is fantastic. Thank you, Margaret. Thank you for listening. This book is so much more than it otherwise would have been because of you.

What do you call such people? Oh. I know. Friends. Not to say that others aren't, for in fact they are, but these surely were The Golden Few.

Love and kisses,
Charlie

PROLOGUE

As I lie here, nearer life's end than its beginning, looking out upon the beauty of the Bush River just off the Chesapeake Bay, its borders crowded with trees iridescently bejeweled in the rust, copper and gold leaves of fall, I wonder what you will think of what I have to say. I am writing this book to walk the walk and not just talk the talk of what I am about to share with you. I'm writing it for all of you: my children, nieces, and nephews, and their children and, as importantly, for any strangers, yet my brothers and sisters in humanity, that happen upon this text and recognize it for what it is – a story of the follies and wisdoms of the human condition or at least one man's version of it.

I write to encourage you to take responsibility for your happiness. If there are two counter-intuitive things I've discovered in my wending journey as a man and as a psychotherapist, it's that it takes great courage to be happy and that most of us are as happy as we can stand.

Years ago, my eldest daughter Keeley gave me a book of questions for grandparents to express who they were for posterity. Although the idea of the book held great appeal, the structure did not. I didn't care if people knew what my favorite color was: Green. It would not have conveyed the sense of me. Then, some years later, my son, Chandler, asked me what I thought it [life] was about. His work and home life were going well, and with the resulting prosperity he was wondering, "Is this it?" I answered something along the lines of "It's about the pursuit of happiness." But my explanation was not well-thought-out nor compelling to either of us. Nonetheless, *it was true.* I just had to build the case for it.

When I started writing this book, I soon realized that I was responding to these two challenges, each of which had been stirring within me for years: "Who am I?" and "What's it all about?" However, along the way, the writing became something else, something more, as I said a story of the human condition. It details my experiences from the Gathering Darkness of my early years, marked by feelings of loneliness, isolation, inferiority and confusion, to a growing sense of fulfillment and hard-earned wisdom in my maturity.

Eventually, I came to appreciate that my struggles continue to this day and, to my surprise, that this is a good thing. It's the struggle itself that fosters a continuing sense of adventure and discovery, and depth, and texture to living, both within ourselves and with our others. Where I would have felt the struggle as a burden years earlier, I now understand it as life itself, a catalyst of self-discovery and self-expression, and of ongoing aliveness. To my surprise, I also discovered that despite the discomfort it often entails I would not have it any other way.

So I will tell it all, the journey that has been my life: the uncertainty, the low self-esteem, the egotism, the mistakes made and then made again, the lessons learned and then forgotten, the failures and successes, the joys and heartbreak. Along the way, I hope to convey the key ingredient to a personally meaningful life: that is striving to embrace *all* your thoughts and *all* your feelings, both the *good* and the *bad* and *then* to think about them. Herein lies one's of life's many paradoxes, although embracing one's thoughts and feelings is essential to the pursuit of happiness, it is not easy.

Indeed, the psyche actively recoils from such activity. Like any organism, it uses all kinds of tricks to distance itself and us from distress and anxiety. But the psyche is not a surgical instrument. It does not cut out and eliminate single undesired thoughts or feelings. Rather, it is a blunt instrument, which represses the capacity to think and feel in general. In other words, denial and repression are not local anesthetics but wide-ranging ones. They numb not only the ability to feel painful feelings, such as shame, sadness, or anxiety but the capacity to feel in general, including positive feelings, such as the joy and happiness entailed in drinking in the colors of a beautiful sunset or the varying textures of a tender kiss.

But that is not the worst side effect of rejecting our troubling feelings. There is a second even greater problem. Where do these feelings go? Certainly, they are pushed from consciousness, but that doesn't mean they are gone and do not have an impact. Rather, what begins as a slow gathering of darkness, ignored over time and ever growing as more negative thoughts and feelings accumulate within, turns into an increasingly ominous mountain range of nameless storm clouds. These, in turn, stir and threaten to break through the repressive barriers in vague feelings of anger, depression, anxiety, and dread or general feelings of emptiness and isolation, and bodily complaints. In this world of the repressed, cut off from the light of consciousness and the spring-fed tributaries of openness to the world, the growing darkness only feeds upon itself.

And that's not the all of it. This self-devouring inner world travels with us wherever we go and seals our fate. For, at the end of the day, there is no running from the repressed feelings; there isn't even any hiding. They only clamor ever more insistently to be heard. And, after all, why wouldn't they? They are part of us; messages from us to us, alarm bells tolling in the night.

Of course, feeling *all* our feelings and thinking *all* our thoughts is not always a happy business, but why would anyone believe that it should be? Life and relationship *can* be scary and depressing.

Confronting distressing thoughts and feelings does not always lead to the semblance of a neat and tidy life, valued by so many. But it does lead to being a more fully self-accepting human being, with all the messiness that this entails. And, at the end of the day, despite how tarnished we human beings can be, I would suggest that being human, feeling both the good and bad of it, is our greatest gift.

The awareness of conflict within the human mind has been with us for a long time. In Cherokee lore, it is captured in the tale of the Chieftain telling his grandson the story of the two wolves. He said, "Within me, two wolves are constantly at war with one another. One is the Evil Wolf that feeds on anger, envy, sorrow, greed, arrogance, self-pity, resentment, inferiority, false pride, superiority, and ego. The second is the Good Wolf that feeds on joy, love, serenity, humility, kindness, benevolence, empathy, generosity, truth, compassion, and faith." Looking into his grandson's eyes, the Chieftain said, "You have these two wolves in you as well. Everyone has them." The grandson, eyes wide, considered this then asked his grandfather, "Which one wins?" The grandfather laughed and said, "Whichever one you feed."

Cherokee Indians are not alone in speaking of the dark side of the human condition. The psychoanalyst Carl Jung called it the shadow and warned that one either reconciles with his shadow or is swallowed by it. Psychoanalyst Melanie Klein, who pioneered the analysis of children, asserted that the feelings of love, hate, jealousy, greed, lust, envy and so on are all part of human experience and that it is harmful to try to eliminate rather than integrate them. Freud spoke of the Id as that part of the psyche that houses a person's primitive and base impulses. Fairbairn posited the existence of an anti-libidinal ego, which houses all repressed negative experiences, comprising an internal world of sadistic and hostile relationships that can take us over if not taken into account.

Whatever the theory, the point is that from the earliest age, while the human brain is in the nascence of its development, there is an ongoing gathering of darkness. Whatever we choose to call it, the Evil Wolf, the shadow, the Id, the anti-libidinal ego, or even original sin, it's real. And if we deal with it through denial, it will only call out louder in its insistence on being heard, troubling us in ever more profound ways throughout our lives, radically interfering with our becoming whole people and damaging our capacity for, and tolerance of, happiness. And, this will prove true no matter how successful we may become in the external world. We see this all the time: fame and fortune protect no man or woman from their personal demons. You see, The Evil Wolf, unconfronted, never stops biting.

Erik Erikson warns that not dealing with issues leads to the experience of stagnation in middle age and despair and bitterness beyond. If you do resolve your conflicts, he assures a life of integrity, generativity, and fulfillment. In other words, the struggle between the conflicting aspects of being human lasts throughout life—it is not a one and done thing. However, how well we meet this ongoing challenge directly determines the degree to which we may live happily, versus a life full of anxiety, depression, and despair.

William Faulkner once said, "The past is never dead. It's not even past." This insight references one of the major characteristics of the unconscious—that it is timeless. In the unconscious, everything is *now*: There is no past or future; there is only the *Interminable Now*. The good news is that in consciousness there is a past, present, and future. Thus, making things conscious affords us the opportunity to put our pasts behind us, both in and outside of awareness, never forgotten but shorn of its tendency to cling to us, like Ivy strangles a tree.

None of this is to suggest that insight is the be all and end all: Even if necessary, it is not sufficient. Insight must be felt not just intellectualized, and other strategies often must be brought to bear to overcome habituated forms of feeling and thinking that date from childhood. Yoga, meditation, and mindfulness are all useful tools to help us stop feeding the Evil Wolf and start feeding the Good one. In using every means at hand, we lessen the power of the shadow world to over-shadow the present and foreshadow the future, while never making the mistake of denying its existence within us.

The title of my book, *Hatching Charlie*, is intended to represent this ongoing struggle. My story is the description of birth, but one that is ongoing—a lifetime of trying to break out of the encircling shells that constrained me like a Russian Nesting Doll. Hatching Charlie is the story of my struggling in the darkness, confusion, and despair that characterized much of my early years and, in truth, continue to cast a pall, albeit a much fainter one, to this day.

The verb "hatching" also speaks to the importance of healthy aggression, the inner work of pecking away at what confines us, a refusal to accept the world as if we're passive participants rather than active subjects, functioning as both playwright and actor in the story of our own lives. I don't care how you do it; hatching is not always well organized—watch any chick fighting its way out of its shell to the outside world. Hatching can be quite random, but nevertheless, with persistence, leads to the end goal, the cracking of the shell to access the freedom and the privilege of living one's own life. You will notice acts of aggression throughout this book, both mine and others and, as horrid as these can sometimes be, it is important to keep this possible motivation in mind. As the psychoanalyst Winnicott noted, delinquency is often a railing against the present and a sign of hope that things can change.

Before we begin, I would like you to understand that this is *my* version of events. Perception and memory are notoriously malleable and unreliable. Parts of my story will meet with agreement with those who have lived them alongside me; parts will not. Each of us lives a life of illusion as the protagonist in his or her own often too polished and too edited personal play. I have no qualms with this. We can each have our truth. The important thing is to leave room for the truths of others.

In that we are all wired differently, perceiving, relating and reacting to the world in ways unique to each of us, my view of my upbringing differs, sometimes sharply, from those of my siblings. As Adam Phillips once wrote, "None of us get to choose our parents, but each of us gets to create them." In just such ways we each create narratives that guide our lives. As I tell my story, you will come to see that my self-perpetuating story line was the cause of great suffering. You will also come to understand that none of us are immune from such folly—not even psychotherapists who have spent much of their lives thinking about such things.

From the beginning, I was fascinated by my relationships, to myself and others. I was always trying to make sense of my world, to pin down how it worked and my place in it. I've essentially failed in this, now understanding that it was a largely impossible task. However, I have made headway.

What you should know from the outset is this: *Everyone* has an interesting story to tell. Unfortunately, most of us tend to take our personal story for granted and fail to recognize how remarkable it is. Here I'm reminded of the story of three fish, two swimming one way and a third going the other. As they pass, the single fish courteously calls out, "Hello. How's the water today?" Once past the solo fish, the pair of fish look at each other, and one puts his puzzlement to words, whispering, "What's water?"

I've spent a large part of my life helping people tell their stories and arrive at answers to the question, "What's water?" in their own lives and discover personal meaning. In part, this occurs by fostering their autobiographical memories. Interestingly, research suggests that the ability to remember our histories is directly related to our capacity to imagine different futures. Accordingly, if one's autobiographical memory is deficient, so too will be the capacity for such imaginings, thereby limiting the ability to bring them to life. Think about that. In this circumstance, where the imprinting experiences of our early years have been blotted out, our yesterdays become our tomorrows. Tragically, this impediment to the imagination can lead to the experience of life as a given, a stark and barren landscape in which things just happen to us and where we feel like passengers in our own lives. In such a world, absent personal agency or responsibility, one can only be born, live and die. Who would not be depressed feeling that way?

Fortunately, remembering is possible. Once we begin to remember, more memories come tumbling out, and the connections between the various puzzle pieces of our lives reveal themselves. Epiphanies occur, leading to a deepening understanding of ourselves and how we came to be the way we are, the highlights and the lows.

Consequently, I would say to you, take an interest in your story and think of it as you listen to mine. Revisit your puzzlements and confusions, and try to put them into words. Words or some other way of symbolizing things, such as dance or art, are essential. Thinking is a symbolic process. Only when you put your feelings into words can you think about them: Without words, or some other symbolic process, we are deaf and dumb to ourselves.

Pay attention to how you tell your story. Do you frame yourself as a martyr? Or a saint? Are you a victim or are you an aggressor? Are you helpless or are you powerful? Are you creating your destiny or are you living life as a passive participant? Are you generally happy or sad, anxious or upset?" Then ask yourself: "Is this the way I want the book of my life to read? Is this the role I want to occupy? Is this the way I want my children to remember me? Is the way I'm writing my life making it meaningful and relevant to me?"

I have organized my story essentially into four parts. The first chapters set the table, describing events that contributed to the gathering darkness within. These are the stories of my early years in which I am absorbing and reacting to what is going on around me. Nevertheless, as a sentient being, I am inevitably drawing conclusions before and beyond words about life and relationships, and forming simple strategies, largely outside of my awareness, for how to stay safe and get through it all.

The next chapters describe my pecking away in random fashion, essentially floundering, sometimes lashing out, trying to make sense of my confusion and despair. I try to stumble across some reason, meaning, or purpose to my existence. I don't discover one, but I keep trying.

The third part of the book tells the story of more focused Hatching, of coming to discover in psychoanalysis my self-limiting and self-defeating story line, deriving from childhood, that I continued to perpetuate. I have now found a purpose in my life; I want to rid myself of these self-written life scripts to see who I can become.

The last chapters detail an emerging sense of wisdom and fulfillment that derives from my unrelenting, if often ineffective, struggle toward meaning. As I reconcile myself with my past, I become more self-compassionate, I laugh more and learn how to write a happier last quarter of my life. I become more spontaneous and with the help of my grandchildren more child-like, more in the moment, feeling a renewed underlying optimism in a happy ending.

I feel like I'm living proof that it is never too late to have a happy childhood. What I have come to understand is that we must fight for it and give it to ourselves, and we have to accept that it won't meet the often perfectly unreasonable demands of a child, who not yet well formed and near totally dependent often equates disappointment with disaster.

Play along with me. Consider yourself the supervising therapist and me the patient. This book is the case presentation. I, the psychotherapist, am *your* patient. With mischievous glee, I ask, "What could be better than that?"

PART I

A GATHERING DARKNESS

The psyche is like a tree trunk, early experience forever imprinted on the tender flesh of the inner rings. And just like the tree, the inner rings become the foundation upon which all else rests. Amazing. Such an important time and at a time that is both before and beyond words. Incomprehensible.

CHAPTER 1

VIOLENCE AND BELITTLING—THE

FAMILY

I grew up in two families: one when my father, John McCormack, an artillery officer of Irish descent, was there; the other when he was not. The family of my father's teachings was tyrannical and sadistic, interspersed with manic moments of humor and gut-splitting laughter, fueled by all the tensions and anxieties that had preceded it. Born to a prominent Memphis, Tennessee family that boasted black servants and field hands, along with a distinguished history of military service, Dad was of devoutly Southern traditions and beliefs. His mother was a socialite, once written up in the newspaper announcing her presence in the United States Senate. His father, who died at the age of fifty-four, had a distinguished military career, serving as an aid to General Black Jack Pershing while he chased Pancho Villa and during the Meuse-Argonne campaign that brought an end to WW-II. Military values of honor, bravery, toughness, and endurance were touted. Nevertheless, my father's day-to-day actions were more those of a spoiled ten-year-old in a man's body.

What he constantly went on about were not the human capacities to think or feel, to be curious, or to question, but the machine-like ability to do what you're told without question or complaint. In other words, to unthinkingly do whatever he said. His favorite saying, which he pronounced each time as if it was original, was "If I tell you to jump, the only thing you need to ask is how high." Questioning was equated with "back talk" and could easily earn a slap.

Dad was forever the disciplinarian. I think he fancied himself another General Douglas MacArthur. He loved nothing more than to line us kids up like soldiers at parade rest whenever he was upset with something we had or had not done, real or imagined. Our hands firmly clasped behind our backs, Dad would harangue us with our perceived inadequacies. But, in that he suffered from a terrible stutter, it was difficult for him to pull the whole thing off—it's hard to sell a commanding role when you're strangling on your words. As he marched up and down the line, he would lecture us interminably before finally resorting to slaps to the face when words failed him.

The lectures were far more painful than the slaps. Being forced to watch for what felt like forever as Dad strained mightily, face contorted, to push his words up his throat and out his lips was excruciating. Also tormenting was the attempt to focus on his meandering rants to avoid being caught for not listening. For someone else I would have felt deep empathy, but not for Dad. His behavior did nothing to invite it.

Despite efforts to control myself, I would occasionally blurt out a word upon which he was foundering in the vain effort to speed the grueling experience to a conclusion. All was well if I got the word right, but Lord help me if I got it wrong; that only added to the growing volcano of his frustrations. Paradoxically, I came to look forward to the slaps for they typically heralded the grand finale of my dad's meandering tirades. Nevertheless, despite their predictability, these disciplinary sessions only added to the feeling of craziness and *d—d—d—dread*. What did I learn? If there's no avoiding a slap, better to get it over with.

My father relished courage in fighting and, as with most things in his life, to mostly mythical proportions. He loved telling heroic tales of his ancestors and of his battlefield accomplishments, stories that rivaled the Legends of Daniel Boone, Jim Bowie or Davy Crockett. In praise of fighting, he would sometimes tell a story of me swarmed in a throng of kids when quite young, only to rise pugnaciously undaunted out of the scrum. I have no recollection of this less than epic event, but the story drove home the point: you never give up.

Such an attitude might sound admirable, but trust me, it's not. In fact, it's idiotic if you, like me, are *not* a good fighter. Outside of intramural wrestling in which I went undefeated—for the most part because I took it far more seriously than anyone else—I can honestly say I have never won a fight. I have however taken a severe beating, largely due to my continuing to get back up until my opponent quit for fear of killing me. I showed him!

Please do not entertain the idea that such tunnel-vision thinking was mine alone. No, plenty of company there. My siblings joined me in this unintelligent relationship to physical pain and confrontation. My youngest brother, Mark, by far the most athletically gifted among us, once ran for 250 yards in a high school football game. My father touted this achievement, so much so that one might have thought it was his own. I remember Dad proudly showing me the newspaper clipping that he carried in his wallet extolling this athletic feat; I was surprised he hadn't laminated it. Curiously, what he never mentioned, indeed it seemed to reside outside his notice, was that the pounding of being repeatedly tackled to the ground by the opposing team's defenders neurologically damaged Mark—an injury that forever impaired his ability to smile. From that time on his smile looked more like a sneer. I admit his sneer looks pretty cool, but it is still a shame for a guy who smiles, now sneers, a lot.

The darkness of my father's sadism and brutality also cast itself upon my brother Ed. Ed played linebacker in high school until he was kicked off the team. Why? He battered the coach's face with his helmet during practice. The coach had made the mistake of unknowingly impersonating my father. Ed had been pushing a two-man sled in the Virginia heat far beyond when the whistle had blown; Ed had not heard it. The coach then made his fatal error. He chortled sadistically, "Great, Ed! You kept pushing that for two minutes after the exercise was over. Way to go." He wasn't laughing after that.

My dad had a callous over his heart—a large callous, a small heart. Once he bragged of putting puppies into a bag and tossing them in the lake, valiantly (from his perspective) preserving the bloodlines of his hunting dogs—Let's all stand up and cheer. Can you imagine the terror those puppies must have felt, shoved into the dark and claustrophobic constraints of a burlap bag, compounded by the confusion of being tossed into the air and then sinking into the lake, cold water seeping in from all sides as it filled their noses and mouths choking them to death? "What a guy!"

I remember another of my father's heroic achievements.

We'd been out hunting. More accurately, Dad had been out hunting; the kids along only to keep him company. We had been nestled in bushes in the early afternoon as the heat of the day reached full stride and were finally getting ready to leave. Hot and parched, that's all I wanted. But at the last minute, Dad spotted a hawk perched majestically on a treetop in the far distance and like a boy ridden with attention deficit disorder who had just found a sudden distraction had to shoot it. I hated that idea. The bird was beautiful, and my heart opened itself to it as I understood what he did not: his impending fate. I railed angrily in my mind. *What's the point?* But I was helpless. I had no say. My dad was going to take the shot no matter what, and my heart shriveled as I resigned myself to it.

The report of the rifle was startling, even though anticipated. But miraculously, off in the distance the bird remained silhouetted upon its tree and then a moment later, to my delight took flight. Charged with the joy of its escape to live another day and with my dad's being deprived of his ill-imagined glory, a happy yelp escaped my lips. But then, shockingly, the bird seemed to crumple in on itself and fell like an old work glove, lifeless, to the ground.

I then understood. I had been fooled. The bird hadn't been taking flight; it had been lifted in the air by a projectile traveling over a thousand feet a second. The bullet had taken a couple of seconds longer than I had expected to traverse its course. Bile filled my heart where joy had been, and the sour mist of melancholy settled upon me. This beautiful creature and innocent soul was forever gone. The truly appalling thing was that this death was inflicted as easily as the snapping of one's fingers and with as little concern. The brutal cold-heartedness and shamelessness of the act staggered me. All this destruction and for no other reason than mindless self-aggrandizement and because Dad needed a distraction. As we left, Dad cautioned us not to say a thing about this incident, noting that the bird was on the protected species list. Wow! What a parental lesson that was. Are we all ready to cheer again?

Dad was smart and knowledgeable and a prolific reader; He would read a book every two or three days. Consequently, he knew a lot about a lot. Indeed, Dad could be brilliant. He was the head of his division at the Foreign Science and Technology Center in Charlottesville, VA, an expert on Russian armaments, and respected in his field. Unfortunately, his was the classic case of having a head without a heart. Without the compass provided by empathy and compassion, which entail the ability to identify with others—rather than needing to be superior to them—he was short on wisdom. Do not misunderstand; my father had feelings. The problem was that to him only his feelings mattered.

Then there was our mother, a French Canadian, Madeleine Turgeon McCormack, born and raised in Quebec in a family that was wealthy until her father's lumber business went bankrupt. Similarly, to my dad, she came from a prestigious and well to do family. Her cousin, Roger Lemelin, was the author of four novels and a TV series writer and producer in Canada. The winner of multiple awards, including the Legion d'Honneur for his contribution to Canadian culture, he won a Prix David for a book entitled *The Town Below* which was partly based on his observation of my mother's privileged family, who lived in the celebrated Upper Town of Quebec. My mom's brother, George, became a millionaire in his own right, creating and selling frozen meat pies. I remember him as a Kennedy-esque type figure, handsome, trim, tanned with silver hair swept back. But not all had been well in her family either. Her mother suffered from depression so severe that she underwent multiple hospitalizations and her father, an alcoholic, was so hung over that he missed her wedding. Another brother hung himself while playing cowboys and Indians at age six. The problems in that family were so extensive that the last remaining child living at home, Guy, was taken away by social services. It took them a long time to get Guy back.

Mom and Dad met at a gala at the Belgium embassy, where she worked. He was there with his mother, Dee, the Washington socialite. He tells the story of seeing my mom coming down a staircase, pointing her out to his mother and saying, "That's the woman I'm going to marry."

My mother, nicknamed Mutti (German for mother), was an off-setting influence to Dad whenever he was losing all control and things were getting seriously out of hand. Then, out of a mother's love and to take the heat off the kids, she would speak to him in sarcastic tones that would score a hit and distract him. As I grew older, I noticed something I hadn't recognized before—that sometimes she would egg him on, seeming to hunger for the fight, usually if they both had too much to drink. She would implicitly challenge his manhood, oddly playing her part in the continuation of an ever-repeating, highly predictable, and ultimately insane one-act family play entitled the "Cycle of abuse." The lyrics would change, but the melody always stayed the same.

I fear that I may be unfairly giving the impression that everything was bad when Dad was around; this was not the case. When he was in a good mood, we all breathed more easily and rode the coattails of his fun and gregariousness. He always cooked Sunday morning breakfasts. Corn beef hash, grits, fried eggs, bacon, and French toast were all on the menu one week or the next saturating the house with their aromas. And he could surprise you, unexpectedly exhibiting traits or talents you had not known he possessed. Once, he took us to a farm. There, in the barn, was a beautiful black stallion. I remember standing in wonder and fear as I watched Dad, his black hair slicked back, polished knee-high riding boots reflecting the sun, and carrying a riding crop, mount the prancing beast, who seemed ready to launch into flight if only given his head. The scene hummed with raw power, making Dad all the more a dashing figure as he sat upon the prancing horse, clearly in his element. And then, without a word, Dad spurred the stallion into a breakaway run across the meadow, rider and horse melding into one. Until that moment, I had no idea he could ride.

My parents also loved to party, and my Dad prized the opportunity to put on a good show. He was the one to cook on those special occasions; a forty-pound roast baked to perfection was no problem for him. Christmas and Thanksgiving were always sparkling events, the house alive with formally dressed people and the buzz of conversation, wine-filled crystal glasses glinting with ruby light as music played, rendered clear by the top of the line sound system. All came together to make the song of people having a genuinely good time.

Upon such occasions, I felt pride in my parents, each of them socially adept, effortlessly moving around the room with class and elegance. Dad, standing erect, five-foot-eleven inches tall in his well-tailored suit, with prominent forehead, trim build, and brown eyes flecked with gold, glimmering from his love of social interaction. For her part, Mutti stood five-foot-four-inches tall, willowy, with buttermilk skin, her delicate face, elegantly framed by lustrous, shoulder-length auburn hair, and ears and neck adorned with pearls, all highlighting her sapphire eyes. Floating about the room with beauty and grace, she embodied a femininity only made more captivating by the warmth of her smile and voice dipped in the honey of her French accent.

Also, upon occasion, my dad would say the most profound things. He gave a toast at a family reunion that was so polished and thoughtful I was awestruck. I can't remember what he said, but I do remember feeling confused, wondering, *Who is this guy? Is this my father? Why isn't he like this more of the time?* I didn't know the answers to those questions. It wouldn't surprise me to find out that he had plagiarized the toast and practiced it in front of a mirror. Still, it was a great toast, far exceeding any I have ever made.

What made it so confusing was that dad was often completely obtuse when it came to anything requiring emotional sensitivity. My sister, Michelle, tells a story that illustrates this. She was fifteen, the only child still at home, when Dad asked to speak to her on the back patio on Brentwood Lane in Charlottesville, Virginia. Standing within its brick surround, marigolds in the planters, Michelle knew something was up because Dad did not usually seek time with her to talk. Her apprehension only grew as Dad appeared uncertain. He started talking about the University of Virginia Basketball team. Then about the upcoming ACC Championships. Michelle writes, "God bless him, but even at fifteen, I knew he was floundering. He finally explained that Mom had cancer and that her chances of survival were less than ten percent. He stated the UVA basketball team's chances of winning the ACC tournament were also less than ten percent. From this, I worked out that UVA had to win the ACC championship...oh, and Mom had to survive."

From this point on, with mother relatively incapacitated, Michelle and Dad developed a routine. He would have his two-martini lunches, then arrive home at 4:30 PM and expect Michelle to have another martini ready and waiting for him. He would then ascend to his bathroom to sit on 'the throne' for hours while having Michelle wait upon his every need. Michelle, who later became a nurse, believes Dad, in his mid-fifties at the time, was suffering from congestive heart failure, perhaps similar to that of his father who, as I mentioned, died of a heart attack at age fifty-four. In addition to having difficulty clearing his bowels, Dad suffered leg cramps, chest pain, arrhythmias, and shortness of breath. Amazingly, he lived until age eighty-three, dying the whole way.

Michelle illustrates how Dad was obtuse to the sensibilities of others. She reports he had no idea how to cope with an adolescent daughter. He took her to the doctor and asked specific questions about nodules, breasts, menstrual cycles and so on. I could readily imagine this. It would be exactly the approach he would take in interviewing a veterinarian about the best methods for maintaining the health of a bitch dog that he planned to breed. Understandably, Michelle found the whole experience embarrassing and demeaning. When she angrily confronted Dad, he just didn't get it. To him, it was just information, and Michelle was too sensitive.

Michelle loved Dad. To be sure, all the kids did, each in their way. I loved him in mine, like any child loves a parent, feeling that if love was slow in being returned that it must be my fault. But that was before I differentiated who he was from who he could have been and more to the point who I wanted him to be. Strangely, I never saw Dad grow or evolve in any way; He never changed, he never grew as a person. He didn't learn emotionally from experience; accordingly, he didn't develop or mature. Of course, in hindsight, this makes perfect sense. How could he grow if the only emotions that mattered to him were his own, and these were sparked solely by the satisfaction or frustration of his immediate desires? Thus, for me, my dad was always a final product, valuing others only to the extent they served his egocentricity and grandiose image of himself.

But this did not stop me from trying. In my mid-twenties, I strived to connect with Dad in different ways. When I phoned, I deliberately tried engaging him for longer periods before allowing him to pass the call off to Mother. I got him all the way up to 90 excruciating seconds.

Another time, I intentionally bought him a Christmas gift that would outshine the one I had gotten for mother, a turning upside down of the usual course of things. I wanted to see how it would affect him. While I gave Mom a bathroom dish set, I bought him a gold golf tee, a ridiculous golf hat bestrewn with outrageous golf ornaments that were sure to be a topic of conversation on the links with his cronies, and a new pair of golf shoes.

I was not with them that Christmas, but Mutti phoned, laughing, saying, "Charlie, you've created a monster. Your dad is walking around the house in his golf shoes." I can't say I was surprised; after all, his being the object of special attention was right up his alley. But I was pleased, feeling good that I had been able to make him happy, at least for a moment, in some small way. As was his way, he never thought to thank me. Why would he? *The generosity of spirit* and the *capacity for gratitude* are opposite sides of the same coin. Consequently, he had neither.

Another time I bought him slippers, which boasted the head of a Disney character above the toes. He loved those slippers for all the attention they brought when the grandkids were around. In these he cut a hilarious figure in that by this time his body and face had developed to Hitchcockian proportions and gravitas, contrasting sharply with the silly-looking slippers.

So, we did have some good times. But sadly, at the end of the day, I would use my father more as a model of what not to be as a man or as a father. I remember him at the beach on the Delaware Bay near the end of his days. Suffering from dementia, he sat hunched on the screened-in porch, hollowed out and shorn by age, stick-like legs protruding from his swimsuit like toothpicks from a withered olive. Facing the incredible beauty of the bay, watching freighters make their way in the distance, he repeatedly asked in mantra-like fashion, "Is this for real? Is this for real?" In an aside, my brother Mark tearfully expressed how sad it was that Dad had come to this. Genuinely perplexed, I asked, "What are you talking about? Dad is a perfect example of addition by subtraction. Dad's a much nicer guy now than he's ever been." Mark gave this some thought then, with that smirk of a smile, said, "You know what? You're right!"

When my father was not around, we were in my mother's family. Here it wasn't all about her; it was all about us: the kids. In this family, I was transformed from a cog in the wheel of my father's universe to being the second born of four brothers and one sister: Jacques, me, Edward, Mark and Michelle, each with a valued identity.

My mother's family was a warm and happy place. Mutti ran a tight ship and might yell at us, but we would go unconcernedly on our way, forever held secure by the knowledge that she loved us to the depths of her soul and would never do us harm, or so I thought.

Mutti was an incredibly strong individual, feisty and deter-mined, and she would muscle her way through most things. Nevertheless, as time passed, she also came to enjoy her two mar-tini evenings. In her middle years, Mom contracted the cancer that I mentioned earlier and suffered third-degree burns from the primitive radiation treatment of that era. Her buttermilk skin, now hideously swollen and red, peeled off if she scratched. Sometimes she was overcome with moments of despair which, every once in a great while, she would allow Michelle, but no one else, to see. Michelle remembers those times. Mom sitting at the kitchen table, sobbing, sometimes weeping bitterly, shouting and lashing out in anger. Other times, she would sit stoically, gin and tonic, and cigarette in hand, as smoke coiled in front of her face. Mom eventually gave up the cigarettes.

Mutti was an active woman. She had to be, raising five kids, often completely alone while my father was away during the Korean War, on maneuvers, or being transferred from one post-ing to another. As he went ahead, my mother followed behind, tasked with closing down the house and transitioning to a new one. Her job was the home, as my father's was being an army officer—he got the better of that deal. He never helped around the house. Indeed, he was more burden than blessing, calling my mother or one of the kids to wait on him in ridiculously petty ways. I can still hear his voice, "Charlie! Bring me a martini," or, "Charlie! Come here. Turn on that light." Of course, the lamp would be well within his reach. Somehow, the Great Man could not be reduced to doing these things for himself. The curious thing to me was that he thought nothing of this kingly behav-ior, nor did my mother. They acted as if this infuriating sense of entitlement was the most normal thing in the world. In this way, they were like pieces of broken glass that fit perfectly together.

Mutti was a determined and imaginative person, possessing a vision of the future sorely lacking in my father. As they neared retirement, she was entirely responsible for buying a house at Lake Monticello, a gated community outside of Charlottesville. There they built a split-level gray aluminum sided home that became a meeting ground for the entire family for years to come. Sporting an open floorplan featuring a fireplace in the wood-ceilinged A-framed great room and a large deck upon which to sit and observe the beauty of the tree-encircled lake, it soothed the spirit.

A devout Catholic, Mutti prayed nightly, hands together in the classic position, head bent as she knelt beside her bed. Small of stature, seeing her like this invariably reminded me of a young child. Indeed, this ritual dated from her girlhood days and ran like a thread from then till now. In the best Christian sense, Mutti was very much other-oriented, genuinely interested in people and concerned about them. In these ways, she was the opposite of Dad: while he focused on himself; she focused on others. Even near the end of her life, which wouldn't arrive for another twenty-five years, Mom was all about others and specifically taking care of Dad. Fighting nausea and fatigue issuing from her second and final bout with cancer, she ramrodded a move to Aiken, SC, to ensure that Dad would be near Mark and his wife Carol Ann, devout people themselves when she passed.

Of course, I can't speak of early family life without talking about my siblings. There was my older brother Jacques. Born twenty-one months apart, we were wedded together in time and a love-hate relationship—Ed followed four years later, then Mark and Michelle four and six years after that. So, Jacques and I had a unique connection and yet very different roles in the family. While Jacques garnered attention on the stage of family events and worldly successes, I lived in a world of my imagining, daydreaming and fantasizing my way through the day, and received attention in thoughtful conversations with my mother. I believe these helped shape my inner life in a way that later benefited me as a psychotherapist. She would say, "Charlie, you think too much," or "You're too sensitive," but never derided me for it. Conversely, my father, if he took any interest at all, would call me "Egghead" or "The Owl," this latter in part for the thick glasses I wore—he was often in the business of raising himself up by putting his kids down.

With my mother, I sometimes shared a mental play space. At about age eleven, sitting with her in the kitchen, I told her that I wanted to be either a farmer or a priest. She laughed delightedly, blue eyes twinkling, asking what those two seemingly divergent callings might have in common. I had no answer, but it does strike me as oddly foretelling, given that I have spent much of my life hearing peoples' confessions in the privileged relationship of psychotherapy while trying to help them grow into happier, more personally meaningful, lives.

My tendency to "think too much" and to "feel too much," sometimes called "too sensitive," started early and stayed with me. I not only lived in two families, but also in two worlds: the external world, with which I was in largely rebellious relationship which helped to reduce its frightening power over me, and the internal world of my private thoughts and feelings. To the latter, I would naturally retreat when too stimulated by contact with others, to play by myself or ruminate about events. I always had a need to make sense of things, and my mind was the one safe place I could do that. There *I* was in control. Or, so I imagined.

Before this chapter concludes, I must tell you of two memories that have stuck with me like thorns over the decades. Probably this is because they distil the essence and the atmosphere of that time. Both occurred when I was about age seven or eight.

In the first, I'm playing in the honeysuckle scented backyard in Montgomery, Alabama, when I felt an urge to connect with my mother. I did not know what gave rise to this wish; all I knew was that it was compelling. I climbed the worn wooden steps to the kitchen, entered the screen door, and found her cooking at the stove, her back to me. I approached and reached out to touch the hem of her skirt, but then suddenly apprehension stayed my hand. I felt vulnerable and vaguely afraid. The act I had been about to engage in unexpectedly felt too exposing, perhaps even shameful. I didn't understand these feelings. I stood there a moment, pulled in one direction by want and another by fear, then silently turned and left the kitchen. Mother never knew I was there.

I do not know what this means, but I do have ideas. The memory suggests that I felt unsafe to be vulnerable or perhaps needy with my mother. I could not put the why of it into words. I remember many times crying or feeling sad about something and her providing comfort. But what about when feeling fine, just wanting a hug? I was not accustomed to such spontaneity. I did not know and did not dare to find out. Perhaps I sensed a distinction between my mother's being responsive to my glaring needs versus being responsive to me. I would not have been requesting her to perform a task but to engage in a moment of tenderness for tenderness' sake. Perhaps I feared she might not understand or deem me weak and be annoyed by my distracting her from her focus on her ever-present chores.

At that moment, I fed the Evil Wolf. I succumbed to the fearfulness of my internal world and did not allow my mother to have her say in external reality. Invariably, the pursuit of happiness and fulfillment takes courage, not because it's risk-free, but because it isn't. Years later as I realized my mother couldn't relate to my depression and sense of all-aloneness following my divorce, perhaps due to her being defended against similar feelings within herself garnered during her childhood, I suspected that the apprehension I felt all those years earlier was not entirely misplaced. To be sure, given the events that followed in the years to come, including the stoicism with which she bore her cancer,

I grew to believe that my mother defended against any feelings that smacked of anything but strength.

Or perhaps the cause of my fear of rejection was related to my second memory. This memory illustrates a characteristic of my mother that contributed to her great strength but as such things often go was also the source of her greatest weakness: Her tendency to compartmentalize. In her early years, once she held a feeling or belief, it was unshakeable and evidenced not only in the way she loved but in the way she hated.

My stepbrother, Cris, was five years older than me and the product of my father's first marriage. As the story goes, my dad's first wife was a party girl and fooled around after she and Dad were married. They divorced, and she rejected custody of Cris. My father's mother, the socialite, whom I met only a couple of times, had already raised one narcissist and now was raising another. In fact, Cris came to be a *Mad Magazine* (a comic book of the day) caricature of my father. Unlike Jacques and me, Cris looked like my dad but in a rather strange and asymmetrical way: skinny as a blade of grass, bird-eyed, shrunken-chested, sporting a large head miscast upon his body and a receding hairline that only accentuated his bulbous forehead. He acted like Dad in his constant need of attention. Upon occasion, Cris would come to live with us for months at a time. My mother hated him.

In his teen and adult years, he would show up for holidays and invariably do something outlandish. He undermined one Christmas evening, by appearing at the party wearing a beret and sporting a worm-thin mustache on his upper lip. Clearly, under the influence of drugs, he took the hand of each woman when introduced, kissed it, and whispered "Enchante'"—a truly bizarre performance and probably the only French word he knew. Mother, forever invested in the social rightness of things, was mortified.

The thorn of memory I wish to speak of occurred on a sunny summer day in Montgomery, Alabama. A kiddy pool was set up in the backyard, directly under a tree. Cris, maybe thirteen, skinny framed, with trunks hanging limply from his non-existent hips, had gotten in and muddied the water. When Mutti noticed this from the kitchen window, she shouted furiously "Get out of the pool and stay out. You're not a child." Unfortunately, driven by his need for attention, Cris then opted to climb the tree and literally out on a limb. It was only with a cracking sound that we all realized the limb would not hold.

At first, it was a slapstick moment, Cris's elongated frame wrapped like a bony snake around the limb as bit by bit it began to bend and then to break. The law of gravity showed no mercy. He was pulled down, head first, until his head, eyes bulging, hung ludicrously below his legs and just above the pool. We were all laughing hysterically, recognizing that his strength could only hold so long, then the limb broke.

Choosing this moment to look out the kitchen window, perhaps investigating the electric excitement of our laughter, Mother went apoplectic. Outraged, when Dad got home, she confronted *him* with the misdeeds of *his* son and demanded Cris be punished. Such happenings were not infrequent, but this time, she was unhinged and seeking blood. To appease her, my father took Cris to the upstairs master bedroom with its four-poster bed. I snuck along behind to see what was happening. Peeking through the bedroom door, I watched as Dad ordered Cris to strip to his underwear and then to put his hands over his head and grip the bedpost. Bony torso now fully exposed and unprotected, Dad ominously took off his belt and without saying a word, only grunting with the effort, laid into Cris, whipping him mercilessly from head to toe, again and again, striping his body with white and red welts.

Though my brothers and I had been slapped and spanked with belts and with a swagger stick, we had never undergone this kind of strapping. Aside from Dad's grunts, there was no sound other than the whooshing of the belt and the sharp crack of leather against skin. It was the worst beating I have ever witnessed, yet Cris did not cry out. Skinny face knotted in agony, eyes squeezed shut, hair rumpled upon his head, he cried silently, tears tracing the outline of his face, falling like raindrops upon his bony hairless chest.

Cris was being the good soldier and was, as always, desperate for my father's approval, whatever the cost. Unfortunately, Dad's approval was always in critically short supply. But for Cris, it was even worse. At least the rest of us had our mother; Cris, confused, proud, mismatched boy, had no one, no one at all.

In the years to come, Cris would be banned from our house and our lives. He turned to drugs and worked a variety of jobs, finally settling into road work where he eventually became a supervisor. He married, had two kids, and divorced several years later. He would occasionally invent reasons to visit my dad. He showed up on one occasion in motorcycle gang colors with a friend named Spike to show off a long barreled 45-caliber revolver that he extolled as a collector's piece. My mother wouldn't allow him in the house. My father met with him briefly outside and sternly, only steel in his voice, told him never to return.

Cris would visit me upon rare occasion, sensing my empathy for his plight. But these meetings were always awkward, Cris continuing to be a parody of my father, engaging in self-aggrandizing stories of derring-do and acts of social inappropriateness that only made me sorry to be with him once again. But I never told him to go away, and I never told him not to return. I just couldn't. I later heard that Cris died in his fifties from a heart attack. I hadn't seen him for years. His ex-wife (whom I met once when they were first married) and children have no relationship to the rest of the McCormack family.

As you can see, everyone has his or her low-light reels. My mother, by all accounts a religious and loving woman, had glaring gaps in her compassion. She had triggered this near-murderous assault; Dad had only done her dirty work.

It is important to know that it is not only the victim of abuse that is traumatized but also those who witness it. I took in the brutality of that beating and all that had led up to it: my mother's homicidal rage; my father's subservient going along with it; the bloodlust; the lesson that when such behaviors are perpetuated by those who are supposed to keep us safe, no one is ever safe.

All in all, I think I was better off having a father in my life; I just wish it had not been the one assigned. Children need both nurturing and discipline. Whereas my mother provided nurture in good measure, she was not an effective disciplinarian. And though my father was extreme and erratic in his discipline, there was still enough cohesion to it that we all had a good idea of the rules, which isn't saying that we obeyed them.

It's just unfortunate that my father stood out in ways that would have seen him imprisoned in today's world, and rightly so. He is not the kind of guy I would ever aspire to be. Indeed, for me, he's a model of what not to be. Consequently, I rarely ask anyone to do anything for me that I can do myself. I usually clean up if my wife, Janet, cooks, and I cook if I'm home earlier than she. In truth, I'm uncomfortable having people wait on me. I still feel a twang of discomfort along with the pleasure of feeling her care when Janet unexpectedly brings me a drink or plate of food. Thus lays the fingerprint of my father's presence upon my life.

What I learned from these family experiences is that it is important to be fair in relationship and to pull one's weight. I also learned that we are all flawed and that the most dangerous of all people are those who don't see the flaws within themselves. Such blindness has deleterious effects, one of which is that it prevents learning and growing from experience, my dad being a case in point. Such denial also serves as the underpinning of self-righteousness and results in the tendency to project onto others those characteristics that we deny in ourselves. But perhaps the greatest cost of all is that denial of our faults interferes with our ability to identify compassionately with others, that is *empathy*. We cannot very well recognize ourselves in others or others in our self wherever we reject aspects of our own personhood. And here I'm not just talking about empathy for others that are like us, but all others as brothers and sisters in the human condition.

Obviously, my childhood was not well constructed to foster security or independence. Quite the opposite—an emotionally chaotic and physically violent environment promotes feelings of insecurity, mistrust, shame and doubt. Maybe this is why I developed the autistic self-soothing behaviors of headbanging and nail biting. Of course, when you are living through it in the early years, where your family is all that you know, you're not aware of the causes of such things, or even that there is any such thing as a cause. In that, it is all that we know everything is felt as normal—just the way things are—the unnoticed water of our lives. As the saying goes, "When you grow up in a blue world you don't know the color blue." I can tell you with certainty that when you grow up in gathering darkness, there are few colors at all.

CHAPTER 2

VIOLENCE AND RACISM—THE WORLD

M y memory is far from a continuous thing. It does not lend itself to the weaving of a seamless story with a beginning, middle, and end. Rather it consists of snippets of my life that often arise unbidden, like shards of glass, and sometimes equally cutting. At first, they emerge as fragments, only later, if at all, to meld into recognizable shapes.

One of the things about the memory that I'm about to relate is that it speaks to hidden violence, or the potential for violence, which is an abiding presence for anyone who steps outside the cultural norm. This threat of violence is all the more powerful because you can feel it but rarely identify its source.

I was age eight. Suffering under the sweltering heat of the Alabama sun. I walked down a parched dirt track through what was known then as the colored shanty town just across the highway from my home. It was only a few hundred feet distant but an entire world apart. Comprised of ramshackle hovels of gray, aging wood, buckling tin roofs and tilting wooden porches, the shanty town seemed ready to be swept away like leaves in the first winds of a thunderstorm.

Curiosity had brought me here. I was like a tourist visiting the spellbinding unfamiliarity of a Third World country. I trudged along, inhaling the clay dust rising from the path and the aroma of fried chicken and collard greens cooking in the shadowworlds beyond torn screen doors. As I went deeper into this new world, my own receded. Untethered, I was on my own. Around me, black men in sweat-stained wifebeater t-shirts talked together in twos and threes as the discordant sounds of angry shouts and laughter punctuated the soupy late afternoon air. Bizarrely, no one spoke to me nor acknowledged my presence. Some stared coldly; others turned away.

My little boy brain registered hostility but did not understand it. Had I done something? Was I misreading the situation? So, on another day, I returned, thinking *Maybe I got it wrong.* For some inexplicable reason, it felt important to know. Now, like reading a novel for the second time, I discerned more detail. Under the hostility skulked fear and anger. What was going on? I didn't know. All I knew was that not only was I not welcome but somehow represented a danger to these people—I never intruded in their world again.

The first time I went to the movies in Montgomery, I noticed that the "coloreds" got to sit on the balcony while the whites sat on the ground floor. I was offended: *Why do they get the best seats?* To me, sitting up high was a lot more fun than sitting below. Only dimly did I recognize that the whites and coloreds are kept apart, something I later learned was called "segregation."

After the movie, thirsty, I looked for a water fountain, spotted one, and walked towards it. Then stopped as a sign on the wall claimed my attention. It said, "Colored." I was puzzled. I knew who Coloreds were; I just didn't know why the sign was there. The realization started slowly, then arrived—this fountain was reserved for Negroes. I'd never seen such a thing. I was indignant; it was unfair. I was thirsty, why were they the only ones who could drink from the fountain? That was just not right.

Baffled, I looked around and to my relief spotted a second water fountain on the opposite wall. It also boasted a sign: "Whites." Ah! I realized I was being told to drink from this fountain and quickly sipped away. Thirst sated, I looked back and forth between the two fountains, trying to discern the difference. The fountain labeled "Whites" was newer and cleaner. The one labeled "Colored" was older and rusty in spots. That was when I knew. It wasn't the whites getting the short end of the deal; it was the Negroes and in an offensive and demeaning way.

Innately, as innocent children are wont to do, I felt the wrongness of this. Why should the Negroes have to drink from the rusty water fountain while the whites enjoy a new one? Why should anyone be able to tell anyone else where they can drink water? The injustice of it roiled through me, the intensity of my response likely fueled by my negative feelings regarding my dad's sense of entitlement and tyrannical dictates. I felt a defiant urge to drink out of the fountain reserved for Coloreds as if doing so would change wrong to right, or at least spare me from participating in it. Even at this young age, I knew without knowing I knew that you either rise or get quashed.

As I took a step toward the fountain reserved for Coloreds, I noticed for the first time that scattered around the lobby and out on the sidewalk were clusters of white teenage boys, all James Dean look-alikes, packs of cigarettes rolled up in the sleeves of their tight-fitting t-shirts and cigarettes drooping loosely from their mouths. They were a raucous bunch, radiating sinewy strength and aggression, like roosters displaying in a barnyard. At that moment, a dark glistening fear coiled tightly within me. I knew without knowing how I knew that for a white boy to take a drink out of the Colored fountain would bring unwanted and potentially dangerous attention. I could readily imagine being yelled at or even beaten up. I could hear their angry challenge, so loud in my mind that it might have been shouted: "Who the fuck are you? What the fuck are you doing?"

Suddenly, my urge to drink from the Negro fountain only frightened me. Just that quick, the idea of changing wrong to right evaporated as fear overwhelmed courage, and shame grew in place of pride. In seconds I was wrenched from my brave, upholder-of-the-right feeling of myself to a sneaking, cowardly, mouse-like me. The amazing thing was that this transformation, so pitilessly wrung from within, occurred without a word spoken or anyone, outside of me, noticing a thing.

Later that evening, I asked my parents about the two fountains. My question troubled them; they appeared uncomfortable. Just as clearly, I could tell that they were not discomfited by the existence of the fountains, which they seemed to accept without question, but by the fact that I would question the *rightness* of that arrangement. As they groped for an answer, I could tell that my mother was afraid. As I puzzled upon this sense of her, I realized for whom she was afraid—it was for me. At this point, Dad donned the head-of-the-family-role and took an authoritative lead. Without using these words, he explained there was a caste system, and that Negroes were lesser than whites. With this less than compelling bit of data, really only a pronouncement offered without supporting evidence, my parents seemed to rest easier, unmistakably done with the topic.

Years later I would learn that Mother was as equally prejudiced as my father. Ed and his wife Ellen, of Filipino descent, visited the parents to announce their plan to marry. Dad pulled Ed aside to warn of the problems of interracial marriage, predicting it would affect his social standing, limit his job opportunities, and end in divorce. Mom later asked if Ed had had the father/son talk, clearly knowing they had, then, watching the comedy show *Sanford and Sons* on TV, complained that all the shows were now about blacks.

Over the ensuing months, whenever I went to the movies, I glanced at the fountains but forced myself not to dwell on them. I told myself, *I have to accept that they just are; they always have been and always will be. By what arrogance does a nine-year-old dare question the rightness of this situation? What is wrong with me that I cannot accept this basic truth that no one else, including adults far more experienced and wiser than me, seems to have a problem with?*

Then one day, I made an important discovery. I was bending down for a sip of water from the "Whites" fountain when I sensed that something was different. I carefully looked around but could not discern what it was; the two fountains were still there, and the coloreds still sat on the balcony. As I continued to puzzle upon this feeling, I realized something that struck me as incredible: what had changed was not outside of me but within. I was beginning to feel that not only was the Negro water fountain dirty and repellent but so were the Negroes themselves. Their bigger lips and wider noses, which had once appeared different but not ugly, now seemed repulsive.

I felt ashamed. I had changed in a way that had been outside my awareness, that I did not consciously choose. Then I understood. *Oh! This is how you catch racism. It's sneaky. It creeps up on you through pressure, implicit threats, and suggestions.*

I now understand that racism, or any prejudice for that matter, begins in feeling, not in thinking. The thinking follows unhurriedly behind to rationalize the feeling. I can only imagine that for me the peer and cultural pressure to fit in, in conjunction with my parents' obvious endorsement of the cultural norm, was just too corrosive to my allegiance to the disquieting weight of the wrongness of the situation. In deep recesses, my feelings were changing, moving from the pain of disquiet toward the rewards of belonging and the path of least resistance. Now, I fit in. Now I belonged. Lucky me.

It occurs to me, in telling this tale, that I may not have recognized the wrongness of this situation had I always lived in that Southern town. If I had been exposed to two fountains in the movie theater from birth, along with all the other explicit and implicit messages, I might never have noticed the ignorance of racism. I might have accepted it as readily as I accepted the existence of air and maybe have given it as little thought. Perhaps, it was only the fact that I had moved five times in my first eight formative years and experienced different cultures in various parts of the country that provided the contrast necessary for me to recognize that something was different here.

Now I understand the anger and fear emanating from the people of that colored shanty town some sixty years ago. Aside from whatever I represented to those people, what would have happened to them if some accident befell me through no fault of their own while I was in their midst? Would they be subjected to an unreasoning "punish first and ask questions later" reaction from the white community? Conceivably.

Another thing I had noticed but not questioned in my visit to the shanty town was a strange awareness of power implicit in the fact that absolutely no one spoke to me. Even though they resented my presence, none of these adults acknowledged or challenged me in any way. Why would this be the case? I could imagine white adults confronting me if I was someplace they felt I did not belong. But now I understand or at least think I do. They didn't dare risk the charge of being an "Uppity Nigger" any more than I would dare challenge my dad or the existence of two fountains in the movie theater.

What the totality of this experience helped me appreciate over the ensuing years is that in just such tiny ways our deepest afflictions, disturbances in our relationship to ourselves or our others, develop in the supposedly protective confines and cultures of our families regardless of their social prominence or level of education. They worm their way in and are often what we notice least. Of course, there will always be people who are aware of something wrong. Children, in particular, have an innate sense of what's fair. But, make no mistake, such afflictions, large and small, occur in *every* family. No matter how wrong or destructive these beliefs or behaviors might be, they can feel increasingly normal, even if the feeling of normalcy never fully arrives. Comprised of thousands upon thousands of major and minor fibers of interaction they form the fabric of our daily lives, passing uncommented upon if not largely unnoticed. Indeed, they are so much part of our existence they can come to feel a part of us, making it all the harder to notice them, much less to question them, or, for that matter, to give them up. Instead, people say, "That's just the way I am." Or, "It's just the way things are," if they notice those "things" at all.

The question becomes "Who is to confront that less than compelling answer?" It usually takes somebody from outside the group to notice the flaw and question the norm. As a case in point, I remember a woman who grew up being molested by her grandfather. This abuse did not occur on the sly, but right in the living room with other people present. He would have her sit on his lap and fondle her as they watched TV while the other adults in the family, including her parents, stood around in the kitchen. Everyone knew what was going on, but no one said anything. She would even tell them she didn't want to go into the living room, but she was pushed into it anyway. This family behavior went unchallenged until the new wife of one of my patient's uncles witnessed what was going on. She immediately took issue and determinedly confronted everyone with the wrongness of it, insisting that they go out and tell the grandfather to stop. The fondling stopped; unfortunately, the damage had been done, on many layers and levels. The historical ring of that experience, not just the fondling itself but the nature of relationships that would allow it to happen, became the foundation upon which future rings built.

In just this way, despite all evidence to the contrary, I felt I had grown up in a "normal family," even an exemplary one. I was proud to be a member of my family, and I still am. It was not until later, in my mid-twenties, when I truly began questioning my family relationships in therapy, feeling terribly disloyal for even presuming to do so, that I realized normal does not always mean healthy and certainly doesn't mean right.

I once read that the human brain processes ninety thousand stimuli a second. To avoid going crazy, we each possess a stimulus barrier that protects us from the resultant cacophony. Therefore, it takes energy for thought, feeling, or sensation to reach consciousness. That understanding alone should give us pause. The fact that a thought, feeling or sensation reaches consciousness should alert us to resist the impulse to ignore or minimize it. Instead of ignoring these niggling warning signals that something is askew, we should try to discern what they are referencing.

Thinking for ourselves is foundational to the privilege of owning our own lives. Many people don't do it because it takes courage to stand outside the throng and have a mind of your own—it can be a dangerous thing. A sign I once read now comes to mind, "The worst thing a man can do is nothing at all."

With this said, the idea is not to try to change anyone's opinion. In more than forty years as a psychotherapist, I haven't changed anyone, much less his or her opinions. But what I have done is asked questions and presented alternatives that fostered a person's coming to ask their own questions and sometimes change their opinions. The important thing is the willingness to share one's thoughts or feelings without blaming, shaming, or attacking those of another and without demanding change, unless, of course, abuse or neglect is occurring. At the same time, it is important not to allow others to shame, blame or attack you; one must hold one's ground without invading the ground of another—that's worth fighting for. It's just not easily done in childhood, a time of extraordinary vulnerability and marginality. The role of a child, romanticized in fantasy, yet demonstrated as one of weakness and ignorance in many interactions with the adult world—and often associated with the animal, unruly or dirty in adult words—subtly induces the child to accumulate worldly darkness within herself. It is on this stage and according to these rules that darkness gathers in the world of the child and becomes a felt part of herself as if it were second – or first – nature.

CHAPTER 3

ROAD WARRIORS

Our family moved a lot. By the time I was age eight, we had lived in Tennessee, Oklahoma, California, and two places in Alabama—there might have been more stops along the way that I do not remember. Here, of course, I am just reciting facts. What these facts do not convey are the disruption and upheaval: the ending of many relationships, leaving one school and entering another, leaving behind another place called home and then having to grow accustomed to a new house, before it too morphed into another place called home. These moves meant repeated uprooting and resulted in little contact with extended family: grandparents, aunts, uncles or cousins. These people, the ground of our origins, we barely knew. And there was no such thing as a hometown. We were not from any place nor was there any place to which we would return. It was a wandering journey with no destination in mind.

It is amazing, the imprint of early experience. I suspect that my life-long difficulty in remembering peoples' names may be an unconscious strategy to minimize the impact of the radical temporariness of every relationship in my life outside the immediate family. Perhaps my thinking was, "If I don't say hello,

I don't have to say goodbye. That way it hurts less." What I do know is that despite having lived in the Baltimore, Maryland, area for nearly forty-five years, I still feel ready to move at a moment's notice. To me, this suggests that I've never fully arrived, never fully relaxed, never fully committed: I'm always waiting for that next move.

I don't think it should be surprising that my brother Jacques went on a tour visiting his family and friends in various parts of the country and England following the passing of his wife Christine or that he spent much time considering where to live. What was interesting was that all the places he was considering were overseas. His reasoning was that these places were less expensive, giving little importance to a support group. He dismissed such concerns, noting he could make friends anywhere, and he did. I'm not sure these connections would meet my need for friendship, but they met his. He had been able to do the same during our travels as kids. Now, I wondered if he was returning home, *home* being the nomadic life we had all lived. *Home* being the experience of making your way alone as a stranger in a strange land. But, all that said, Jacques says he's happy.

I don't think it was by accident that I engaged in the autistic self-soothing activities of nail-biting and head-banging. My introversion poorly suited me to the fear engendered by my father's invasively chaotic behavior combined with the insecurity induced by a nomadic life. I developed an intimate understanding of instability and the temporariness of all things. Both behaviors, nail biting and head banging, occurred outside of my awareness, only recognized when someone, usually mother, brought them to my attention. For a long time, Mutti waged war to break me of these habits, painting my fingers with foul-tasting liquid—but that did not deter me. An abiding feeling of anxiety had set up house in my body and the power of those autistic behaviors to soothe and comfort me trumped all.

Aside from the continued threat of emotional and physical violence at home, and of racial and cultural violence around me, I remember my time in Montgomery as a comparatively secure and happy one. There were a routine and order to my world then, a rhythm that lent structure and stability.

One memory that stands out, illustrating the wonder of that time, is of flitting through the shaded woods with my friend, Greg Cook. We came upon a dilapidated shack in a small clearing. On the rickety porch sat an old, wizened black woman, head crowned with gray steel wool hair, and spittle-laden lips framing a mouth of a few tattered, yellowed teeth. She was a sight drawn straight out of a Grimm's Fairy Tale. Her dark eyes gleaming in the dim light, she called out, "Dayawantyafortunered." Neither Greg nor I had any idea what she was saying. I kept asking, "What?" and she would repeat, "Dayawantyafortunered." After several attempts, I deciphered her message: "Do you want your fortune read?" This was exciting stuff, the possibility of magic at hand.

We approached cautiously, ready to bolt if anything the least bit threatening stirred the air. But nothing did. She asked for a coin, and I fished a nickel out of my pocket. Using a cane, she heaved her thin body out of her creaky chair and, faded dress hanging loosely upon her frame, limped through the door behind her, into the gloom of the inner recesses of her shack that spoke of secrets as yet to be known. Warily, I followed, my eyes struggling to acclimate to the dusky interior. Within this world of shadows stood a small wooden table with a thick, worn paperback book closed upon it, a large needle laying alongside. Abruptly, in one fluid movement, the woman picked up the needle and drove it into the book. Startled, ready to take flight, we jumped back. Cackling in delight, the soothsayer opened the book to the last page the needle had penetrated and revealed that therein lay a verse proclaiming our fortune. Unfortunately, it was to remain hidden from us for we couldn't understand what she read and had no desire to shuffle nearer in an attempt to see for ourselves. I just remember the aliveness of that moment, enchantment sparking through my body. God, it was great!

Those summer days in Montgomery, were some of the happiest of my life. Hours spent playing red light, green light until dusk turned to night and walking to the A & W Root Beer stand in the glare of the sun and the pulsating heat of the day—the root beer served in frosty mugs sure to give us headaches. Another memory happened on a Christmas morning—a sparkling red bicycle waited under the tree. To my disbelief, it was for me. I had never received a more wonderful gift. I felt loved, special and filled with a joy that I remember to this day.

Ten days later I was hit by a car while riding my bike. I remember a motorcycle police officer's helmeted face staring down at me from above, then waking in the hospital suffering from amnesia and with both knees injured. Not only did I lose my beautiful red bike; I felt the added disappointment of not being able to see the Barnum and Bailey Circus that the family was going to that weekend.

The strange thing about this incident is that I vividly remember arriving safely home. My mother was on the front porch waving warmly in greeting as I neared, my chest filling with the warmth of her love for me and mine for her. But this did not happen. My mind created it. Perhaps this was my psyche's way of defending itself from the calamity that had befallen me, trying to tell me, "You're safe. Everything is okay. Life is as it should be." I later learned that I was hit by the car at the top of the street and taken to the nearest neighbor's house, then transported by ambulance to the hospital. I never made it home that day, and indeed, as I examine that false memory, I realize it ends before I ever reach my mother.

On balance, my life was good; My life was full. "Therefore," the internal story line that was just beginning to coalesce within me choruses, "you should have known that your life was about to change: Bad always follows good." In later life, such story lines would interfere with my capacity to enjoy the moment, but at that time, in a state of general happiness and belonging, they hadn't yet firmly rooted. Then, one night at dinner, my parents made the announcement: "We're moving to a place called Hanau, Germany."

I was beginning to learn that life, like the ocean tide, continuously brings things in and takes things away. I was starting to understand that everything, including each of us, will one day be swept away, that nothing is guaranteed, but the tide and the tide is unrelenting.

I was grief-stricken. I said my sad goodbyes to my friend Greg, and then, like magic—poof!—we were gone. Goodbye school, goodbye friends, goodbye Montgomery, goodbye home, those times, and Greg, gone forever, like a beach swept clean of footprints by the tide.

CHAPTER 4

CHAOS—WITHIN AND WITHOUT

After seventeen hours on a propeller-driven plane, stomach rising to throat, vomit splashing onto my lap during the landing, too queasy to feel embarrassed, I arrived in Hanau, Germany. Once arriving at the hotel, I collapsed onto a bed without the energy to undress. Seconds later, or so it seemed, my dad awakened me: It was time to eat.

All I wanted was to be left alone, to sleep forever. Despite that, hunger soon supplanted the nausea of fatigue as the tantalizing smells of stuffed cabbage and quartered potatoes wafted through the air. I was now fully awake for the first time in Hanau, Germany.

Ensconced in this hotel, situated on the T of the forested road that pointed like an arrow to the Army Fort where Dad is a battalion commander, I had a front-row seat to the early morning maneuvers. These entailed deploying tanks and 8" howitzers, each weighing 60,000 pounds, in practice for war. The maneuvers always began with a forewarning. A sound like the bass growl of lions on the prowl arising in the distance, slowly growing menacingly louder as, yet unseen, they stalk closer. The floor begins to vibrate, sending an electric tingling up through the soles of my bare feet. Even as the behemoths draw near, they remain invisible, and then, as gray as the early morning fog that swirls around them, they begin to come into view, like wraiths materializing and de-materializing in the swirling miasma of their passage. At last, one by one, they emerge once and for all, as grand as tall ships sailing across a leaden sea.

The sound, a physical thing, thrummed through my body as these mammoths slowed to make the turn at the T below my window perch. There, they hesitate, as if sniffing the air for danger, before once again gathering speed and disappearing ghostlike back into the murk. A primeval silence is all that is left in their wake. No matter how many times witnessed, this spectacle never failed to awe.

This hotel was our home for the next nine weeks. We then moved to a stone house attached to a burnt-out factory situated alongside a narrow river. The river froze over in the winter and beckoned us to skate, as best we knew how, ankles buckling under the weight of our bodies. In the spring, the river, flooded by melting snows, roared its assent to the change in seasons. The sky winter gray, with an occasional sunny day thrown in, made all the more glorious because of its rarity, found us playing for hours within the factory walls. Running like cheetahs, or so we liked to think, through cavernous rooms and sodden light, stubs of burnt floor beams peeking out overhead like gargoyles as we spun our fantasies into life.

The custodian, a bedraggled man, his scruffy gray beard perpetually in need of a shave and dressed in overalls, kept a cow and a pig. Each morning, he picked up a metal bucket and milked the cow. The milk resounded with a pissing-like sound, adding its music to the pungent odors of straw and dung, so thick in the air they seem draped over my face. With solemnity, the man offered us a sip from the bucket; the thick milk steaming in the frigid morning air speckled with dark fallings from the cow's hide. This stew of sights, sounds and smells weighed heavy. We hurried to decline. He guffawed good-naturedly.

One morning, as I entered the cobblestone courtyard, the custodian was conversing with another man in the doorway of the shed, the pig at his feet, then there was a sharp pop, and the pig collapsed. After several adrenalin-driven heartbeats, I realized the custodian had shot the pig in the head with a small pistol. As I watched in horrid fascination, the two men grasped a chain from a pulley above their heads and wrapped it around the pig's hind legs. Grunting with effort, they pulled on the chain, jerkily raising the pig into the air where it swayed from side to side. While the custodian stilled its motion with one hand, he swiftly cut the pig open from chest to pelvis, with the other, intestines spilling spaghetti-like into a smoking pile on the frosted cobblestones.

While at this place, Jacques and I experienced a sexual awakening. My parents were in the habit of going out on the town, leaving a local woman to watch over us. Each night she sent us to bed in our pajamas, and we turned out the lights as instructed. Later, she opened the door to check on us, now dressed in a thin nightgown made transparent by the backlighting from the hall that perfectly silhouetted her. With still breath and partially lidded eyes, we pretended to sleep while waiting for her to finish her inspection. When she again closed the door, we broke out giggling, chattering excitedly, "Did you see that?"

God, it was glorious. She was spectacular—or, at least, *we* thought she was.

Eventually, it became apparent that this was a stressful time for our parents. The soldiers, going on endless maneuvers, were tightly strung and unruly. One night, a riot broke out at the bar next door to the hotel where we had lived. The commander of the fort arrived to restore order, but when he entered, servicemen exited from the rear and turned his car over, his wife inside. Shortly after, my father assumed temporary command.

Many years later I learned that my dad had a "nervous breakdown" during this time and was hospitalized. After years of treating narcissists, I can well imagine the cause. He lacked the psychological substance of being able to handle less than heroic results, results that rivaled the tales told of Jim Bowie and Davey Crocket. Heroic results were nowhere to be found; his narcissistic vulnerability, his unrealistic need of perfection, was exposed.

I also learned that this was only one of several psychiatric hospitalizations. At the time, we knew none of this, which again speaks to my mother's strength fueled by her capacity to compartmentalize. All I knew was that one evening I was told he was transferring to a place called Heidelberg, Germany, and I was going with him. The family would follow behind. I did not understand this; no one had ever accompanied Dad before. But, with no alternative, I did what I was told: Away I went.

For the next several months I lived with my father in a single room in the BOQ (bachelor officers' quarters), sleeping on a cot. We ate at the officers' club, and on warmer days I washed the cars of the other officers for pocket money. The main negative was my dad barking at me daily to "straighten up, head up, walk straight!" Also, there were no other kids around; it was summer, and school was yet to begin. I knew on one; I played by myself. The main positive was that there was a kind of intimacy in sharing dinner or evening snacks with Dad. I grew to love smoked oysters and crackers with cheese. One afternoon we went to play bingo at the officer's club. I won fifty dollars.

When fall came, I didn't attend the American elementary school near us but, along with a few other kids, was sent to a school for the children of the French military located in Spire, Germany. Here we were not allowed to speak English, and for the first time, I was initiated into the confusion, fear, and disorientation that follows not being able to understand what the teachers were saying and or being able to sort out how to please them, as I was introduced to the teaching techniques of rulers striking hands, ears pulled, and teachers—saliva flying—yelling like drill sergeants into my face. In this manner, like being plunged into a tub of ice water, I was introduced to the importance of making sense of things that would forever remain with me, and the danger that arose when one did not.

One little girl, another American, peed her pants. Despite her begging me not to, I told everyone on the bus. I still think about her and what I did. It brought me no joy. In truth, I felt horrible—another experience of me as a lesser version of myself. I suspect I was scrabbling to feel some power and control that would thrust from me, no matter how briefly, the powerlessness of my existence. I was so chronically upset, looking for someone, anyone upon whom I could safely discharge my ire—not unlike my Dad. In her, I found that someone. It was the shabbiest of victories.

The rest of the family finally arrived, and we moved into an apartment in Patrick Henry Village, one of the post's housing developments where we could get back to what was for us normal family life. But we were not there long when my parents had another announcement: Jacques, Edward, and I would be going on a Great Adventure. We were being sent to boarding school in a place called Strasbourg, France. Straight-faced, my mother told us about this fantastic opportunity to expand our cultural horizons.

I could not believe it, just could not believe it. Couldn't things ever settle down, even for a little while? Why was there always disruption, dislocation and upset? I was learning that not only does bad follow good, but bad also follows bad. My parents were impervious to our mewling that even to my ears sounded like the unintelligent bleating of lambs. At one point, my mother, overwhelmed by the intensity of our angst, sent us to appeal to our father. As we begged, literally on our knees, he responded with his usual lack of empathy, irritably commanding, "Stop crying like babies. You're going."

What I was to learn from this experience is that some things you cannot change. Some things you must endure. My life was about to change forever. This time, the tide was going out—way, way out—forewarning the coming tsunami. I was about to get a lesson in how dark, dark can be.

CHAPTER 5

ABYSMAL

I remember vividly the day our Great Adventure began: cold, sunny, and mockingly bright to my eleven-year-old eyes; I now knew the way of the world, it was smiling at my misery. Stiff with apprehension, slotted alongside my two brothers in the backseat of the car, I felt betrayed. Always before I had felt the car to be an extension of my home. It had taken us many places throughout Europe and kept us safe. But today it hummed along, impervious to my despair, as it collaborated with my parents to exile us far from home.

To be fair, the car was only following the lead of my parents; its imperious attitude only mirrored theirs as they chattered mindlessly in the front seat. Their refusal to acknowledge what was happening, couched in their single-minded pretense that we were setting off on a Great Adventure, left no opening for discussion, much less connection. Worn down mentally and emotionally, I tuned out their babble. Turning inward, I sought refuge in the only warmth I had: the blanket of my despair.

After traveling many miles, I was pulled out of the cocoon of my depression by a burgeoning awareness of urgency emanating from the front seat. I struggled to grasp what was going on and soon understood that my father was concerned about car trouble, telling my mother that he was feeling a recurring jolt through the steering wheel. I could see a look of apprehension cross her face, as conversely, hope flared in mine. I thought *The car hasn't betrayed me; it has only been biding its time to make its move.* As I nurtured this notion, I became aware that I was rhythmically thumping my head against the back seat—to my horror I had discovered the source of the car trouble. Embarrassed and fearing ridicule, I willed myself to be still; it was not easy.

The car continued to carry us along the two-lane road winding its way through postcard German towns and villages, across bridges spanning churning streams, and alongside dung-scented fields upon which farmers labored in the distance. It carried us on and on, ever further from our home, toward a town that for me, despite its inherent beauty, would always be cold and gray as burnt coal—Strasbourg, France.

Collège St. Etienne was three stories of slate-roofed stone building in the shape of an H. The ends of the H were closed off by fifteen-foot-high walls, crowned with green and brown broken bottle glass cutting like incisors into the sky. As we approached the maw of the main entrance, I wondered, "Are the walls to keep people in or to keep people out?"

Inside the belly of the courtyard stood an old church under reconstruction, surrounded by mounds of dirt from which scattered bones jutted out like spikes on a sea urchin—the remains of an ancient cemetery disturbed by the digging. Adding to this surreal experience was the jabber of French parents and children excitedly bidding their farewells, a festive mood starkly in contrast to my own. Panic-stricken, heart thumping, I turned back to my parents, only to be painfully reminded that they were already gone. Not physically but in their continuing refusal to relinquish, even for a moment, the story line that this was a Great Adventure and all was fantastic.

Another appeal to stop this madness was scrambling up my throat when I clamped down on it, finally acknowledging the futility. As resignation set in, I turned to questioning myself. *What's wrong with me? My brothers don't seem to be feeling this way, though they are unusually quiet. Am I the only one? Why can't I, too, see it as a Great Adventure? My parents wouldn't leave us in a bad place, would they? Why don't I trust them?*

Then, I reasoned it out. *I don't trust them because I'm standing here, hours from home, trapped in a cobblestone courtyard, amidst piles of dirt and bone, cloaked in the frigid shade of stone buildings, in a foreign land, amongst strangers, none of whom speak English?* I concluded, *There's nothing's wrong with me!*

The long-dreaded moment arrived and passed with shocking indifference. My mother hugged me. I held on tight, face buried in the scratchy wool of her stylish gray coat. She pulled away; my cheek slapped by the cold air rushing in. With dead eyes, I watched her follow my father out the gate and out of my life; she never looked back. From that moment on, I would never fully trust my parents again.

I stood silently with my brothers, Jacques, thirteen, standing tall and handsome, a Clark Kent look-alike, with his dark hair and fair skin, and Ed, only age seven, small and vulnerable, quietly trying to disappear, each of us encompassed in despair. A movement caught my eye. A priest, about forty, with pale skin, light blue eyes above cold-reddened cheeks, and dark hair slicked back from a high forehead, strode energetically toward us, black cape fluttering spookily behind. This vampiric figure began pushing my brothers and me unceremoniously in different directions and into different lines of students that, I would soon discover, went different places. Silenced by the language barrier, I felt lonelier than I could bear.

I numbly followed the line of boys into a hall filled with worn wooden tables set with plates and utensils. Mimicking the other kids, I stood behind my assigned chair, waiting for what I did not know. After several moments, there was a sharp tap on my shoulder. I turned and looked up into the eyes of a young man who seemed unremarkable in every way, brown hair, average height and weight, eyes observing me with indifference. He spoke, the sounds a garble to me, his tone as neutral as his appearance. I smiled tentatively, hoping I was signaling friendliness, as I attempted to discern his meaning. Wishfully, I decided he must be asking "Are you okay?" Smiling wistfully, I said, "Wee."

The next instant I was knocked to the ground and kicked around the floor. After an eternity of seconds, his thumping feet drove me back to my chair, and he motioned me to stand. Shocked, disoriented, dizzy, I rose on unsteady legs, holding onto the back of the chair for support. He angrily pointed at my arms. I was alarmed, still not knowing what had just happened or what he wanted. Frantically, I looked around and then realized the other children had their arms crossed, and I didn't. Quickly I crossed them, giving up my grip on the chair. Deprived of my steadying hold, I did the next best thing—I stared at the back of the chair. Strangely, even in this dimmest of hours, I realized something curious: something as small and meaningless as the back of a chair had become the most precious thing in my world. As insignificant and lifeless as it was, its weathered features and scratches, formed a world unto itself, free of dangerous people, and provided me with a point of focus and balance. And, something even more important, something known, certain, stable in a world otherwise gone crazy mad.

Several minutes later, The Priest entered the cafeteria. Leading a procession of faculty, he self-importantly ambled to the dais that occupied one end of the room. Upon it rested a long wooden table. After a short prayer, the faculty took their seats, and we were now permitted to take ours. Kitchen help entered and placed large metal bowls on the tables. The one nearest me, filled with pieces of meat, each boasting the severed end of an artery sticking out like a rubber tube; I had never seen such meat before. My mind scurried to name it, stumbling upon the likeliest answer given the shape: tongue. Another bowl contained white mush, drowning beneath a layer of filmy water; I guessed mashed potatoes. I did not eat that night, except for a piece of bread and two squares of chocolate that served as desert.

Following dinner, The Priest, his black cape once again fluttering dramatically behind, shepherded us up wide marble stairs and along high-ceilinged, darkened hallways echoing coldly with the sound of our passage. We arrived at a large rectangular room with an uneven planked wood floor containing three rows of beds, maybe thirty in all. One long wall held windows overlooking a canal and a fountain. The short wall, nearest the entrance, featured a metal trough that ran its length. A row of faucets, like the beaks of black birds, poked their heads out from above. The short wall at the opposite end of the rectangle contained a small flimsy cubicle for the surveillants—those creatures charged with keeping us in line, one of whom had introduced himself to me earlier that evening with kicks.

I was assigned a bed near a window, thankful, not just for the view and the light, but that I was not surrounded on all sides by strangers, thus providing me with the tiniest illusion of privacy. The bed was covered with an enormous pillow serving as a quilt. The window looked out upon a fountain, which I would discover had a life of its own as it danced to the tune of the changing weather, and transitioned from one season to the next. In winter, its waters seemingly frozen in mid-air, it stopped dancing altogether, patiently awaiting the music of spring.

At the foot of the bed, sat a locker, a wash rag perched on top. My belongings were next to it. Following the example of the others, I put my things into the locker and, braving the cold, stripped to my underwear, grabbed the washrag and waited in line for my turn at the trough. There I discovered that each faucet boasted only one handle—there was no hot water. In the months to come, the faucets would freeze, icicles hanging like the fangs of saber-toothed tigers from their beaks. To compensate, once a week we would be taken to the local swimming pool. That would serve as our bath.

As I lay in darkness in the unfamiliar bed at the close of that first day, my feelings caught up with me. I sobbed, struggling to remain silent for fear of drawing unwanted attention. Bereft and hurtling into this first eternal night away from home, cut off from all that was known and familiar, I realized I was thumping my head against the pillow. My last thought: the forlorn hope that this was only a nightmare.

A cacophony of light and sound jerked me from sleep. The bright ceiling lights had snapped on and the noise of faucets angrily spewing water into the metal trough joined noise of sharply clapping hands, as the surveillants ran up and down the aisles, maniacally shouting, "Allez vous! Allez vous!" My racing heart began to slow as I realize this was no life-threatening emergency, only the surveillants taking sadistic delight in ushering us into the pre-dawn. The first full day of my Great Adventure had begun.

I was never a victim of Collège St. Etienne. Ah, that's not true. My feelings—aside from depression—unnamed, scampered like feral children, dark eyes hooded. But, if someone had known to give them a name they would have shared one thing in common: fear. But, I did fight back. I rebelled, I broke the rules. My transistor radio with earpiece was confiscated when I was caught playing it during the first day of class. On another occasion, in the middle of the night, an accomplice and I crept out of the dorm, down the hall, down the stairs and out into the courtyard that housed the old church. Sneaking within, we snooped around. The moonlight, streaming through the windows, provided just enough light to see. Behind the altar, I found a hole filled with bones, selected a large one, what I assumed was a leg bone, and threw it out the window into the public street beyond, earning a yell of shocked surprise in return. My accomplice and I broke out laughing, our own journey into the spare joys of sadistic humor, and snuck back to our beds.

Another time I brought back a large bag of marbles from a visit home. I had noticed that the dorm floor canted toward the cubicle in which the hated surveillants slept. An hour after lights out, I crept to the top of the room near the trough and quietly eased the marbles onto the floor. With a gentle push, I sent them on their way, quickly returning to the shelter of my bed, excited to see what would follow. Slowly, the marbles gathered speed, click-clacking their way downhill over the ancient floorboards toward the doorway to the surveillants' cubicle. Soon, a surveillant stepped out to investigate the clatter, and I smiled with satisfaction as he cried out in pain, cursing, having stepped on the marbles in his bare feet. The lights were turned on, and the students rousted from their beds as the furious surveillants began their investigation. We were made to strip our beds and empty our lockers, in search of evidence that would point a finger toward the culprit, but there was nothing to find. Since no one had witnessed my actions, there was no one to turn me in.

Even so, my rebelliousness had garnered me a reputation. So soon, despite the lack of evidence, I was convicted of the crime and forced to stand outside the building, in the cold, in pajamas and bare feet. I imagine this was supposed to frighten me. All it did was make me cold and temporarily distance me from my persistently depressed mood. Indeed, on the ivory chimes of my chattering teeth, my spirit soared. Once again, for a fleeting moment, I felt free, alive, unburdened from the feeling of being a cog in someone else's universe.

A final perversity was visited upon me by The Priest when I became ill with La Grippe (the flu). Feverish, I was taken to the infirmary, which had the luxury of a working radiator, and allowed to sleep there out of the cold. That night, The Priest entered, bathed in the devilish glow cast by the naked red light bulb above the door. Exuding a false joviality that did nothing to hide his scaly soul, I watched through feverish eyes as he approached and unbidden sat on the edge of the bed. Then he bent over and whispered in my ear, "Oh, La Grande American. You're not so grand now are you?" and proceeded to take a few minutes of this night to mock me. He obviously relished my exhausted state as I could not even rise in response. I did not understand any of this because I had never felt like the Great American. I did not know who he thought he was talking to, but I did know it wasn't me. I was merely a stand-in, an available representative of hated Americans. Despite my sickness, I felt a twang of pleasure and pride. Even I knew that for this perverse fool to take the time to visit me, an eleven-year-old, in a sick ward, in the middle of the night, to perform an act of such petty sadism was proof certain that this Grande American was under his skin. Happiness nestled inside me as he continued to seethe. I slept well that night.

It was also at Collège St. Etienne that I was introduced to some of the marvels of France: Gaulois cigarettes, intensely flavored ice creams and pastries, the smell of roasting chestnuts wafting from small kiosks along city streets, and steak au poivre (peppered steak). But aside from these temporary delights, I was alone and afraid, bereft of care and connection.

It was at Collège St. Etienne that I made a most interesting discovery: One can grow to hate something precisely because it is loved. In this instance, I'm thinking of my parents' visits. These occurred about every six to eight weeks. During warm days, they would take us out for a picnic, serving my mother's oven-roasted chicken and potato salad, re-igniting memories of a home I had begun to forget. I loved the food, I loved my mom, and I hated these visits. All they did was excite a desire they never fulfilled. They became a cruel tease; a reminder of all I had lost and could never have again. Each brief visit cut unerringly through the thick wall of my defenses and re-ignited grief, at first upon my parents' every departure and later upon their every arrival.

After eighteen months at Collège St. Etienne, I was returned to civilization. What words and tears had been unable to accomplish, my body was able to effect. For months I had been suffering from bouts of stomach pain so acute they bent me over and sometimes dropped me to the floor, curled into a ball, and unable to move. The prescription of powdered milk recommended by Army doctors did nothing to help. Curiously, though, I did find the nightly ritual of putting the foul-tasting powdered milk together with water in a jar and shaking it vigorously in preparation for drinking strangely grounding. It provided me with a routine, a mooring, which helped hold my embattled spirit in the turbulent seas of this abysmal existence, providing something, however small, that was all my own. The fact that I grew to like the taste of it tells all.

Later in life, as an adult, I discovered that such rituals and routines, seemingly so small in nature, often loom large in providing anchorage in times of emotional upheaval.

My condition had grown such that the doctors feared I would develop an ulcer: my lucky wound, my ticket home. My brothers' ordeals lasted several months more but came to a full stop when, during a visit, my mother found Jacques' mattress lying in the cavernous hallway rather than in the dorm—his punishment for some infraction. This act by the school finally breached the walls of even my mother's compartmentalization and denial. Furious, she yelled at The Priest and with my brothers in tow indignantly quit the school forever.

You might ask why my parents kept us in this place. I certainly did. It is a question that gnawed at me for years. My mother's protestations that it was to expand our exposure to other cultures was not sufficient to explain her blind insistence that we continue to go despite the complaints we were making.

I puzzled on this for years. I did not care that my siblings and their spouses groaned whenever I raised the subject with my parents; they wanted to brush aside the topic and leave it in the past as if this were possible. That did not stop me because I could not stop. I knew that because something was not understood did not mean it was not understandable. I needed to make sense of things to trust again. I needed to get beyond my mother's obfuscating answers.

Over the years, I never did get a compelling answer from my parents, but I didn't fail. I pieced together a story from circumstantial evidence that made sense of things and calmed my questioning soul. Part of me wishes I could talk to my long-dead parents about my beliefs, but at the same time, I am confident that even now they could not or would not answer my questions.

What I pieced together is this. From Michelle, I learned that while she was touring Canada with my mother, Mutti had spoken about being raised in Catholic boarding schools from age four. This information gave historical context to many of her behaviors. I readily imagine four-year-old Mutti in these bastions of structure, stricture, and faith. There the nuns would have been a source of validation from whom she could garner approval with her other-oriented, self-less behavior and steadfast devotion. Always her nightly ritual of kneeling at her bedside, hands prayerfully clasped in front of her, eyes closed and saying her prayers, had reminded me of a little girl. Now, I could see the thread that wove its way back to her childhood, and that would wind its way forward to the day of her death. She had discovered her own rituals, ones that held her throughout her life, where her parent's' arms would not.

From my mother, I knew that her father was an alcoholic, a one-time millionaire who lost his fortune in bankruptcy. Moreover, I knew her mother suffered from depression and had a history of psychiatric hospitalizations. Given a depressed, often absent mother, and an alcoholic father, absent in his way, I could well imagine that for my mom, boarding school could serve as a positive contrast to a sad and debilitated home life. Sending Jacques, Ed and me to boarding school uncannily recreated her early life experience. It is plausible that, either inside or outside of her awareness, she was protecting us from the psychiatric disabilities of our father, as she may have felt protected from similar difficulties afflicting her parents.

Another piece of the puzzle that contributed to a compelling argument for me is something about my mother that I knew from personal experience: she *was*, in fact, loving and caring for the most part, but even more so a lioness when it came to taking care of her family. I have no trouble believing that she would have sent us away in service of helping my father recover from his psychiatric traumas by providing a more peaceful home environment than would have been possible with three unruly kids (five total) at home in a relatively small apartment. Perhaps it was during our time in Collège St. Etienne that my father had undergone further hospitalizations. I'll never know. She was strong that way, doing what had to be done, at least as she saw it, while my father was frail, over-identified with the exoskeleton of his personality rather than with any substance within.

Thus, outward appearance notwithstanding, we see that my dad was not the strong one in the family. Under his brittle veneer, he was weak and dependent on my mother to serve as the buttress to the fracturing walls of his psychology and ultimately, right up until the end of her life, as his protector. He could not empathize with his children because he could not tolerate in them what he could not tolerate within himself: human frailty. For my mother's part, she would have seen her support of her husband as what a good wife should do to protect her family. I just wish that if this were the case, she had told us so; that, at least, would have given meaning to our suffering. But my dad would have been absolutely against that, against anything that did not uphold his need to maintain an image of himself as a heroic figure. He was like a bald man with a comb-over: Everyone knows it's a comb-over but the bald man.

Unfortunately, since we did not have this information, my mother's insistence on keeping us at Collège St. Etienne made little sense and fueled my suffering. Not being able to make sense of what was being done to us was the cause of much of my anguish. Looking out for family was a value to which I could subscribe, and paradoxically it was exactly that value that appeared to have been breached when we were consigned to that Kafkaesque existence far from home without a convincing explanation or a sympathetic ear. How ironic and sad that my mother's attempt to look out for the family might have been the primary cause for our not being looked out for at all.

CHAPTER 6

UN-CIVILIZATION

I once heard war described as an experience of days, weeks or
months of boredom shattered by a few seconds of violence.
That description seemed to fit my life. I wasn't being shot at, but
I was repeatedly turned inside out and upside down, with little
warning. An unanticipated slap, a sudden change in living situation, a kick in the back, or being exiled to a foreign land where
I knew no one and could not speak the language did the trick.
I had come to understand the world as an ever-changing and
dangerous place.

Even after Collège St. Etienne, this continued to be the case.
But there was one difference: I was older and more hardened; I
had adapted. I was no longer grief-stricken by the loss of parental care. Now, I was twelve going on thirteen—or was it forty? I
had developed a fundamental sense of my agency. Where for-
merly there had been an "us" I felt I could rely on; now there was
just "me" and the world with which *I* had to contend.

I now understood that I was on my own and nothing took me
by surprise; I was always ready for the worst, forever expecting it.
I had been in the Abyss and survived. Or so I thought. What I did
not yet understand was that the Abyss had taken up residence

within me. On the inside was an angry, dark, brooding soul with little respect for authority. Where once I experienced the world as a place in which things were constantly being done to me, I had now partially broken out of that shell of ignorance and realized I could also do something to it.

Home represented civilization, and civilization was in Patrick Henry Village, Heidelberg, Germany. My father, for reasons known only to himself, lobbied to have me admitted to the ninth grade rather than the eighth grade, where I belonged. He argued with school authorities that French education was superior and that to place me in the eighth grade would only hold me back. So instead of entering school with same-aged peers, I was once again thrust into a foreign environment, this one called high school in the middle of the academic year. I began floundering right away, but that was okay, that had become my normal.

I joined the high school soccer team because it was the one thing I enjoyed playing at Collège St. Etienne. I was by far its smallest and slowest member. I remember playing a German team comprised of six-footers. I begged the coach to put me in. He reluctantly granted my wish with several minutes remaining in a game we were losing badly. I ran out on the field, expecting to heroically save the day, only then realizing that I was a dwarf among giants. But I did not let that deter me; I just gritted my teeth and ran as hard as I could. To my embarrassment, my body did not follow my mind. The harder I ran, the more my limbs flailed in all directions, forward movement seeming to slow to a crawl. People began laughing, including members of the German team, who, smirking, looked contemptuously down upon me. But that was not the humiliation it once would have been. I had had plenty of experience being scorned.

Ironically, my biggest nemesis academically was English; I was failing. After struggling for so long to learn French, I spoke and dreamt fluently in it. But, in the meantime, I had lost three years of schooling in English between Spire Academy and Collège St. Etienne, with no remedial teaching offered. I then lost the fourth year when I hopscotched into the ninth grade. I didn't care. I was used to failure; in fact, I was good at it.

But I was concerned with my father's wrath, and I had learned that when you have nothing to lose, strike preemptively. Based on that timeless wisdom, I set out to steal the 9th-grade final exam. While I was so engaged, another student happened upon me. Sulkily insisting on inclusion, he threatened to give me away if I did not give him a copy. I instantly didn't like the guy and should have paid attention to these feelings for some days later I was called to the principal's office and confronted with the theft. Like any good soldier or thief for that matter, I stoically denied all until a small voice behind me squeaked, "I've told him everything." It was the other student. Bastard. Apparently, he had not gotten the memo. Whatever happened to only giving name, rank and serial number, not to mention honor among thieves and never being a rat? What a dweeb! He had begged me, and now, in payment, he had gotten himself caught, then sold me out. Dad kicked my ass, again.

All was not negative in Heidelberg, though nearly so in that I had no friends. The kids in high school were not only older and bigger, but the kids my age went to a different school. Consequently, I spent my time alone. Of course, it didn't help that I was dark on the inside and socially inept. I entertained myself, playing alone or going to the local pool, where I lounged on the grass under the heat of the sun, pretending not to watch or envy the camaraderie of the other kids, a sense of fellowship that eluded me.

My twelve-year-old self lay on the grass looking up at the diving platform soaring into the sky, watching as kid after kid climbed the rungs, rushed to the edge of the platform, and threw themselves off screaming with delight as they rocketed feet first into the water below. I thought *I could do that.*

As I made my way up the ladder, I noticed that what did not look very high while lying securely on the grass below became more Mount Everest-like with each rung ascended. It felt like the air was thinning. In fact, it was my chest constricting. Thirty-nine rungs and thirty feet later, white-knuckling the ladder, I was seriously wondering what I had gotten myself into as I crawled ignominiously onto the diving platform, suffering vertigo, dizzy and unbalanced from the loss of perspective entailed in standing on a pinnacle, surrounded by open air. Security rail clenched tightly in hand, panting with anxiety, I looked around my new domain then reluctantly pulled myself as if by rope, hand over hand, to the far edge to look down upon the pool below.

One of the many things I had not anticipated was that without my glasses, the pool was just a blur. I could see its outline, but not the crystal-clear water within. How was I to prepare myself for entry if I couldn't see it coming? As I stood there, wrestling with fear, seconds morphed into minutes and minutes into handfuls of minutes. Kid after kid worked their way by me, each giving a questioning look before joyously leaping into the void.

Sick to my stomach, I considered exiting the way I had come, back down the ladder. But I imagined myself being the object of scorn, my cowardly descent on display for all to see. That way out cut off by my fantasy peer pressure; I once again approached the edge of the platform. As I readied myself to jump, I envisioned cartwheeling out of control in mid-air and landing face first on the surface of the invisible water below. Thus, I moved like a metronome, tick-tocking back and forth between ladder and edge. Shame on one side and terror on the other. Finally, I could stand no more. I went to the lip of the platform, took a deep breath, and leaped feet first: *my* scream held no glee.

Before I knew it, flats of feet stinging, I plunged into the water to the bottom of the pool. Clouds of bubbles rose past me, and I followed them up, thinking *That wasn't so bad!* I climbed to the platform again, then again and again until I had crushed the fear that minutes earlier had been crushing me. I learned three things that day. One, things look differently depending on where you stand. Two, that if you face your fears, they are almost always less frightening than what you imagined. And three, point your toes when jumping into water from a height.

Combatting my abiding sense of isolation was an ongoing challenge. I had not yet turned the magic thirteen, the "teen" part of the word holding all the magic. But that did not deter me; I began sneaking into the Teen Club.

It turns out I had a natural eye for shooting pool and after several months of practice could make difficult shots, albeit not consistently. Nonetheless, sometimes, as the law of chance would have it, I would string shots together, beating a series of the older players. The problem was there was only one pool table, and it was center stage. All the testosterone-filled boys milled around, impatiently waiting their turn to play. The winner of each game held the table while the loser, chastened, had to make the walk of shame back to the end of the line. Losing to me, the smallest of the small, tended to be unusually galling to my older, more ego-driven, and physically bigger opponents.

One such brute, a member of the high school wrestling team, went into a rage. He pressed a pool stick across my throat, choking me from behind. Angrily, pushing against the stick, I hissed, "Get off me, you half-breed." This insult giving him the excuse he needed to challenge me to a fight. I knew I had no chance of winning, but refusing a fight frightened me more than losing one. So, outside we went, and this fellow proceeded to beat me to a pulp. However, he's the one who quit. I made him afraid. Not of me—I never laid a hand on him—but of the damage he was doing: my face distended, eyelids like golf balls, one eye swollen shut, the other almost so, an ear torn, my lips split, and bleeding all over the place. Again and again, I kept getting up and going at him until, a look of growing worry cascading across his face, he waved me off and nervously walked away.

When I stumbled home, my mother screamed. She applied cold compresses to my face and demanded that I tell her what had happened. Jacques wanted to know as well—family honor was at stake. He took off to find the guy but returned having done nothing. The guy had explained that I had called him a half-breed. Somehow the rest of the story had been edited out. I said nothing: Jacques' honor as the older brother had been maintained. Dweeb!

Several other memories stand out for me during my time in Heidelberg. I hitchhiked a lot, sometimes going to Heidelberg Castle overlooking the Neckar River. Skinny enough to squirm through the bars of the security gates, I played within its walls and dungeons. Occasionally, I would stop to take in the view. The Neckar River and the town of Heidelberg situated on its opposite bank were breathtaking from the Castle's promontory.

Another time, I rented a rowboat and almost went over a three-foot-high damn I didn't see until I was upon it. That got my adrenaline going. Looking back, I find it amazing that a twelve-year-old was allowed to rent the boat, much less take it out on the Neckar, a substantial river, all by himself.

Two other incidents impressed themselves upon my memory. One involved hitchhiking to NATO headquarters to see my father, the reason long forgotten. After a brief visit, I had no luck finding a ride home. Finally, after more than an hour, a car stopped thirty yards beyond me in the middle of the road. This was peculiar; usually those picking up hitchhikers stopped closer by and pulled to the curb. Even so, unwilling to risk losing a ride to indecision, I rushed to the car, swung open the back door and jumped in. Only then, in mid-leap, as words of thanks spewed from my mouth, did I fully take in the situation.

Inside the car were four visibly startled, pop-eyed African American soldiers. The one in the front passenger seat had been looking at a map. I instantly realized they had not stopped for me. They were only trying to find their way. Desperately needing a ride, I ignored my understanding and continued thanking them for stopping. Pushed by the weight of my gratitude, they reluctantly agreed to take me home.

As we started off, they asked if I knew where they might find a fun time. This question concerned me, for I realized that if we maintained the current route, we would pass a town square which was a marketplace for prostitutes. The other thing I knew was that if the soldiers saw them, my ride was over. So, hurriedly, I gave directions circumventing the square. At the same time, I remembered that an Octoberfest was taking place at Patrick Henry Village and directed them to that. So, we all ended up with our needs met, though, I will admit, perhaps some more than others.

A second memorable occasion also involved hitchhiking. I had gone into Heidelberg having saved enough money to order a green lasagna that I had fallen in love with when visiting the restaurant with my parents. Hitchhiking back after enjoying lunch, I was picked up by an African American male driving a car, with a Caucasian female in the passenger seat. Good looking, they were made more attractive by their warm and gentle demeanor. All was good until, as we approached the Village, an MP (military police) jeep pulled us over. It soon became apparent to me that the two helmeted white MPs were intent on giving this couple a hard time, not only the African American male daring to be with a white woman but the white woman who was low enough to accept his attentions. The MPs were derisive and didn't bother to give any reason for having pulled the couple over. Anger arose within me—more bastards with power and authority. These people had done nothing wrong and were now being made to suffer. Enraged, as if used to the exercise of power, I arrogantly interjected from the back seat, "Excuse me. These people are giving me a ride home. My dad, General McCormack (I gave him a battlefield promotion), is waiting for me. He won't be happy if I'm delayed." The two MPs looked at me with dagger eyes, but their uncertainty was also plain to see. Unwaveringly, I held their gazes and, after some hesitation, they finally backed off and drove away.

We drove on, no one mentioning the encounter, but the atmosphere in the car palpably changed. A few minutes later the couple dropped me off at my apartment building. As I entered the front door, I turned to wave goodbye, only to discover to my dismay that the MPs had returned, their jeep crowding behind the couple's car. Clearly, my claim of my dad being a general was blown: generals do not live in apartment buildings. I wish I had gone back to the couple's car and bore witness in some way, but instead, I crept inside, changed from heroic warrior to a frightened twelve-year-old once again.

So, after a few months in Heidelberg, my dark view of the world continued to be confirmed, somehow having more power than the acts of kindness I had also known.

Two weeks later a new announcement at dinner: We were returning to the United States, someplace called Virginia. From my point of view, staring out at the world through jaundiced eyes, it didn't matter: Every place was the same; they all sucked. The good news was, given that they were all the same, I knew how to deal with them; I knew how to make it through. The question that hadn't yet occurred to me was, "Through to what?"

PART II

PUSH BACK—HATCHING 101

I was tired. Tired of feeling like an object to which things just happened. I didn't know what to do, but I had to do something. And I knew one thing: I wanted to do more than existing, and to do that I had to continue to push back.

CHAPTER 7

MAD PECKING ADOLESCENCE

In truth, I do not know why these particular memories come to mind when I think about my formative years. But maybe that's the point. I was blindly hammering away, like a punch-drunk fighter, trying to make a way in the world, but with no destination in mind. In my teen-hood, I felt confused, aimless, adrift, carried along by the prevailing currents of the moment. My hormones raged, right alongside an abiding loneliness that exhausted me. I did not know what I wanted or where I was going; I didn't even know how to find out. I was stupid with anger. I assumed this was just the way things were, and that was simply that.

In 1963, at age thirteen, my family returned to the United States via the ship the SS United States. One of the largest ships in its day, it boasted marble stairways and hanging candelabra, as well as uniformed waiters ready to discern needs before needs arose. It was a five-day crossing, which allowed time to appreciate the immensity of the ocean and the importance of *not* spitting into the wind.

Having failed the 9th grade at Heidelberg High, I entered W.T. Woodson H.S. in Fairfax, Virginia, as a freshman, as fate would have it back where I belonged age-wise. I was astonished by its size: three thousand students, over seven hundred in my graduating class. A city unto itself, it even boasted a planetarium. It was here that school prayer had been challenged and ruled unconstitutional by the Supreme Court just a year earlier, in June 1962.

Crazily, by the end of my freshman year, I had unwittingly earned enough credits, when added to those carried over from Heidelberg High, to qualify as a junior, and leapfrog a year again through no academic achievement of my own.

I hated high school. I did not study. I didn't want to study, and I didn't know how to study. I performed okay in classes I was interested in and daydreamed my way through the rest. I fidgeted with boredom until the last bell rang, then, magically, my malaise would lift and, energized, I could finally embrace the day.

One class was distinctly noxious: typing. It was both hard and boring, and I discovered that boring makes hard ten times harder. The worst part was the teacher. Not she in particular, although a bit stern and perfectly cast: a frail, bent, bird-like figure, repeatedly pecking away at me in ways disconcertingly similar to my father: "Straighten your back. Don't look at the keyboard. Touch the board lightly. No, that's wrong." But I could forgive her all that. What was unforgivable, truly intolerable, was her breath: she had gag-worthy halitosis. During her corrections, she would lean down and speak into to my ear, enveloping me in a cloud of gangrenous breath.

I responded to this aversive conditioning in my usual brilliant way: I stopped going to class. First one class, then another and another, like magic, until I ended up skipping twenty-one days in a row. It was a perfect example of wishful thinking. I talked myself into believing that because I got away with it one day, I could get away with it the next, and then the next, and so on— it's impressive how self-delusional I could be, seeing the world how I wished it rather than how it was. At this point, an acquaintance who volunteered in the principal's office warned me that

I was about to be called in for cutting class and would be facing suspension.

Forever fearful of Dad's retribution, I sought a way out. Desperation fueled creativity: Again, I would strike pre-emptively. You know, that old strategy that had already served me so well. I would turn myself in, claiming an unbearably guilty conscience demanding I confess. I hoped such purity of soul and palpable self-flagellation would help mitigate my punishment. I hurried to the principal's office, fearful that the administration would find me before I found them, thus robbing me of the initiative so necessary to selling my tale. Straightaway, I asked to speak with the vice-principal and, hat figuratively in hand, eyes downcast, studying the toes of my shoes, voice infused with the veracity of the worry I was feeling, I put on a world-class performance of Catholic guilt incarnate. If I had known how to cry tears of blood, I would have gone for it.

The principal, apparently impressed by the strictures of my harsh conscience, compassionately advised me that he had to tell my parents. My heart filled with claustrophobic anxiety as I anticipated another interminable lecture punctuated by the staccato drumbeat of my father's stuttering and slaps to the face. I was also worried about my mother. I knew she would be upset, and I hated disappointing her. Noticing my despair, the principal hurriedly assured me that he would personally speak to them on my behalf: Hope found, lost and found again.

That evening, my mother did all the talking. On this rare occasion, it seemed my parents had spoken about how to handle the situation beforehand. Their response was thoughtful rather than reactive. In truth, Dad didn't have a response at all. In this land of nuance and human complexity, he was out of his element. Mom remarked that my skipping class was "not right." Then, with ill-disguised pride, she praised me for having done the right thing in turning myself in. She went on to note that she and the principal were proud of me. With those words, I transformed from sinner to saint. Hallelujah. Grounded for two weeks, but I had avoided the crucifixion of suspension and Dad's endless lecture and slaps. Also, I had won favor from my mother. All in all, a good day.

My brothers and I were not model citizens, but I bet you gathered that already. We cut school and stole money from cars in the church parking lot on Sundays. When younger, we threw dirt clods from a cliff at vehicles passing below, thrilling to the game of being chased through the woods by angry drivers. Jacques and I engaged in frequent bloody battles that I predictably got the short end of since he was older and bigger. At one point, he cut the back of my hand open from wrist to small finger with a razor. On another, enraged by something Jacques had done, I threw a knife that stuck in the wall near his leg. And on yet another, I threw a can of vegetables that bore right through the hollow kitchen door as he slammed it shut to shield himself, thereby leaving a perfectly round hole for my father to find. You guessed it: thumped again. I was beginning to feel like one of the three stooges.

I could go on and on, but you get the idea. None of us were strangers to delinquent or violent behavior. We were all channeling significant aggression, which felt perfectly normal to us, in that it modeled our father's chaotic and violent ways.

However, one memory of combat stands out from the rest. Jacques and I, fourteen and sixteen respectively, were fighting in the foyer of the house in Annandale, Virginia. In a one-in-a-hundred chance, I landed a kick to his groin, sending him to the floor, writhing in pain. Fearful of reprisal, I raced upstairs, stopping near the top to see what he would do next. He just kept on squirming and crying. Perched there atop the steps, I heard my mother enter the foyer. To my surprise, she responded with disgust to Jacques' whimpering and irritably demanded that he get up and stop crying. At this moment, I felt an unexpected and confusing wave of empathy for my hated opponent, who lay on the floor below in agony with no compassion to be found.

Looking back, I think my mother treated me differently than Jacques. If it had been me on the floor, I don't think contempt would have laced her voice. I marvel about how we each shape our parents and are shaped by them. I felt that Jacques served as a narcissistic extension for my parents: Tall, handsome and outgoing, he represented them on the public stage. The cost? He was less likely to garner compassion for any perceived flaw while receiving more praise and admiration for any success.

My role was a more thoughtful one. I know, hard to imagine given everything I've told you. But, it's true. I reaped attention in long philosophical talks with my mother while encountering resistance from her to activities such as having friends over. Where Jacques typically brought friends over uninvited to be welcomed excitedly by my parents, when I asked to have a friend over I was told it wasn't convenient. This family dynamic was one of those that was so prevalent that it went completely unnoticed, unquestioned and unexplained for years. Still, such differences in upbringing are internalized and, as you shall see, can contribute to personal story lines and our roles within them that can become self-perpetuating throughout life without a word ever being said.

Jacques and I both internalized our respective roles. Recently, I asked how he was doing after the death of his wife, Christine. He responded, "It's not as if I'm on the floor crying," perhaps referencing in the timelessness of the unconscious the event that had occurred more than fifty years earlier. I, on the other hand, assumed a role on the periphery of the family, sometimes as an advisor, but rarely at the center of family life. It is amazing how these roles, never explicitly stated, function like hypnotic suggestions, shaping our behaviors but typically out of awareness. I later recreated my role in my career.

Between Jacques and I, there was no getting away with any-thing, only delayed payments. I got my comeuppance that night. As I was climbing to the top of the stairs, exactly where I had been sitting empathizing with him earlier that day, his disem-bodied fist came flying around the corner, catching me square in the face. Knocked backward, I struggled desperately to break my fall all the way down the stairs.

Given that he could beat me physically, I exacted my revenge with sabotage: hiding his things and listening in delight to his frustration when he couldn't find them. Or, more directly, in hitting him and running away. I was never very fast, but I didn't need to be; I was always faster than he.

I was not *only* in the business of breaking rules; my actions were far more complex than that. Some teachers were unusually taken by me, apparently seeing something in me that no mat-ter how hard I searched I could not find in myself. My French-5 teacher, on whom I had a crush at the tender age of thirteen, would sometimes drive me home after school and talk to my mother about how much she liked me. Nonetheless, she also sent me to the principal's office if I misbehaved. On one occasion, I used a French cuss word in class when she requested students come up with words that others might not have heard. Obviously, this attempt to be cute was ill-advised. That's how I came to be in the vice-principals office when the calls reporting President Kennedy's assassination by Lee Harvey Oswald came in. His death cast a pall over the nation and me. We all felt the poorer for it.

Another teacher invited me to his home for dinner with his wife and then, at another time, to join them for a trip to Georgetown bars. I declined the Georgetown trip, feeling out of my league and uncomfortable. I was not more than sixteen and didn't have a fake ID. I could never understand why these adults wanted me to hang out with them. I never figured that one out.

During my sixteenth year, something very odd happened that I did not think odd at all. My brother Mark's elementary school teacher and his principal were proposing that Mark be held back in the third grade. Mutti wanted me to meet with them to give her my recommendation. I don't know why she or my father didn't go. I barely gave it a thought. My going seemed perfectly natural, fitting in as it did with my role as advisor, and I felt proud that Mom would entrust me with this responsibility. So, there I was, a pimply, sixteen-year-old, coke-bottle-glasses-wearing kid, meeting with a perplexed teacher and baffled principal to discuss their thinking on the pros and cons of holding Mark back in school. I came away impressed by their concern and their reasoning, confident that they had Mark's best interests at heart. I recommended mother follow their advice. There was no discussion; Mark was held back.

As you can see, my behaviors fell on both sides of the moral spectrum. I did some bad things, but I was not a bad guy. I had a moral compass, actually a very developed one—I knew right from wrong. I just often chose the latter, mainly if it did not involve hurting anyone. I also knew that some things mattered more than others on the moral dimension. I felt sorry for deceiving the principal; he had gone to bat for me. But I chose to look out for myself. I was a guy who had been uprooted much of his life and immersed in different cultures and foreign lands. I had experienced that each locale varied from the next regarding what was and was not okay. Where the high school principal was compassionate and considerate, The Priest was a sadist. Each held sway in his respective domain. I had long since learned that rules and injunctions were not absolutes; I had to weigh things for myself.

The teachings of the Catholic Church only contributed to my irreverence toward authority. In catechism class, I took particular issue with the notion that to think or feel something was the equivalent of doing it. At that time, the church taught that to covet another's bicycle was the equivalent of stealing it. I just knew that was ridiculous. If that's the case, why not just take it? I also knew given all the covetous thoughts I had that if that were the case, I would be going straight to hell. I would later learn that the Church's kind of thinking had a name in psychoanalytic terms: *symbolic equivalence,* the equating of a word or a thought with an action. Symbolic equivalence is problematic in that words and thoughts are symbols, which lend themselves to the symbolic process called *thinking.* To equate words and thoughts with actions destroys their symbolic aspect and consequently the capacity to think. If there is a sin, that is it. To me, the Church sounded like my dad, "Don't think. Just believe what I say. Do what I tell you. Don't ask any questions? If you do ask a question, the answer is "Because God loves us" or "Because God wants us to," so shut the fuck up and believe what we tell you or you're going to hell."

Of course, this God-validated teaching of symbolic equivalence would wreak havoc upon one's soul, fostering a fraught relationship to one's thoughts and feelings, a relationship rife with guilt, shame, and fear. How could it be otherwise? My God, if to think or feel something was the equivalent of doing it, I would be running around screaming all day long, beating myself on the head in the futile attempt to suppress all thought. The truth is, we would all be dead or in jail if our thoughts were the equivalent of our actions. I later learned that the Church changed this teaching, which only proves my point: It is hard to find absolutes, so you better be able to think for yourself.

My father was a further reminder of this. He preached about honor and integrity all the time in his role as Legendary Man, yet abused his children and his wife. I even caught him using a power drill to reverse the mileage on a car he was selling. So, I was accustomed to getting by on my own thinking, as poor as it sometimes could be, in a world in which the rules kept changing.

Nonetheless, I must admit that I too love the absolutist feeling of all-or-nothing thinking, and of moral superiority and righteous indignation that follows. I mean, who wouldn't. It's a great feeling: powerful and iconic. When I'm righteously indignant, I'm reminded of classic movies, like *The Ten Commandments*, wind blowing Moses' robe and hair as he confronts the current target for his ire, be it pharaoh or sinning multitude, pounding his staff into the ground for emphasis. It's such high ground, made all the better by the total absence of self-limiting doubt or uncertainty. What's not to like?

However, once I've come down from such exalted heights and returned to the sobering air of reality, often hung over from the altitude sickness, I know that I have been thinking simplistically. Righteous indignation is always simplistic, leading to that good old feeling of omnipotence, but it is far less accurate, nuanced, wise, and humane than the more considered if less intoxicating approach that entails complexity. It is then I come to suspect that the more often or greater the expressions of indignation, the smaller the man that is exercising it.

As I'm sure you have guessed, my delinquent behaviors served functions in addition to that of immediate gratification. They helped me maintain a sense of self in a world in which I felt powerless. It was certainly an immature sense of self but far better than no sense of self at all. My delinquency served as a revolutionary act against any so-called authority that would wish to suppress me or tell me what to do.

Still, I could not escape my father. Since returning to the United States, he was home most of the time. Under his tutelage, one learned to persevere—there was no alternative. From the day we moved into our newly built home in Annandale, Virginia, he put us to work, clearing the yard of tree stumps and brush and digging a hole for a rose garden unlike any other. For a year we were his slave hands, spending every weekend, including a snowy Christmas Day, working in that yard.

The rose garden was no laughing matter. The Great Man required that we dig a rectangular hole approximately four feet deep, fifteen feet wide and thirty feet long. He ordered us to shovel the dirt from the hole, sift it through chicken wire to take clods and stones out, and then return the soil to the hole with peat moss, lime, and topsoil mixed in. Ah! The joys of gardening, laboring in the Virginia heat and humidity, so overbearing that even mosquitoes stayed home. As usual, Dad was impervious to our complaints: swallowed up in the deep and narrow well of his dreams and desires, as watching us, giving directions, he sipped his cold drink.

We resented him so much that we broke out in sadistic laughter one summer afternoon when he nearly set himself ablaze. Smoking a cigarette, drinking one of several extra dry gin martinis, and engaged in another of his mind-numbing prattles, his captive audience well in hand, he poured gas on the brush to burn it away. As he blathered on, falling further under the spell of the sound of his own voice, he kept pouring and pouring. While he yakety-yakked, it occurred to me that gas vapors had to be spreading along the surface of the ground; he had been at this awhile. A similar thought seemed to occur to everyone but the Great Man at about the same time. Making eye contact with one another, we started backing up, like synchronized swimmers, one small step at a time, without saying a word. We all knew better than to question the Great Man.

Sure enough, Dad eventually got around to throwing a match onto the gas-drenched yard. It ignited with a percussive whoosh, transforming into a voracious fireball that immediately expanded outward like the hot breath of a yellow beast. The look on Dad's face was priceless: Surprise mutated into alarm, and alarm into panic. In a split second, he launched himself into full flight, the wall of fire biting at his heels as he tore down the hill. Even now, the recollection makes me laugh. Despite having run for all he was worth over uneven terrain, we all swore that he never spilled a drop of that martini. At this observation, even he laughed.

Many times my dad, who loved golf, would steal another day from me by insisting that I caddy for him. On this occasion, before play began, he instructed me to not walk on the putting green because I was not wearing golf shoes. This was ridiculous. I was wearing tennis shoes and did not weigh a lot but, as we all know, as his "little nigger," it was not mine to question, only to serve. So off we went down the yellow brick road looking for adventure with a couple of his equally boorish cronies.

A large green eventually arrived in which he was standing next to his ball about five feet from the hole, well away from the green's edge. He barked in command voice, "Charlie! Putter!" Fuming about his treatment of me and about losing my Saturday to his desires without his having any regard whatsoever for mine, I instantly recognized my moment had arrived.

Just think about it. On the one hand, he had ordered me in no uncertain terms not to step on the green, and on the other, he demanded his putter. Last of all, I knew not to ask questions. Oh me, oh my! What to do? I quickly realized there was only one solution that would honor all of his demands. I loved it! I flung that putter toward him like Zeus slinging a thunderbolt. It hit hard, head first on the green, tearing out a large divot just in front of where he stood.

It was a grand tableau: Dad's friends frozen in amazed bewilderment, Dad's mouth wide open in a scream, voice rising to falsetto, as red-faced with fury and incomprehension he shouted, stutter completely forgotten, "Charlie! What the hell are you doing?!"

I had anticipated this question. I promptly reiterated all of his orders in best soldier-reporting-in fashion for all to hear. I finished with a flourish that made me proud, the proverbial topping on the cake, "Sir! Throwing the putter was the only way I could comply... Sir!" He was furious but didn't know what to say. He didn't hit me, hoisted as he was on his own petard in front of his friends. Bam!

Dad enslaving his kids was a common occurrence. Unsurprisingly, we learned to avoid him for once he got ahold of us, he would never let go. One task would morph into another, then another, often hijacking the day.

In defense, we all became proficient at listening for him and charting his location within the house, sneaking out one door as he was entering another—ninjas had nothing on us. We also excelled at deafness when he called, quietly tiptoeing out of the house as if we had never been there.

Is that not a great way to relax in your home and live a life? Is that not the kind of relationship anyone would aspire to with his father? Did my dad not epitomize the generosity of spirit, kindness of heart, sense of protection, and capacity for human relatedness that one would seek in relationship to one's children or spouse?

As you may have gathered, my development was jagged and uneven, like the terrain of my childhood. I was mature beyond my years in some ways and vastly immature in others. I was a mishmash. I couldn't make any sense of it or me. It was like I was in a food processor turned on high, in the process of becoming something, but who knew what as the different bits, pieces and colors whirled by?

I didn't know what I wanted. I didn't have a dream. There was no single version of myself. What form I would finally take was anyone's guess. But most—including me—would guess it would not turn out great. I just knew one thing: I had to keep plodding along, hoping somehow, someday, something would fall into place.

CHAPTER 8

RISK TAKING

U nfortunately, finding a way did not seem to be something that was going to come to me quickly. I stumbled out of high school much the way I had stumbled in, a year early and an education short. I barely had the grades to graduate, but then I ask you, what's wrong with a strong D average? Apparently, Dad thought something was. He lobbied the school to hold me back. What *was* with that guy? Why did he only care when it had to do with skipping or failing a grade? He argued with the school that I needed a stronger foundation and, no doubt, he was correct, but so what? Did he have no faith in my ability to replicate my poor performance? It's not like he took the time to oversee it. Baffled, I could only add these questions to the growing list. Thankfully, the school ignored him.

Going to college, for me, was not some great dream or burning desire. It was just the expected thing to do: the next monotonous step after high school. There was no plan B. Having already done a stint away from home at Collège St. Etienne, leaving home for college was no new point of demarcation. It's main appeal: I would be out from under my dad's thumb. That was good enough for me.

Astonishingly, I made it into the not-so-hallowed halls of Lynchburg College in Lynchburg, Virginia, albeit under academic probation and the requirement I attend summer school. Home of ChapStick and Jerry Falwell, Lynchburg was just quirky enough for me. Basking in the joy of my freedom, I earned A's in summer school. Can you believe that? Who knew? I polished that report card so hard that I rubbed the grades off.

The trouble with Lynchburg was that there was nothing to do, and that became the trouble with me. It was one of those rural towns where they roll up the sidewalks by 6 pm. So, with my usual foresight, I decided to hitchhike with a friend the 220 miles to Virginia Beach over a long weekend. Given my Dad's austerity program, I had a whole twenty-five cents in my pocket and holes in the soles of my shoes; my friend had no money at all. But I was not going to let that stop me… No siree!

What can I say? My cleverness showed forth. I relied on the careful planning of youth heavily dosed with wishful thinking and naive optimism to get me to my goal. The powerful need to get away, bolstered by the irrational belief that "Everything works out"—which rivals the notion that "Everything happens for a reason" in its less than compelling underpinnings in logic—overrode any vestige of common sense that might have argued against the plan. Oh! That's right, I forgot. There was no plan. Well, we'll worry about that later.

Thus we began our journey, thumbs out, trying to hitch a ride on the outskirts of town. After a few minutes, a police cruiser passed by, the officer giving us the stink eye. I thought, *Ummm, maybe hitchhiking on this highway is illegal,* so to avoid trouble we ran and hid behind a small berm, waiting to see if the cop returned. After a short while, when he did not, we resumed our noble quest. Soon, a guy our age picked us up, and we were on our way.

Several miles later, siren blaring and lights flashing, a squad car pulled us over. We were waiting patiently for the cop to run the tags when our driver suddenly became agitated, and in a fear-laden voice anxiously whispered, "What did you guys do?!" His change in demeanor flummoxed me. He had seemed a bit uptight from the beginning, but this was ridiculous. That is until I turned my head to see the officer cautiously approaching the car, squatting low, duck walking, gun drawn. The officer yelled, "Get your hands up! Get out of the car! Keep your hands in sight! Get out of the car!"

For those of you who have not had the pleasure of performing both of these instructions simultaneously, let me assure you, it is no easy trick. For one, how are you supposed to open the door? I was beginning to wonder if the cop wasn't a long lost relative of my dad's. But you'll truly understand the epic nature of this challenge and the yogic skills required to meet it only when you take into account that I was scrunched into the *back* seat of a two-door car, the infamous hatchback AMC Gremlin, that awful green colored one no less, without any room to move. The challenge was to push the front seat up, squeeze through the resultant narrow opening, and then perform a half twist to make it out the door. How was one, anyone, to do that with both hands in the air? I was looking for a golf club to throw. But, yogic master that I was, fervently desiring to keep my body free from perforations, I performed these feats to perfection. Grunting and groaning, I squeezed myself out of the car—like a giant being birthed by a narrow-hipped lizard—while fighting to remain upright.

As I staggered into the bright sunlight I beheld firsthand three of life's basic truths. The first is well known: The small hole in the bore of a gun becomes the size of a mountain tunnel when pointed at you. The second truth is less well known: When that tunnel is shaking, as if its holder bestrides the shifting tectonic plates of an earthquake, the hole gets even bigger, in fact, so large it develops a gravitational pull. The third truth is even less well known: The hole becomes all-encompassing when the gun is held by a jowly, middle-aged cop, eyes bulging, belly protruding, sweating profusely and shaking with fright. In short, the precariousness of our situation was not to be pooh-poohed.

The possibility of getting shot was real, if only by accident— not that I cared much about the reason why. I found myself in the strange position of trying to calm the cop. Hands out, palms down, pressing them again and again toward the ground in my best calming fashion, repeatedly uttering the mantra: "Everything's cool. Everything's cool," while secretly feeling somewhat cool myself, thinking I had witnessed a similar scene on a TV show.

Despite my skilled handling of the situation, the cop— hands shaking, eyes bugging—didn't seem reassured, the possibility of a heart attack and an accidental trigger pull only grew.

Eventually, his body and mind unable to sustain such peak levels of anxiety along with his world-class Lynchburg police training obviously kicking in, the cop became more professional. He had us show identification, empty our backpacks, explain who we were, where we were going and why we had run. Upon this gathering of facts, he ran some complicated algorithm and like Inspector Clouseau came to a decision. Without preamble, he holstered his weapon and relaxed. Now, a virtual Chatty Cathy (a doll popular in the early sixties that talked when you pulled a string), he explained there had been a robbery in town and that my friend and I met the description of the culprits. Our run from the side of the highway had only stoked his suspicion. At that, he let us go, and away we went.

At Virginia Beach, we swam, ogled the girls, and fell asleep on the sand, awoke hungry and bought a loaf of bread with my twenty-five cents. That night we slept under a tarpaulin-covered stack of chairs on the concrete boardwalk, awaking the next morning to the sound of a car passing close. Warily, I lifted the tarp to spy the tires of a squad car roll past an inch from my hand.

We were hungry and penniless, taunted by the smell of food we could not buy. Again, we alternately swam and slept the day away and then, driven by hunger and a lack of possibilities, decided to cut our trip short and return to Lynchburg. Of course, with the usual benefit of my fine planning, it was nightfall. What a great time to start a 220-mile journey, depending upon the good will of strangers for a ride. Brilliant! You go, Charlie!

Apparently, the saying that God loves fools and drunks is true. We were the former and only failed to be the latter due to a lack of resources. Miraculously—the law of random events kicking in—we got a ride right away from a man in a Cadillac: the Cadillac Man. In casual conversation, he claimed he was the brother of the great guitarist Charlie Byrd. Bitter and jealous of his brother's success, he lamented having to grind out a living as a salesman. Luckily, his less than attractive envy was offset by his generosity. He paid for dinner at a truck stop and gave us money to stay in the Richmond YMCA. Cadillac Man is forever okay in my book.

The next morning, I awoke in the YMCA, face sunburned, and eyes swollen shut, sealed tight with dried mucus: the price of two days on the beach without shelter. After painfully prying my eyes open with the aid of a hot shower, we hitched another ride. This time, an old couple picked us up and soon we, or at least they, were having a party. Swilling vodka from a bottle and bickering non-stop, the party went the way of many alcohol-fueled revelries. The bickering grew into a squabble, and the squabble into a squall as the crone took increasingly relentless issue with the man's "drivin' too fas and putt'n dem yung boys in back at ris." I silently agreed but became alarmed when in the middle of her rant she suddenly disappeared from view and seconds later the old man began screaming. Hurriedly, I leaned forward to investigate. To my horror, the crone was on her hands and knees on the floor, bent forward and biting the man's ankle in a determined effort to get his foot off the accelerator. Yelling, kicking and screaming, the man finally relented and pulled to the side of the road. There they continued to argue. Survival instincts humming, my friend and I took this opportunity to beg off from the ride.

We eventually drug ourselves back into Lynchburg safe and sound, if somewhat tattered, our mini-vacation having been successful in providing adventure and relief from small town monotony—so successful that I decided never to do anything like that again.

That fall, I was assigned to off-campus housing, rooming with another guy. He was a talented singer, guitar and harmonica player, and a babe magnet to boot given that he had `the look'— tall, gangly and long-haired—and entertained at the local coffee houses. He introduced me to marijuana and hallucinatory drugs, and before I knew it, a new world exploded open before me—a whole other kind of education had begun. I was a quick study and while watching neon-colored dragons scamper around playfully breathing fire in the brightly lit coliseum of my mind my grades plummeted. Before the end of the semester, we were both expelled from school.

My father picked me up from Lynchburg for the endless ride home, made longer by his usual lecturing punctuated with the customary pokes, smacks, and slaps to the face. I'm telling you; I was starting to believe my name was Curly. But, all jokes aside, I had earned this treatment. My parents were rightfully upset, and it was decided that I would work for a year to get my head on straight before reapplying to college.

That year proved tedious and a huge motivating experience to return to school. I now had personal experience with the limitation of job opportunities one faced without that bus ticket called a degree. The job had been mind-numbing, and one thing I now knew with certainty was that I could not tolerate boredom, particularly if I did not have to, and frankly even if I did—get me on that bus.

I worked in a government warehouse in Springfield, VA, that distributed medical publications around the world. I thumbed through the articles and pictures and learned for the first time about hermaphrodites. When not browsing the literature, my job entailed walking up and down long aisles of the warehouse, collecting books for shipment. I worked alongside African-American trustees from Lorton Prison and became friends with them, earning the nickname "ABC." When I asked what that stood for, they all laughed and said, "Ace, Boone, Coon." Years later my African-American son-in-law, Jason, informed me, in the black dialogue he puts on for such occasions, "You got the ABC's but you missing the XYZ's." Always the wise-ass, Jason comes from a middle-class background whiter than mine. What can I say? My family's a tough crowd.

One fellow, maybe forty-five years old, was nicknamed Rabbit, purportedly for all the children he had sired. Rabbit constantly used lotion to keep his hands soft. As my uninvited mentor in this department, he explained "Da laidies luv dat." One day, Rabbit asked me to join him for a night in D.C. to celebrate his release from Lorton. I tried to find his address, but this was before the time of GPS. I got lost and gave up. He was upset, feeling I should have hired a cab to take me to the address. Frankly, that idea had never occurred to me. To make it up to him I joined him a few weeks later, in a black part of town that made me feel like a vanilla cone in a sea of chocolate.

It was a weird evening. We stood outside, drinking cheap whiskey straight out of the bottle, the only thing missing a brown paper bag. We walked to a woman's house; she had a friend. Each of these ladies weighed in at 250 pounds if an ounce and was not over five foot two. We slow danced together, but try as I might, I could not fan the flames of romance within myself and, thank

God, neither could she. Indeed, my only thought was *How the hell do I get out of this?* It occurred to me that Rabbit's idea of a great night, the stuff upon which legends had been built, might be a little different from my own. I left as soon as was polite and to the relief of all. But I'm glad I went. I never intended to disrespect Rabbit and was successful in making amends.

By the time the year was over, I was desperate to return to college. Fortunately, given my less than stellar record, my Uncle Mac knew the president of Baltimore's Loyola College of Maryland (today it is Loyola University) and arranged for me to apply there. I was accepted under social *and* academic probation, just happy they weren't forcing me to wear leg shackles.

I well knew that if I had not had this connection, my life might have gone in a different direction. I felt sorry for those without such connections and guilty about using mine, thinking that I should have had to make it on my own. But if there was one thing I knew about life, it was: forget fair. However, the least I could do was to make the most of this second- and last-chance opportunity.

Around this time, given the perspective rendering year I had had off from college, I came to realize that my more impulsive behaviors were often an attempt to abort uncomfortable feelings such as boredom, dysphoria, incompetence, floundering, and the uncertainty of not knowing what I wanted to do or where I was going. I was just beginning to awake to the most important of all communications, those from myself to myself. I was just starting to understand that if I sat with my uncomfortable feelings, rather than aborting them, through drugs or action, the feelings themselves would become a gateway to my uncharted thoughts and feelings. In later life, I was to learn that boredom and floundering are in some ways to be valued, constituting the fertile soil from which creativity blooms.

By this point, I had come to recognize that the harder I partied, the unhappier I was probably feeling. Don't get me wrong; I had some genuinely great times. But what I am talking about here is partying in service of escape rather than enjoyment. Excess drinking, drug use, risk taking, all served as rocket engines in the desperate attempt to escape the orbit of my complicated feelings.

But that understanding was only dawning. Though I was determined to make it successfully through Loyola, I was still prone to actions that could get me into trouble if I were caught. Consequently, my brilliance once again shining forth, I deduced the following axiom: if you can't be good, don't get caught.

CHAPTER 9

SOMETHING CALLED THINKING

"What would you do if you were walking down a city street and saw a drunk passed out in the gutter with one finger on the sidewalk?" My response to this strange question ranged from "help him up" to "walk around him." But this craggy-faced priest, so different from The Priest of my previous acquaintance, seemed vexed with the lameness of such pat answers. He impatiently chided in his Irish brogue, "No, no, no... You step on the finger!" Stunned, I pulled back, disbelieving that a priest was saying this. I was also fascinated, intrigued by his outside-the-box assertion.

It turned out this priest was not cruel, but a recovering alcoholic. He explained: "It's kindness to step on the finger. The drunk will grab any pretext to negate where he is. With his finger on the sidewalk, he'll pretend that's where he is, denying that he's in the gutter. He needs to accept his reality to have any chance of changing it."

In such ways, I was introduced to the Jesuits of Loyola College. Surprisingly, it was at Loyola that I learned to question the Catholic Church more actively. It was the Jesuits who told me that the Church at that time was the fifth wealthiest organization in the world, richer than Exxon. This information gave me pause, *Why would the Church hold onto their countless artifacts rather than use them to help the poor?* Years later while touring the treasures of the Vatican I thought Jesus would have wondered the same. As to the Jesuits, they seemed to stand apart, questioning the hypocrisies of the Church rather than doing everything to defend it. It felt like a sip of ice-cold spring water on a parched throat.

At Loyola, I was introduced to a variety of religions and philosophies, from Judaism to Hinduism to Buddhism, from existentialism to nihilism, with courses in logic added for good measure. There, I taught myself how to study, employing as many sensory inputs as I could: reading out loud to take in the sound of the words, writing out key concepts to take in the motor memory of writing them, underlining sentences in books to intensify my visual recording of the information. Whenever my grade on an essay or test was disappointing, I would borrow the same from a classmate who had done well and compared them, often discovering that what was at fault was not so much what I wrote but how I had written it.

I also learned to develop strategies for taking tests. Ironically, this was prompted when I failed a test because I knew too much. I tend to lose track of time when writing. On this occasion, I got so caught up in answering the first essay as thoroughly as possible that I was caught completely unaware when the professor announced only five minutes were remaining.

In another class, I recognized that the instructor graded by taking points away rather than by giving them. In a five-question essay test, in which each question was worth twenty points, he would deduct points from each answer, noting the deduction in the margin, something like -3 or -6. He would then add the deductions and subtract the total from the perfect score of 100 to establish the final grade. Totally stumped on question three, I decided to write the answer to question two all the way to the bottom of the page in the blue composition booklet, starting the next page with question four, skipping completely over question three. I reasoned I had nothing to lose. The teacher had to grade at least one hundred such tests, and I suspected that that wearisome activity would dull his wits and that he might not notice an answer was missing. I was right—at least about his not detecting my ruse—and received a good grade.

In this way, I learned how to learn. It took a while, but over the four years at Loyola, I advanced from a low C average to a B average. I missed qualifying for the honor society in economics by a tenth of a point; that first year of learning to learn had cost me.

I had chosen economics as a major because I didn't know what I wanted to do. I still had no dream, no ambition or burning desire lighting my way, but I had discovered a love of learning in general and of philosophy and religion in particular. Perhaps the only piece of useful advice my dad had ever given me was, "When you don't know what to do, move from minus to plus." In other words, just make sure you are moving ahead. Getting a degree in economics met this criterion. Over the ensuing years, I came to understand that learning is never a waste; everything relates to everything else.

Along the way, I joined Loyola's soccer team where, given my lack of speed, I largely rode the bench. However, I did have one glorious moment. I was playing fullback when I caught the incoming ball on my knee. I gazed at it in amazement as if asking, "Where did that come from?" Realizing I had to do something, I started running toward the other goal. I ran half the distance of the field bouncing the ball from one knee to the other, never allowing it to touch the ground. This feat of agility, worthy of Pelé, brought a roar from the spectators. Little did they know I was as amazed as they. I could not have repeated that feat in a million years. I guess the old saying is true, "Every dog has his day." Woof!

At Loyola, I lived on campus in the Hammerman House dorm. From the roof we all watched Baltimore burn during the riots following the assassination of Martin Luther King. Quietly worried, we watched smoke and flame rising from the city, uncertain as to what would follow. But none of us blamed the African-Americans in the community. We all felt grief, the loss of another great American leader following the killing of President Kennedy, which would only become further exacerbated with the murder of Bobby Kennedy several months later. Much like 9/11, these events became a unifying experience.

Strangely, I had an equally powerful experience of unification, albeit from an entirely different and less far-reaching cause. Having been in near constant motion throughout my life, I had never had an allegiance to any city, much less their professional sports teams. But now, as I joined my compatriots to watch the Colts and Orioles, I became mesmerized by their intense love affair with these teams. Their tribal passion was unbridled. I was soon to discover that this affair wasn't confined to college kids but was city and statewide, and knew no gender, age or racial divide. It was a completely uniting experience and the first of its kind I ever felt. When the teams won, the whole city was happy, and when they lost, the city was in despair. The amazing thing was the power with which these teams brought the whole town together and gave it a sense of pride. To me, someone who had been the perpetual outsider, it was all inclusive and a joy to experience—I loved feeling a part of something so primal.

During the summer, after my first year at Loyola, a friend declined a job at Assateague Island National Seashore as a lifeguard. His father worked for the National Park Service and arranged for me to get the job. Thus, I became, as far as I know, the first legally blind (eyesight 20/450 with my glasses off) National Park Service Lifeguard. I guess we could say they hired me sight unseen.

Of course, this was not a problem until I had to get wet. Clark Kent style, I would whip off my glasses and immediately plunge into a fog of near blindness. This was probably not a good thing, particularly if you were the one needing rescue. As luck would have it, I never had to save anyone or, at least, not anyone *I* saw.

At Assateague, the head lifeguard was Wayne Kirgel. In the next several years he was to become an important part of my story and a life-long friend. Wayne was six-foot tall with light-brown hair that turned blond in the sun. By the end of the summer, he looked like a gay caballero, without the sombrero but with blue eyes. In contrast, I was 5'10" and change, with brown hair, lean, muscled, and deeply tanned, almost black. We were both incredibly fit. Where I was garrulous, he was quiet and unassuming. Neither of us was stunningly handsome or a lady-killer, but nor did we send ladies screaming from the room. We were simply regular guys who were completely out of their minds.

At Assateague, we drilled daily regardless of the weather. During a storm, the sky stained with threatening dark clouds, the ocean flogged by strong winds and high seas, I was ordered to 'rescue' Wayne by the visiting supervisor. Wayne had swum out about fifty yards. Standing on the lifeguard tower with my glasses on, their windowpanes beaded with rain, I could barely see him in the murky light as his head bobbed erratically into view from time to time between the white crests of tossing waves. Upon the signal, I fearlessly whipped off my glasses, leaped to the sandy beach, grabbed the rescue board, and darted valiantly into the chaos. Within moments, the current swept me several hundred feet downstream. Completely disoriented, paddling frantically, with my prestige as a lifeguard on the line, I looked for Wayne far and wide, and wider yet, without success. After a few minutes, panting like an Alaskan Huskie, tongue lolling, I heard a wavering bellow carried on the wind, barely floating above the din of the sea,

"MccccCorrrrrrmackkkkk!... MccccCCcccccormackkkkkk!... YYYYOOoouu BASSSSTTTTTTARD!" The absurdity of the situation struck me hard. I began laughing uncontrollably. When I finally found Wayne, helped by his continuing invectives, I dragged his sodden form onto the rescue board. We were fast friends from that moment on and proceeded to get into a lot of trouble together—as if I needed help!

The ocean, particularly on big sea days, taught me something about dealing with the power of natural forces, such as emotions when they threaten to overwhelm. This was an important lesson, for I had been overcome by emotion many times in my life and would be so again.

On one of those days, a Nor'easter was passing through, sky leaden with churning clouds, wind gusting to 40 mph, sweeping the beach and ocean clear of people. Gray waves were running high and fast, crisscrossing crazily, crashing into one another like locomotives driven by wild men.

I made it out beyond the break, gasping for breath after fighting my way through the incoming mountain range of breaking waves. Finally, exhausted, I sat astride my surfboard a couple of hundred yards from the beach, just outside the enormous break. I paused to gather myself, and fear prickled my chest as I took in the power and the beauty of the tumult that surrounded me. The noise of breaking waves pounded like bass drums, and the wind shrieked like cats flung through the air.

I was waiting, first to catch my breath, then to catch a passing mountain of water before it morphed from swell to cresting wave. It was exhilarating. Like a living thing, each passing surge of water lifted me up and dropped me down like a child on a huge swing. The walls of water crested high as they moved past, hiding the shore beyond. Deprived of the sight of land, I was alone in the foaming, crashing bowels of the beast, both frightened and ecstatic, all earthly concerns scrubbed away.

It was time. I began to paddle, catching a swell as it rolled beneath me, shape-changing into a wave. Tottering, I managed to stand up on the board, adrenalin coursing through my veins as the breaking wave slung me like a sling-shot down the falling mountainside. I couldn't believe it. I was doing it. I was riding the monster.

Holy shit! It's high up here. Whoa! Going so fast. Keep your balance.

This self-conscious patter separated me from the moment and my instincts, slowing my response time and sealing my fate. Down I went into the trough, so fast there was no time to be terrified as the towering wall of water crashed its tons down upon me, driving me topsy-turvy into the muffled silence and darkness of the underworld. Simultaneously, the surfboard, far more buoyant, was launched high into the air.

Now I was genuinely afraid. I was scared of being hit by the board when it returned to earth and of the unrelenting power of the waves that kept pushing and holding me down. I knew to give in to panic, to fight the ocean, was to lose. I suspended the urge to battle to the surface. I focused on conserving air and began taking in my surroundings.

I took notice for the first time of my temporary dwelling. Wonder supplanted fear as I opened my mind to the symphony of sight and sound as waves rumbled like freight trains passing overhead and shafts of light, filtering through the turbulent water, revealed the sandy bottom swirling around me, along with thousands of bubbles equally unable to make their way to the world above. Held firm in the ocean's embrace and rocked back and forth by the ebb and flow pressures of the waves passing above, I unexpectedly felt at peace, a child held in the arms of Mother Nature.

After a few moments of luxuriating in this sensation, I began thinking how odd it seemed given the circumstances, I wondered, *Is this the bliss of asphyxiation?* But quickly reassured myself,

I had not yet felt starved of air. I returned to enjoying nature's embrace. Eventually, I noticed a lessening of pressure and deduced that the current set of waves was passing by overhead. My time was now. I kicked hard toward the surface, moving from shadow to light, from the muted sound below to the fury above, and fought my way to shore, dragging myself, limp as seaweed, up onto the beach.

In later life, I learned to co-exist with powerful emotions rather than trying to defeat them. I learned to sit with them, to suffer them, to observe them, to appreciate their power and their embrace, and their terrible aliveness. I found out that the very fact of observing one's own emotions creates the time and space necessary to being in relationship with them, to learn from them rather than to run in panic, the latter course guaranteeing they would swallow me up.

I learned that observing emotion is the difference between having an emotion and becoming that emotion, the difference between feeling panic and being panicked. Emotions, like waves, expand and contract, ebb and flow, and eventually, given time, dissipate. The only thing to remember is that it is typically not up to you to say when this will be: the breaking waves must run their course.

Despite the lessons learned, I was still not immune—from anything—but specifically from doing things that could get me in trouble. Wayne and I were both fired from the National Park Service when we threw an unauthorized party at the lifeguard barracks. Our crime was twofold: bringing females into a male barracks and charging admission to a government barracks. What they did not know was that Wayne and I had liberated a keg of beer from the Ocean City Police Department. I mean if you're going to steal, steal big. The night before they had had their office beach party. Wayne and I dug a hole on the edge of the light from the bonfire, rolled the keg in, covered it up, and retrieved it the next day. We were very pleased with ourselves: fired, but pleased.

Wayne and I then got jobs at Phillips Crab House in Ocean City where I picked shell fragments out of cans of crabmeat while sitting alongside Mrs. Phillips, the grandmother of the clan and a millionaire businesswoman. All I knew is that if I had her money, I wouldn't be sitting next to me. But of course, I can hear the voice of some party-killing dullard saying, "That's probably why she has the money."

Working in a restaurant was one of the hardest jobs of my life. Caught skipping out of work in the middle of the day to go to the beach, Wayne and I were fired again. After that, we worked at a gas station that featured bikini-clad beauties at the pumps. Somehow, despite, or perhaps because of all our sins, we had landed in heaven, thus proving the adage that "God works in mysterious ways."

All the while, forever restless, we would drive on Wayne's Honda 450 motorcycle back and forth to Baltimore and D.C. to party. On one such occasion, while driving in a downpour that stung like bees, Wayne sped up trying to make a yellow light before it turned red. I instantly saw that we would never make it and uselessly screamed at him to stop; I had the insane urge to bite his ankle. Finally, seeing his effort was doomed, Wayne slammed on the brakes—not a great idea given the wet surface—sending us into a spin. Our feet kicked out rapidly against the road in the instinctive effort to keep upright, looking for all the world like men performing a wild Cossack wedding dance. In this frenzied manner, we went through two complete 360-degree turns, somehow, against all odds, ending up perfectly situated at the stoplight next to a van. The windows of the latter were filled with a now bug-eyed family staring out at us while Wayne and I slumped with relief.

Our exploits seemed never to end. There was a chemistry between us that led to one adventure after another. One time we were pulled over by a police officer outside of Berlin, Maryland, in a random traffic check. The problem was I was driving and did not have a motorcycle license. I protested that I simply could not find it, but the cop insisted we follow him back to the station. The station sported a front office with what I presumed were one or more cells in the back. This proud agent of the law told us to wait and disappeared into the backroom. To my confusion, Wayne immediately began taking off his shirt and urgently whispered, "Charlie, give me your shirt and glasses." In a few seconds, he was dressed in my shirt and wearing my glasses, and I was in his. The officer returned and Wayne said, "Sir, I found my driver's license." The officer looked at us suspiciously and carefully examined the license. He looked at the photo, then at each of us, then back at the photo. Puzzled, he went through these deliberations several more times then said, in his slow country drawl, "I know sump'n goin' on heah; I jus don know wat it is." He puzzled over it again then, shaking his head, let us go. Wayne was like that: quick on his feet and capable of thinking, even in the tightest of spots.

Assateague is a desert-like island, famous for its wild horses, mosquitoes, and horse flies. The latter are unrelenting, even pursuing their prey well out into the ocean. Once, after paddling out, I dove into the water and held my breath as long as I could in the attempt to escape them. But when I re-surfaced, there they were, irritably drumming their forelegs, impatient with having to wait for their meal. In short, these flies would attack until killed.

One such bite became infected. On a visit home, I showed it to my parents, fearing that it was becoming dangerous given that the major artery in the bitten arm had turned dark blue near the bite, and the blue had been traveling up my arm for days. I wasn't sure what would happen if it reached my heart, but I didn't think it would be anything good.

Contrary to my expectations of going to the hospital, Dad happily took this opportunity to demonstrate his army first aid know-how. He had me soak my arm in hot water and Epsom salt for thirty minutes, then, using a steak knife, cut open the wound. He reached in with a pair of tweezers and pulled out a white sack that held the offending pus. All this was very impressive. But, honestly, what impressed me most was that he did this without anesthesia. As per the mores of the family, I gritted my teeth and endured. To give Dad his due, the procedure worked, and my arm was good as new aside from the scar that remains with me to this day. In such ways, history is inscribed upon our bodies.

During one of Wayne's visits to Loyola, he came to watch me in a soccer game. Somehow, he had heard that I was a burgeoning star of the beautiful game. Okay, I confess, he might have gotten this idea from me during one of my shameless episodes of self-promotion. In any event, there I was holding down my usual honored position at the end of the bench several time zones away from the coach. After the game, as Wayne and I were walking away, one of my teammates pulled me aside and asked in a reverent tone, "Is that Killer Kirgel?" *Well,* I thought, *Kirgel was right, but who the hell was Killer?* My teammate went on reverently, like a groupie about a rock star, describing Wayne's dominance as a champion wrestler on the Old Dominion wrestling team. Indeed, that, in addition to wanting to watch the master of the round ball work his magic, was why Wayne was in town.

I had known Wayne was a good wrestler. Whenever we wrestled on the beach, he would lay me down in a heartbeat, and I never knew how—his moves were so smooth I called him Liquid Silk. Well, it turns out he was famous in wrestling circles. That night he had a match, and I was attending. He asked me if there was anything I would like to see during the event. I told him it would be great if he could wait until the third period to pin his opponent thus giving me every opportunity to analyze his game and afford him all of my vaunted insights. He snorted.

That night, during his match, Wayne was repeatedly put into incredible holds by his opponent. Looking like an upside-down pretzel with his head mashed sideways cheek to mat, his feet dangling incongruously over his head, his coach was going berserk, screaming at him, "What are you doing? What are you doing? End this now!" I kept thinking, "It doesn't look like Wayne will be ending anything." To my eyes, he was completely dominated. So much so that I felt guilty for suggesting he wait until the third period to pin his opponent. I feared I had unintentionally put him at risk of losing the match.

At last, the third period arrived, and I took solace in knowing that soon the match would be over. I would apologize to Wayne for foisting this loss upon him. As I thought these thoughts, I watched as Wayne's head, firmly framed by his opponent's arms, was again bent painfully askew to the mat, his appendages impossibly intertwined with those of his opponent. Together, the two formed a bizarre Cubist painting, hinting uncomfortably at a newly discovered position in the Kama Sutra. It was then that Wayne looked directly at me through the tangle of crisscrossing limbs, his eyes boring into mine from his crazy-making upside down position and... winked. I laughed. Within seconds, Wayne somehow got out of his opponent's hold and pinned him. I later learned that his coach was upset because Wayne's national ranking was determined by the speed with which he dispatched his opponents. Typically, Wayne did not care excessively about such things.

All things end, and that magical, manic summer was no exception. During the ensuing summers between academic years, I worked for a moving company, Merchant's International in Alexandria, Virginia, packing boxes and loading trucks. I worked sixteen- to twenty-hour days, carrying dishwashers on my back, occasionally throwing up from the heat and physical demands. Despite this grind, one customer stood out for me. This woman, 5'6" tall with lank shoulder-length dark hair and a face turned roadmap by harsh living, lived in a third-floor walkup, a moving man's nightmare. The day was in the sweltering 90s, and I asked if I could have some water. To my astonishment, she looked at me with dead eyes and said, "No," without nuance or expression. Dumbfounded by her refusal, I exited the apartment and sat down to rest in the shade of the truck. A few minutes later she appeared on the balcony with a pitcher in hand. Waiting until she knew I was watching, she slowly poured water from the pitcher to the ground three stories below. Wow! There was a lady enjoying her day, baking in the acid of her bile. I didn't know this woman and, to my knowledge, I hadn't done anything to upset her—that's what made the whole thing so crazy.

It got me wondering. Why would this lady do this to a complete stranger who had done her no harm? What I came up with is that some people some of the time can feel so small or are so angry at the world that they have a need to try to make others feel the same. I don't throw stones here; I live too much in a glass house of my own. Had I not done something similar years earlier when I had tattled on the little girl who had peed her pants? But, of course, that was typical childhood cruelty, where an adult had done this: that's a league of its own.

Reconciling such events and holding myself accountable for my behaviors, even if I didn't change them, was an important part of who I was and of who I was becoming. Now, I was beginning to understand that to truly relate to another I had to find myself in them and them in me.

CHAPTER 10

LOTTERY

"Three-one-six, Three-one-six." The number rang in my head like an auctioneer's chant. "Going once, going twice, sold!" I felt like dancing. James Brown's voice sang in my mind, "Watch me now!" as I did several tight spins, then broke out into Little Eva's version of "The Locomotive," followed by Chubby Checker's "The Twist," and finished it all off with Elvis the Pelvis' thrusts... at least in my heart.

The date: December 1, 1969, just one month and twelve days before my twentieth birthday. I had just won the lottery. No, not the Million Dollar lottery. No Siree, the Lottery of Life. The selective service had just conducted a lottery to draft men for the Vietnam war. My birthday was the 316th number drawn, which meant Uncle Sam would draft almost eighty-seven percent of eligible men into the armed services, a virtual emptying of America before He turned his baleful stare in my direction. My conclusion: I had just escaped the Vietnam War.

There was just one small glitch: I was enrolled in the Reserved Officers Training Course (ROTC), and that obligated me to join the Army upon graduation from college. I had joined ROTC because as a single male I was likely to be drafted at any time, and

I thought I would prefer going in as an officer rather than as an enlisted man. Furthermore, a ROTC scholarship helped me pay for college, an important consideration given that aside from $1500 my mother had donated from her hard-earned wages as a secretary, I wasn't receiving any help from my parents. Dad begrudged me even this as if the money was coming out of his pocket. But he didn't have a choice about it. On this, my mother stood firm. She had earned the money; it was up to me to fund the rest. So, in addition to working summers at the moving company, I enrolled in ROTC. But now with the number three-one-six, there was a new calculus in play. Consequently, I explored my options and discovered that I could void my ROTC contract if I quit school, so that's what I did.

You can imagine how pleased this made The Colonel, but I didn't care. I was almost twenty years old, paying my way largely out of pocket and making my own decisions. Given his lack of support, he didn't get a say. Then there was the Army captain in charge of the ROTC program. I can still hear Richie Havens singing "Freedom" in my mind as I refused to succumb to his up-in-my face, spittle-laden tirade upon hearing my decision to leave the program. He shouted, "You're not officer material anyway!" All the while I'm thinking, "If that's the case, why are you so angry?"

Upon leaving Loyola, I immediately re-enrolled, but this time in night school. Amazingly, this shell game was acceptable. In night school I learned an eye-opening lesson: it doesn't matter where you go to school as long as you want to learn. And I learned so well that the professor of economics asked me to teach the class. He had a schedule conflict and wanted me to cover for him. I was flattered. My night school classmates were all significantly older, with families and full-time jobs in the business world. I knew nothing of the business world. Fortunately, he arrived early enough that night to save me from what was rapidly becoming a humiliating experience. While presenting to the class I discovered something that I hadn't known—you don't know something if you can't explain it, and until you try to explain it, you can't know what you don't know. While trying to explain various economic concepts, I stumbled upon gaps in my knowledge that I hadn't known were there, effectively paralyzing my capacity to teach. Years later, I was to apply this lesson to psychotherapy, asking patients to explain their thoughts or feelings to me. In so doing, the patient would become aware of the holes or incongruities in his thinking, thereby enlightening himself in the process of educating me.

After one semester in night school, I re-enrolled in day school because it had the prestige that would count in my applying for jobs. It was at this point that a beautiful thing happened. I met Tom Beauchamp, who became a lifelong friend. His brother Randy introduced us and proposed that we room together. Randy felt I would be a stabilizing influence on Tom: Obviously, Randy possessed a keenness of perception.

Tom and I lived together off campus for a couple of years and had our own adventures. He attended Towson State, located a few miles away. One very early morning, lacking a TV in our apartment, Tom and I slipped into the Towson dorm to liberate the TV in the community room. In near absolute darkness, we Pink Panthered on tiptoe over to the TV only to discover it secured with a chain—apparently, others had performed this dastardly deed in the past. As I was intently fumbling with the chain, Tom was looking around. I then heard him whisper from ten feet away, "Charlie." Barely able to discern him in the dark, I whispered back, "What?" He said something inaudible, and once more I whispered, this time with greater intensity, "What?!" Then I heard muffled laughter. My curiosity aroused, I gave up on the chain and moved towards Tom to see what was going on. I again whispered, "What is it?" Choking back fits of muted hilarity, he whispered back, "There's a guy asleep over here." I drew closer to confirm that there was indeed a guy curled up and sleeping on a couch. I didn't know what was so funny about this. Maybe it was all the tension, fueled by the risk of getting caught, or the image of us sneaking around on tiptoes for the last few minutes, all the while not noticing a guy ten feet away. Whatever the reason, the ridiculousness of the situation overcame us. Laughter welled up, the need to laugh only made worse by my every effort to stifle it. We snickered and snorted our way to the exit, barely making it out before our bodies were wracked by paroxysms of laughter, tears streaming down our faces. We returned the following night and, after first checking for sleeping people, completed the deed.

As crazy as this may sound, this was a time when I started to own my life. I now understood that what was important was not whether the decisions were good or not, but that I made them and accepted responsibility for them. Even stealing the TV from Towson fell into this category. If I was willing to do the crime, I was prepared to do the time—at least the sort of punishment a white, middle-class college boy would be likely to receive. I wouldn't complain or blame it on fate.

At the same time, despite a growing number of successes, I still felt like I couldn't quite make the grade. In the previous five years, I had barely made it out of high school, gotten myself kicked out of college, been fired from several jobs, rode the bench on the soccer team, tried unsuccessfully to teach a class in economics, and missed membership in the honor society. Although I had made much progress academically, I still hadn't arrived.

What was my standard for success? Jacques. He was graduating from the University of Virginia with an A average and as the president of his class. Upon graduation, he had been sought after, wined and dined by the most prestigious accounting firms, who paid for him to come to interview with them in Atlanta. He landed a well-paying position with one of the Big Eight companies. I was proud of him, knowing that I fell far short in comparison. But that was the story of my life. That was the way it had always been, and I secretly believed that that was the way it would always be. Without knowing it, I was doing my best to stick with this story line, and it was sticking with me.

CHAPTER 11

STUMBLING INTO THE WORLD

U pon graduation from college, I began looking for work. Meanwhile, Killer Kirgel, in his irritatingly understated way, managed to make it into the *Washington Post* and on National TV: not once, but twice. He accomplished this feat on no less a show than that of the iconic Walter Cronkite, by far the most famous broadcaster of the time. Wayne managed this by turkey-nabbing the National Turkey from the National Zoo, leaving behind a note identifying the kidnappers as The Filthy Five, along with a demand for $250,000 on behalf of the American Indian. That evening, Mr. Cronkite noted the turkey-nabbing at the end of his broadcast, followed by his signature sign-off, "And that's the way it is." The following day Wayne ran into an animal shelter and dropped the turkey off unharmed with a note. The note said he was returning the turkey because it was in the turkey's best interest. That night, Mr. Cronkite bemusedly mentioned this event as well, again during his signature sign off.

While Wayne was making the national news, I was in quest of employment. I visited Atlanta, where Jacques lived. I had none of Jacques' polish, nor his air of confidence. Feeling very much 'the country bumpkin,' I came nowhere close to landing a job. Tail between my legs, I returned to Merchant's International Moving Company. But this time, my job was to run their import/export desk, arranging for the shipment of goods around the world.

In this capacity, several shipping companies invited me to Baltimore vying for cargo. Three sales guys took me out to dinner at the Playboy Club, and then to a strip joint on the infamous Block. While we were at the Playboy Club, one guy went to the bathroom just before the bill arrived. I would not have noticed except the others commented with disgust on the timing of the event. I thought *Wow, sleazy.*

At the strip club, even more sleaze: all the men were solicited for oral sex and accepted. I might have accepted as well except I didn't have any money. Also, I'm not at all confident that my Catholic guilt and discomfort with the whole situation would not have gotten in the way. In any event, I politely declined the woman's offer. She, probably old enough to be my mother, responded, "I didn't think so, but I thought I'd ask." I imagined she detected the straw poking out of my young ears.

In the car after leaving the club, someone produced a joint, and shortly after that, internal filters down, I tried to make a deeper connection with these guys. In doing so, I managed to suck the air out of the evening. Apparently asking whether or not they liked their jobs was not the way to go, specifically when it turned out that they hated them. I then compounded the problem by wondering how it felt to have oral sex with one woman while married to another. I wasn't moralistic; I was naïve, genuinely curious as to how one navigated those rocky shoals. I was being the worse kind of idiot, the kind that does not know he is an idiot until it's too late.

That night, drunk and stoned, I stayed over at one guy's house and awoke the next morning to a family breakfast. I met the guy's classically beautiful and warmly welcoming wife, and two delightful, elementary-school-aged daughters. While breakfasting with them, I kept thinking *Why?* and wondered about the forces that drive us, about the secrets we keep, the disconnections below the surface and the difference between how things look and how things are.

Similar human dramas were being played out at the moving company. The manager, blustering, fat, married, and a Mason was banging one of the secretaries. She, a full-figured Hispanic woman, strutted around the office in stiletto heels, short black skirts and tight white blouses with buttons straining to hold in her considerable charms while arrogantly treating everyone else as if they were the help. It was both absurd and tragic, as she blatantly enjoyed her moments of fleeting power on this smallest of stages.

This was a time when I also was being tossed about by my primitive impulses; in fact, they were driving me crazy. I was using Ed's Honda 450 motorcycle for transportation and my dad's Pontiac GTO whenever I could. I discovered that youth, hormones, and powerful vehicles were dangerous combinations, especially when combined with sexy women.

One Friday evening I was leaving work, amped about having the weekend off. I got on the 450 and turned the ignition. *Varoom!* The vibration of the Honda tingled my groin, rumbled its way up my spine, and exploded in my crocodile brain. *Varoom!* Revving the engine, kicking that sucker into gear, popping the clutch, I screeched away. Feeling great, thinking song fragments to myself *Get back, Jack; I'm the King of the Road.*

Mist had been falling throughout the day, casting an oily sheen atop the asphalt road, the detritus of countless moving trucks over the decades. A car pulled out of an alley seventy-five yards ahead. *Plenty of time to slow down while the driver speeds up* I thought. But, amazingly, she didn't. Instead, she stopped in the middle of the road. *Jesus, she's fooling with her makeup. Unbelievable.* It was already too late.

Brakes locked tight, hydroplaning like a speedboat across the oil-slathered tarmac, my first thought was *Oh shit*, which then crazily transformed into the lyric, *"Slip sliding away,"* then converted into the *"Going, going. Gone!"* of an auctioneer's chant, the last *"Gone"* punctuated by the sound of bike meeting car: *Crunch!*

Lying supine on the wet road, looking up as mist falls on my face, I struggled to push the bike off, trying to avoid the burning hot engine and exhaust pipe. As I lay there gasping, a concerned Asian female face, in crazily upside down relationship with mine, framed by long straight dark hair, appeared above me, backlit by the overcast sky. As I looked at this apparition, she leaned down as if to get a better view, her face a picture of concern, almond eyes worried, and said, in a singsong voice, "Hello. My name's Sunshine."

Perhaps because of the absurd juxtaposition of her name immediately following the relatively terrifying event that had just broken my motorcycle and left me lying crumpled on the wet ground laughter bubbled up in me. However, I made a manly effort to stifle it as erotic possibilities whizzed through my mind. *Varoom!* I replied, "You're certainly the Sunshine in my life." Somehow this shining witticism fell short of either evoking a smile or getting her phone number.

The following week, having grieved apocalyptically the loss of my never-was and never-to-be relationship with Sunshine, much less the loss of the Honda 450 to the repair shop, I stood before the next new-and-true love of my life. I had seen her many times. She was perfect: sleek and curvy, skin unblemished and glistening, with a throaty voice that rendered me weak-kneed. She was the embodiment of power and confidence. I hungered to be inside of her, to claim her as my own, all the while fearing: *Am I up to the task? Can I push her limits without exceeding mine, resulting in a devastating and humiliating loss of control?* Well, time to find out. *Varoom!*

She was my dad's midlife car: a shiny dark blue Pontiac GTO with white racing stripes, hood manifold, front and rear stabilizer bars, roll bar, and a Hurst four-on-the-floor stick shift. Her engine, crowned by three deuce carburetors, generated 360 horsepower. Given my previous week's encounter with Sunshine and the resultant lack of a ride to work, Dad let me borrow her. As I left that morning, he called out, "Ignore the oil gauge. It's broken."

Throughout the day, I looked forward to getting together with another new-and-true love of my life with whom I had a date that evening. This love was also built for speed, and indeed, we had already been around the track several times together. She was sleek, blond, and blue-eyed, pure sex poured into head-turning outfits: completely out of my league. She was used to dating suits on Capitol Hill, who knew how to order wine. I didn't know why she was hanging with me; I just hoped she wouldn't ask herself that question anytime soon. *Varoom!*

That evening, enjoying titillating fantasies as I drove the Washington beltway in a light rain on the way to her house, I felt the GTO falter. It was a fleeting sensation and so threatening to my evening's plans that I passed it off immediately as only my imagination. All the while another part of my brain was imploring, *Oh God! Not now! Not* this *night.* The engine stuttered again in response. I prayed more fervently, *Please, God. Be the kind, compassionate, change-water-to-wine, party-down, New Testament God. Let the car hold together long enough to get me there.*

Deciding to cover my bases, I also went secular. I reasoned: the oil gauge was bottomed out, but Dad told me it wasn't working—ergo, it couldn't be the oil. Despite such faultless logic, the car faltered again, basically replying, "Hey, idiot, it *is* the oil." My lust-driven brain could not bear this thought, for it would be the end of my erotic aspirations. Face scrunched up in concentration, hands death-gripping the steering wheel, I fiercely attempt to hold the car together by sheer force of will. *Bang!* I coast to the side of the highway.

Although sick at heart about the car, my carnal desires continue to rule. I quickly reasoned that I couldn't do anything about the car at this hour, but I *could* salvage the evening. I stepped into the rain and stuck my thumb out. Two hours later, nerves stressed to the max, wet and smelly, having basted in a marinade of misty rain and carbon monoxide winds from thousands of passing cars, I arrived at her townhouse. She opened the door, red lips spread wide in greeting. Her bright white smile told me it had all been worthwhile; visions of sugarplums danced in my head. Well, okay, maybe they weren't plums. *Varoom!*

Tragically, this euphoric state vanished as I looked over her shoulder to spy a guy sitting on the living room couch. *Plop!* What was this? My fevered hopes for the evening, repeatedly splinted and propped up against all the odds, could take no more. I slouched on the couch, accepted a beer, and tried my best to affect nonchalance. My rival pulled out a joint. Soon, glasses slipping askew down my wet nose, I was inert, unable to move or speak, while acutely aware through glazed eyes that my new true love and my rival were chatting animatedly and completely ignoring me. I sat slack-jawed, inwardly suffering a rending agony of humiliation and shame as she moved on from me without ever saying a thing. My last thought *I wonder if I'm drooling?* as my head lolled to one side and my mind faded to black. *Varoom. Crash. Bang. Plop!*

Of course, take this jokey rendering of the tale and turn it upside down and you'll appreciate how eviscerated and heartbroken I felt that evening—as if someone had reached into my chest and squeezed the life out of me, thus my need to defend against it. Nonetheless, that incident represented the story of my love life. Not that I didn't have successes. I did; in fact, many. But the successes were due more to persistence than to charm. All I can say is, "Thank God for persistence."

Meanwhile, back at work, the manager kept stringing me along with promises of salary increases that always seemed to remain just over the next horizon. Accepting this long-denied reality, I quit Merchants International. In its stead, I accepted a three-month contract as an accounting technician for the Department of Defense (DOD): Moving on up!

My workplace at the DOD was a cavernous room filled with row upon row of desks. Each morning, as I enter, I marvel inwardly at the wooden faces of my co-workers, blanched by the harsh fluorescent light, lacking any sign of spirit or playfulness. These people, not unlike the salesmen in Baltimore, were resigned to their fates and their jobs as necessary evils. They were so inanimate that I secretly questioned whether they went home at night or remained frozen in place at their desks until someone came along, took pity, and dusted them off to begin another day just like yesterday.

Almost certainly their lack of liveliness could be understood by the work we did. Every morning what awaited me at my desk was a two-foot-high ream of computer paper, laden with two columns of very long numbers. My mission, if I chose to accept it, was to ensure that the figures in the right column matched the ones in the left. If not, I was to circle the offending digits. I had no idea what these numbers represented.

I learned fast. I became proficient at running a ruler down the pages looking for any hint of deviance, like a sheriff on the prowl. Finished after a few hours, I would pick up a book, such as D.T. Suzuki's *Zen and Japanese Buddhism*, and begin reading. Some weeks into my job the supervisor stopped by my desk as I was reading and asked: "What are you doing?" I thought it obvious, so the question confused me. He elaborated, "Why aren't you working?" "Oh!" I exclaimed, now understanding his interest, "I've finished." Then helpfully added, "If you have more for me to do, I'll be glad to do it." Vexed, he said, "I don't have more for you to do, but you can't read a book; you have to look busy."

I thought about this for several moments—he obviously hadn't got the memo about my intolerance of boredom—then responded truthfully, "I'm sorry, I can't do that, that's too hard. If you have more work for me to do, I'll gladly do it, but I can't do 'looking busy.'" He appraised me silently, trying to discern whether I was disrespectful. Finally, my eyes steady upon him, he correctly concluded that I was neither rude or insincere. He grunted and left without another word.

More weeks passed, and my contract was nearing its end. My supervisor approached my desk once again and said, "We would like you to enter our fast-track management program." He explained this entailed receiving intensive management training over six months and then being squeezed out the other end of the process as a GS-9. I would get a substantial pay increase and more challenging responsibilities. I was surprised and appreciative, even excited, thinking, *This is a real opportunity, the possible beginning of a career. I, too, can be legitimate. I, too, can be respectable. Take that, Jacques!* But, as my brain is wont to do, as one side of my mind was thinking these thoughts, another was looking around the room. And what did I see but these timeworn people, doing their jobs day in and day out, without joy or fire in them. I then understood staying would bleed me dry, as it had done them, and would not fit with some ill-defined need or image I had of myself. I expressed sincere appreciation for the offer and crazily, given that I had no other job opportunities at hand, declined it. Two weeks later, contract expired, I was unemployed.

But I was not alone. I had met Jane at a friend of mine's girlfriend's apartment in Washington, D.C. She was petite, had an excellent figure, pretty face, and a quiet and gentle personality. I was immediately attracted and hopeful that something would come of this meeting. I felt fortunate that we hit it off right away with the help of the girlfriend, Irene, who seemed interested in using me to help Jane separate from a previous boyfriend. The latter arrived later that night, banging on the door demanding admittance. Jane sent him away. I wasn't complaining. I was hopeful about developing a relationship with her. From that moment on, we were like gummy bears, glomming onto one another. I was happy as could be. We moved in together within three weeks and had been together for about six months when I entered the newfound freedom of the recently unemployed.

I decided to do something that virtually everyone was against. Though I could appreciate that my decision would do little in the way of career advancement, what they couldn't understand was that I didn't feel like I had an option. I felt driven by my heart, not my head. I was in search of something without knowing what that something was. I just *knew* I would know it when I found it.

Jane and I cashed out our bank accounts, paid the penalty for breaking the apartment lease, packed up my VW Beetle with tent and supplies, and drove out of town without a backward glance or any destination in mind. My plan—yes, by golly, I had one: Go until the cash runs out; go for broke.

I felt good. I was making my decisions, right or wrong. I knew I was drawing outside the lines and had no idea what form if any, my scribbles would take. What I did know was that I had to follow my heart. The trick was figuring out where it lay.

CHAPTER 12

ESCAPING

I carried a pistol. Great idea, right? Everybody needs a gun. Don't we all need to protect ourselves? There must be hordes of people, so many that I must know some personally, who have needed a gun within the last five years or so to protect themselves. Let me list them: Ummmm. I can't think of a single one. I think harder. I extend the time frame. Ten years, twenty years, thirty years, a lifetime. I don't personally know anyone who has ever needed a gun to protect himself unless you count war. Yet, people are so afraid. The whole headline grabbing, "If it bleeds, it leads," strategy worming angst into our souls. Still, everyone had been worried about our safety, including Dad. He insisted I take his .38 revolver. I secretly suspected he's hoping there will be some kind of gunfight at the OK Corral, another story he could tell, this time about his brave, now dead, son. I wondered if *that* newspaper article would be worthy of lamination.

Soon enough Jane and I have camped alone on a hillside outside of Atlanta, Ga. In the middle of the night, awakened by the arrival of a group of rowdy, drunken guys, I discover that the decision to bring a gun provided troubling options. My mind started whirring. *What if these guys in their drunken state decided to cause trouble? Jane was attractive and the only female around; there was only one of me. Okay, I had the answer: I'd shoot the bastards. But under what circumstances would I do that? Someone telling a risqué joke? Someone's threatening talk or posturing? Or would it have to escalate to the laying on of hands? Then there were the questions, Where should I keep the gun so I could get to it easily? And of course: if I pulled the gun, must I use it or can I bluff? I decide I had to be ready to use it. Otherwise, they could take it from me. Then we would be in real trouble.*

I recognized that my brain had immediately moved to considering the when and how of using the gun, strangely forgetting that I had other options, such as my wits. In thinking about the weapon, I'd gone from one to one hundred in a heartbeat; I was feeling the whiplash. I didn't like it. What had seemed like an easy enough decision in the light of day was proving difficult to sort out in the dark. Here fear was magnified as sound traveled great distances and giant shadows were cast long by the yellow beams of truck headlights bouncing erratically along the uneven terrain, the comings and goings fueling the boil of anxiety. The stress, noise, and fatigue only blurred the lines and amplified my uncertainty. The chance of making life-ruining mistakes very real.

Fortunately, I never had to answer those questions. But I decided to put the gun out of sight and mind as best I could. The way of the gun, as much as I had played Wyatt Earp in childhood, was not the way for me: it complicated rather than simplified. I could only think of using it if I was already in the shit, not in fear of it, and then I would use my wits to find a way to get to it. With that decision, I hung up my gun forever, and a legend was never born.

We drove to New Orleans. It was miserable, raining for five days and nights. Clothes and tent soaked through, we gave up on the idea of waiting out the storm and pushed on toward Texas, driving until we hit sunshine.

We stood on the beach in Corpus Christi, basking in the sun and the buffeting warm wind. Camping nearby, we met a couple from Pennsylvania and decided to cross the border into Mexico together the next morning. I explained the gun. They offered to hide it in the panel of their van, hanging from a string. Strangely, this offer does not reassure me. What it made me realize was that these people were as crazy as me.

That afternoon, I met an old man. He had just returned from fishing and was cleaning the fish at his picnic table. He explained he was a "snowbird," traveling south each winter to escape the northern cold. As he established a comfortable rhythm scaling the fish, he told his stories as old men are given to do. I found it hypnotically soothing and transporting as he spoke slowly, his aged voice sounding like the rustling of dry leaves. In the telling, he remarked that of all the things he had learned in life the most important had been that ninety-eight percent of whatever he had worried about had never come to pass. I left him behind that day, but never his words. They stuck with me, and they come to mind whenever I find myself mindlessly worrying about *things*.

The next morning, we drove across the border into Mexico, like everyone concerned about the dangers. We had heard the stories. The tales of corruption, the police who would plant drugs and the gun-toting soldiers who would coerce money. We had heard of the drug dealers who would kill you and of the locals who would slide under your car when you stopped at a light, cut your fuel line, and later come along to *fix* your car at an exorbitant price. Upon crossing the border, the couple with the van grew nervous and opted out of going further south. They did, however, agree to keep the gun until I could visit them at their home in Pennsylvania.

Jane and I soon discovered the stories were partly true. There were police, gun-toting soldiers, and machete-bearing peasants walking to and from who knew where given the miles and miles in which no buildings were in sight. Perhaps they were going to set an ambush along desolate landscapes. There were banks within which armored pillboxes stood with gun barrels protruding through the slits as if waiting for a return of Butch Cassidy and the Sundance Kid. But our experience was fantastic. The people warm and friendly, and we were never bothered by anyone. That is with one exception, and that may have been brought about by my fears. Over the years, I would discover that fear summons psychological defenses that often bring about exactly that which was being defended against.

During our journey, we would travel miles across flat, arid landscapes, plateaus sometimes appearing in the distance, but no towns or villages in sight. Jane and I wondered together about where the occasional person walking alongside the road, machete on shoulder, could be going. Then, an hour later, the road would meander between unusual geological formations, plateaus replaced by a series of tall, treeless, pointed hills, each standing apart from the others, upon which a single wooden shack would rest on high, like a wooden nipple. We were delighted and intrigued by a landscape new to both of us, and a way of life only hinted at. For several days, we stayed at a small fishing village near Tuxpan, Mexico, and camped in a grove of coconut trees just off the beach. We swam in the Gulf of Mexico, and for a peso, small boys would climb the trees and bring us fresh coconuts.

One evening, we dined with a couple of commercial deep-sea divers, tough-looking young men who repeatedly eyed Jane as if she were on the menu and gave off a bad vibe, but otherwise did nothing wrong. We would sleep late into the morning in our tent and then go touring on foot. We would engage in conversations with the fishermen, rife with laughter and powered by sign language, sometimes to comedic proportions. Here I was informed that shark blood was the fountain of youth and offered a pull from a plastic bottle. I couldn't do it; I declined as they laughed and guzzled it down.

In another small town, just off the dirt road that was its main street, we inadvertently stayed in a hotel that doubled as a brothel, making this realization only after the night's activities had begun. It was a noisy, sleepless night, as Mexican music and laughter echoed off the plaster walls, and especially after seeing the dark silhouette of a man spying in through our bedroom window; He ran when I called out.

At some point along our travels, I arranged to buy marijuana and left with a couple of guys for several hours one evening to obtain it. I had not been thoughtful of Jane and the fear she would be feeling in my absence. She was furious when I returned. I could not blame her, but in my youthful obliviousness, I minimized her concerns.

We kept traveling farther and farther south. On the way, we encountered our trouble. In a small town, I turned the wrong direction on a narrow one-way alley of a street, failing to notice the little faded blue arrow painted on the wall of an old building that was pointing the other way. A young police officer standing nearby motioned for me to stop. I could not understand a word he said, but he made known through gestures and by pointing to the arrow the nature of my mistake. He then crouched down and began removing my license plate, triggering fears fueled by all the stories of extortion, incarceration, and ransom.

My head began to spin as an electric current traveled from my brain to my bowels. Rational thought became difficult, the instinct for survival taking over, only intensifying as I told myself, *I cannot let this happen. The longer I wait to do something, the farther down the road to being trapped Jane and I will be. Without the license plates, we will be stranded. Helpless.*

I ask sharply, "What are you doing?" But he didn't understand me, and I couldn't understand him. I kept saying, "No, leave the license plate alone," my voice rising with each utterance while emphasizing each word as if that would help him understand. But he just kept at it, ignoring me. Becoming more frantic I gently pushed him and demanded in a loud voice, "El Capitan? El Capitan?" I didn't know where I got that from, probably too many late-night cowboy movies, but I didn't care. I kept shouting, wanting to attract the attention of people nearby.

I was interrupted by a shout from behind and turned to see a middle-aged, heavyset police officer in the distance, what appeared to be a commandant's hat upon his head. The younger cop angrily pointed to the older, gesturing for me to go to him. I asked, "El Capitan?" He irately responded, "Si. Si."

As I approached El Capitan, the alley opened into the town square, dotted with park benches, and people taking in the late morning sun filtering through the trees. The claustrophobic feeling of being trapped, so pronounced in that shadowed alley of a street, began to recede as I entered this tranquil, sunlit atmosphere. A sense of liberation came over me, and once again I could breathe and think.

My concern with being held for ransom and the antagonism between Mexico and the United States very much in mind, as I walked toward El Capitan, I decided being a Gringo was not in my best interest. Accordingly, as I neared him, I called out in my rusty French, "Parlais vous Francais?" He beamed in response, thankfully saying "No" and, in his broken English, asked me if I was French. I responded, "Non. Non. Je suis Canadian Francais," never considering that he could easily check my driver's license. He responded enthusiastically and in a few minutes' conversation concluded that I had hired his cousin as a guide in the last town. After we spoke for several more minutes, El Capitan amicably, through words and gestures, indicated I was free to leave, calmly waving aside the angry protests of the young police officer.

The latter, furious, spit words at me—something derogatory about Americans—as I got in the car. For my part, I was willing my rubbery legs to work the clutch well enough to put the car in gear and make my escape. All I wanted was to get the hell out of there. The nightmares of my inner world had rubbed against the nightmarish possibilities that exist in the external one, and I had escaped without harm, but the warning was heard: be careful!

Finally, the landscape becoming ever more lush, turned to jungle as we arrived at the Yucatan, eventually winding up at the Inca Pyramids. There we took tours and climbed the steep structures in the heat and humidity. We had a good time, marked by lots of laughter and love-making, and full of interesting sights and historical teachings. Nonetheless, after several days, the novel became routine, and enough was enough. We turned our sights north once again, deciding to travel through the center of the country on our way to Mexico City.

During this stage of the trek, we discovered that Mexicans made great soup and that soup had the further benefit of being simmered, thus helping to guard against illness. The staff at the casual restaurants were gracious and welcoming, curious as to our culture as we were to theirs, and laughed along with us at our often-failed attempts to communicate with one another as we each took turns gesturing like mimes.

Despite the richness of these experiences, the nomadic life was beginning to take a toll. The new and novel was becoming ever less new and novel. One of those people who is a reader, almost never going anywhere without a book, I returned to spending more hours of the day reading. This time it was the works of Carlos Castaneda, whose stories were set in the actual terrain in which we were traveling. As he was recounting his shamanistic journeys, often under the hallucinatory influence of mushrooms, I was in some way living mine, moving along the same scorched landscapes and staring up at the same starry nights.

I then stumbled upon the works of Joseph Chilton Pierce who, like Castaneda, also challenged the assumed order of reality and the nature of the extraordinary. Such readings stimulated my imagination and filled the surrounding landscape with wonder and enchantment. Such writings got me thinking and stirred me with the feeling that I *could* live a life beyond that in service to what often felt to me like an over-constricting reality. They expanded and reinforced my love of religion and philosophy, the power of spirituality, and the importance of living a creative and perhaps sometimes even inspired life. I could begin to see where the possibility of new realities could be creatively perceived and even brought into being. Years later I would discover this concept, or a version of it, had a name: *creative apperception.*

As we neared Mexico City, the VW broke down. There Jane and I stood, stranded on the side of a narrow, paved road that wound up a hill, on the outskirts of town. As we were discussing what to do, a car pulled in, and a thin Mexican man in his forties, with short-cropped brown hair, just beginning to gray, got out and, speaking fluent English, approached. His name was Juan. Juan and I hit it off right away. As we chatted, he revealed he had a PhD. in psychology. Over the years his work had become far more administrative than clinical, and he had tired of it, given up his practice and started a business servicing Volkswagens at peoples' homes. I was impressed with Juan. He was such a gentle soul and intelligent man, and he had had the courage to forsake his career to follow his heart. Juan proposed that we stay at his ranchero while he fixed the car. We were happy to accept.

His one-story ranchero was situated alone in the middle of a vast field that went on as far as the eye could see. In the waning light of evening, an archetypal sight would unfold. Women of all ages, faintly backlit by the failing sun, wrapped in dark cloth, with shawls covering their heads, moved as shadows, in isolated groupings of ones and twos, across the fields toward a farming village in the distance, disappearing as silently as ghosts as the last light of the sun winked out. Where they had come from, I have no idea. It was a scene that could have taken place two hundred or a thousand years earlier. There was nothing around to indicate modernity.

After dinner, Juan and I smoked cigarettes, drank tequila, and shared stories. He told me of the troubles in his country. Five hundred students had been massacred several years earlier in Mexico City. He noted that, given the tyranny of the government, the crime had never become international news. As our time together neared its end, Juan asked if I might have a gun he could have. I assured him I did not, and, instead, gave him a strobe light used to tune my VW's engine. He was happy with the gift.

By the end of the third day, we were ready to leave. Not only was the car fixed, but I could no longer tolerate being in the house when Juan's wife was cooking. It had nothing to do with her. She had been welcoming but, not an English speaker, less inclined to the struggles of attempted conversation. The problem was the peppers. Everything was festooned with hot peppers from the garden: breakfast, lunch, and dinner. By the third morning, the pepper-infused air created by the high temperature of cooking sickened me. I had always thought I loved spicy-hot food. I had believed I knew what spicy-hot food was. In Mexico, hot ratcheted up to a whole other galaxy of meaning.

Upon our return to the US, we were stopped at the border. The customs agent asked if we were related. Jane, typically quiet, chose that moment to pipe up "No," at the same time I was saying, "Yes." With this discrepancy, we were pulled over for inspection.

Here, we were kept apart, made to empty our pockets, turn them inside out, and watch from a distance as they search our car. A busload of tourists arrived and began taking pictures, some using home movie cameras. I could imagine the stories they would tell when they showed the film at home: narco-traffickers apprehended at the border.

As one customs officer emptied the car, another circled it with a drug-sniffing dog. The search was exhaustive: the air filter was taken off, and the manifold inspected. Thirty minutes later, grinning triumphantly, the border guard approached holding a single marijuana seed between his thumb and forefinger. He said, "I knew there was something." He let us go.

That evening, Jane and I became ill, Jane deathly so, with a severe case of Montezuma's revenge. Earlier in the day, we had made the mistake of buying undercooked chicken tacos from a street vendor and were now paying the price. Jane was in excruciating pain and suffered repeated bouts of nausea and diarrhea. I was worried; this part of the US was little different than Mexico—there were no clinics near. We traveled fifty miles, Jane suffering all the way, before finding a clinic where relief was found.

We continue north, across New Mexico and into Colorado, driving the steep hairpin turns through gorges, up mountainsides, and across towering bridges that spanned the chasms of the Million-Dollar Highway. Fall was turning into winter, and the mountains had grown crystalline beards, ice crystals fashioning a sparkling snow globe Alpine Christmas scene. We visited Arizona, passing through the red hills of Sedona, the Juniper trees supposedly twisted by the energy vortexes for which the area is famous. We moved on to the gaping divide of the Grand Canyon, riding a small plane into the Canyon, swooping past towering waterfalls coming directly out of the rock and over herds of wild horses, manes whipping in the air as they stampeded in front of us. We passed through the Painted Desert, its colors coming alive with the morning sun. And then, the Petrified

Forest, its fallen tree trunks, turned to stone, scattered like the ancient pillars of Stonehenge across the desert floor.

Each night we went through our usual routine of setting up the tent. I called out "positions!"—referring to snuggling in our sleeping bags—and invariably got a laugh from Jane. One morning, on the rim of the Black Canyon, we awoke to discover a landscape newly painted by several inches of snow. Its muffling silence lent an unearthly quiet, which only added to the dark and chiseled beauty of the craggy canyon. Finally, we drove across the unending flatlands of Kansas into the rolling hills of Missouri, and then on to the monuments of Washington, D.C., and home.

The trip had lasted almost three months by the calendar, but light years in experiences. We'd been going for broke, and we'd arrived. We weren't sad. We had grown fatigued by the nomadic life. I had learned that everything could become routine, even non-routine. Wanderlust sated and feeling the need for a more personally meaningful goal, I wanted a destination and now, for the first time in my life, had one in heart and mind.

During this trip, the universe had conspired to help me understand the paradox of freedom. I was free to choose among many options but was free only until I did—once committed; I was on a path. By the same token, if I refused to choose, I was also not free—I would be committing to a directionless life. I realized that, at some point, we all commit, whether we want to or not, and that commitment did not have to be a trap. I was happy and excited. I wanted to commit to something, and I had now figured out what that something was.

The trip had been enormously successful. The immediacy of the experiences, never knowing what was around the next bend in the road, seeing everything for the first time and the last, all worked like the ocean waves of long ago, scrubbing away the daily demands and concerns of life while imprinting powerful memories that remain to this day. The journey had provided a play space free from the need to respond to the muddling impact of external pressures. In this space, I could more easily discern the roots of my desire, dare I say ambition, which had always been within me but until now never recognized. It felt like hunger and brought to personal meaning a quote by Blaise Pascal: "Love has reasons that reason cannot understand."

Juan's courage in following his heart had inspired me. Curiously, what I discovered had been in front of me all the time. It was evident not in dramatic moments of enlightenment, but in a growing awareness of the little things—the fibers that made up the fabric of my existence. It was evident in my myriad curiosities that had for so long pulled at me and in the places to which I would naturally go when the demands of the world became too much. It was speaking from my need to make sense of things, whether of two water fountains in a movie theater or of being abandoned by my parents in a foreign land as a little boy. It had called out when I was a freshman at Loyola, loving the study of religion and philosophy, and as a mediocre business guy being taken out on the town by salesmen, asking those ridiculous questions. It was manifested in my continuing attraction to books on philosophy and religion.

During this trip, with the help of Juan, Carlos Castaneda, and Joseph Chilton Pierce, I had come to realize that what I needed wasn't a job; for that, I could have stayed at the DOD. What I needed was a calling, a vocation that sang to my spirit, indulged my need to wonder about life and relationships and was bigger than myself.

The idea of becoming a psychologist seemed the answer. I had never considered that possibility before. The whole idea of psychotherapy was antithetical to the culture of my family. In all my years living at home, words such as psychotherapy or counseling had never been uttered. But the more I thought about it, the more sense it made. As a psychotherapist, I could earn a decent living while pursuing my heart's desires. Thus, I now had a destination in the twisting journey of my life.

In one sense, I was starting completely over; in another, I was finally going to a place I belonged. A shell, almost unseen, had cracked, and I had fallen through to another world: I was going home to a world for which I had always been looking but never known. I was going *home.*

CHAPTER 13

WAYLAID

Night splintered into day. A sense that something was terribly wrong had flared within my chest before consciousness was once again ripped away, and I was propelled into a midnight sleep. When awareness returned, it was in fleeting and fragmented images. Disoriented, confused, I realized I was in a strange vehicle, a succubus clinging to my face, then I was gone again. Cognizance returned. Jane's voice, receding even as she spoke, is saying something about a car accident as I was once again washed away on a frothy sea of unease. Awake yet again, now certain: I was in an ambulance, and an oxygen mask squeezed my face.

I awake on a gurney, white walls passing by, fluorescent lights flickering overhead, nostrils assaulted by the astringent smell of antiseptic. Pushed along by strangers in a hospital hallway, I worried for Jane; was she okay? I must have spoken aloud, for her voice responded from behind, "I'm okay. I just have a fractured wrist." My thought: *just?*

I awake again, now in a large room. A stout, gray-haired man needing a shave was asking, "Do you want to buy some grass?" as he thrust a clump of sod toward me from his adjacent gurney. Unbidden, he explained, "I rolled a tractor over myself."

Now I woke looking up into a circle of faces, none much older than mine. Guys with ponytails. One asking the others, "Who's going to do it?" I'm wondering, "What is *it*?" then notice the long thick needle. Understanding breaks—these guys were residents or interns or whatever you call them, trying to decide who was going to shove that thing into my torso. In growing amazement and dread, I listened to the debate, each pothead squeamishly trying to avoid the task. These superstars of medicine didn't realize I was awake. Irritated, I blurt out, "For God's sake, somebody do it!" not believing that I was actually telling them to shove that thing into me. Embarrassment flitted across their faces, then disapproval—the hard cold quill slid eerily into my body. Fluid pumped in, then pumped out. I inflated, then deflated, reduced to a human balloon, a sack of skin holding fluid and flesh together. The verdict: no internal hemorrhaging.

I resurfaced to yet another debate: "Who's going to hold him [me] up?" They were talking about x-rays, the fear of radiation exposure writ clear upon their faces. They were annoyed with me; I was the guy putting them in this situation. Had I no concern for others? They gruffly commanded me to hold myself up. I would have loved to. But my stomach muscles were in mutiny, refusing to obey the commands shouting from my brain. Finally, one guy, an expression of resigned compassion flitting across his face, grudgingly donned a lead-lined jacket.

I was now in a hospital bed, tired of the shifting kaleidoscope of confounding experiences, each one demanding that I make a new sense of things. A doctor, a real one this time, given his gray hair and professional demeanor, was gently speaking to me. "We are going to hold you overnight for observation, but we think you will be fine."

I awake. It is the middle of the night. I wonder, *what woke me?* Gradually, I realize it's the sensation of filling up again like a balloon. Was it my imagination? I sit with the experience for a while. *I think not. Best mention it to a nurse.*

Minutes later, an aide is shaving my torso from chest to pelvis. *Uh-oh!*

Wheels clickity-clacked and fluorescent lights flash by overhead. An enormous black man in a bulbous green shower cap is pushing me along. It had been explained: I was going for a major laparotomy, exploratory surgery to determine the cause of my hemorrhaging. Dumbly, I note that the descriptor "major" meant it was a big deal.

Not wanting to be alone during this wheel-clacking journey, I look up into the attendant's face and say, "Wow, this reminds me of a scene from General Hospital." He is unresponsive, staring straight ahead, his face made of stone—I was just a package to be delivered. Then he spoke, his baritone voice resonating in the hallway, like a B-movie rendition of God's voice, "Yeah, man. But this is for *real*." During this brief interchange, he never looked at me. He didn't say another word. He just relentlessly trudged on, pushing me down the hall and toward my fate. My chest tightened. I felt terribly alone. I didn't know anyone here, and no one here knew *me*.

In the midst of this cheerless realization, an amazing thought occurred to me. A bit of a showstopper: *I could be dead soon.* Paradoxically, having voiced this thought to myself, my anxiety ebbed. I wondered, why would this be? I supposed it was because whatever was about to happen was completely out of my control. I could fight it, or flow with it—flowing seemed wiser.

As this unforeseen calm encompassed me, I was struck by two thoughts and one observation: *I may be dead soon, and if so, I will soon know the answer to The Big Question: what, if anything, follows death?* My single observation was that I was a *strange* guy: who else would be having such a thought at a time like this? Who else would be genuinely curious to see what comes next?

That weekend, I was waylaid. It was October 22, 1972, and I was age twenty-three, on the way to visit my parents in Charlottesville, VA, with Jane. I was napping in the passenger seat of our trusty Volkswagen Beetle and Jane, as was her way, was white-knuckling the steering wheel while following what for her was the Eleventh Commandment: Thou shalt never exceed fifty-five miles per hour. All was well until she T-boned a much larger car that pulled out in front of her without warning. She felt guilty, confessing that she froze and never used the brakes. From 55 mph to zero in a second—a hard stop in anybody's language—and I had not been wearing my seatbelt.

Exploratory surgery revealed a fractured spleen. Fortunately, adults don't need a spleen. What wasn't discovered was that a blood vessel to a kidney was also damaged. That kidney would atrophy—a fact undiscovered until some twenty-five years later.

Post-surgery was when all the fun really began: the most painful experience of my life, at least on the physical plane. I was split open like a frog in high school biology class, the incision held together by almost two hundred stitches, the outermost layer comprised of strong thread encased in plastic tubing. As my body swelled from the surgery and during the to and fro process of healing, the ungiving stitches cut into my flesh. The large, round tubing provided some protection, dulling the thread's ability to cut, but even the tubing couldn't follow the thread where it entered my body, and that was where the cutting and pain occurred. The most painful part was when I laughed; then the thread tore into my flesh, turned humor into agony, and tears of laughter into beads of blood. None of this was a laughing matter.

To make matters worse, mucus was gathering in my lungs, making pneumonia a growing concern. In the attempt to loosen the phlegm, the nursing staff pounded my back twice a day. They seemed unaware of the fact that opposite my back was my ruptured stomach. You know, the one that had just been cut in half, and now was only held together by threads that cut into me anytime my stomach moved. During these thumpings, I clasped a pillow to my front, in an attempt to keep my stomach together. I was certain that my stomach was in danger of breaking open, the physical sensation so real that one day I adamantly refused the thumping. I just *knew* I was going to split apart and begged them not to do it, explaining why. They held a conference, called the doctor, and agreed to delay the beating that morning.

Despite their tender ministrations, pneumonia had its way. That evening, extra morphine coursing through my body, I entered the blissful world of Morpheus, a warm and wondrous place amongst cotton clouds so soft that I felt assured everything would be okay. That feeling was torn from me as they forced a tube down my *throat* and into my lungs to suction them out. I gagged and choked as the guitar strings tight along my stomach screeched their terrible tune.

Now, as I lay in my hospital bed, I lived in dread of the nursing staff and their *helpful* efforts, their infinitely creative capacity for torture. I lay minute after minute, day after endless day, unmoving, on my back, in pain, wondering how long it would go on and how could I possibly endure? Only in living through it did I discover the answer which was: *however long it takes*—I had no say in the matter. Time took on another dimension; I had found *forever*.

During the days, my family visited. Everyone was there. Mom and Dad, Mark and Michelle; even Jacques and Ed had flown in from Atlanta. Dad had told them I might not make it. After a visit, Dad snuck back into the room: "Charlie, I can see you are in a lot of pain. You can't hide it from me. But you never complain; I'm proud of you."

Jesus, does he always have to make it about him?

Several days later, Mark and Michelle visited. They told me Jane had returned to Baltimore after being berated by Mutti for having sex before marriage. I was furious. What a way to treat your son's girlfriend while she was dependent upon you for safe haven as a guest in your home. What a terrible thing to do to a gentle and kind person like Jane. I was enraged. Fuck them! They had fucked with the wrong guy.

I called Jane and asked her to get me. I was scheduled for discharge in a few days, so I wasn't too worried about leaving. All I knew was that I needed to be gone before my parents visited again: *payback.* I left the hospital against medical advice but armed with a prescription for Percodan. Thank god for that. Pain-wise, I was nowhere near out of the woods.

I would not see nor talk to my parents for six months and only then to invite them to our wedding, which they begrudgingly attended. They give me three hundred dollars as a wedding present—no card. How thoughtful.

Jane and I bought the cold cuts and beer for the reception at her father's apartment. Unlike Jacques, who eloped to marry but still got a well-laid-on reception, Jane and I got nothing. We were citizens of the second rank, members of a lower caste, and there wasn't even a balcony to put us in.

But then, miracle of miracles, Jane and I were changed from water to wine, from least to most, from last to first—a position of honor to which I was entirely unaccustomed and which made me uncomfortable. Our achievement? We had sex. Oh, yeah. We also got pregnant, and nine months later their first grand-child was born. Not any grandchild, mind you, but their first grandchild. Jane and I didn't stop there: not only a grandchild but a *grandson*—Chandler. He was the Messiah, and Jane and I, by extension, held the honored roles of Mary and Joseph in the McCormack family. Now, there was always room at the inn. Isn't it amazing how values change, often in perfect tandem with self-interest?

So, I became a father.

CHAPTER 14

CHILDBIRTH

I was out in the back yard. Jane was in the house in the pains of early labor. She called out in exasperation from the upstairs window, "Charlie! What are you doing?" It was a damn good question. What was I doing? I had no clue. It was patently stupid, but I couldn't help myself. I felt a compulsion, a primal need, driving me to work feverishly on completing the building of a fence to protect my backyard. After all, we could come under attack at any moment, couldn't we? And, I needed to plant something. A tree, a fucking tree. Planting the tree felt like an imperative, almost like a flag, taking a stand, marking ground I will defend, proclaiming the impending birth. I thought *Won't it be great that our child can return thirty years from now and see this tree that was planted on the day he was born.* "Christ, what's wrong with me?" I chided myself, "I am out of my mind. Jane's having contractions, and I'm out here in the backyard trying to complete these projects that are so completely peripheral to the moment." I took myself into the house, shoulders hunched, into Jane's recriminating stare.

Years later I shared this experience with a child psychologist. She explained: "You Idiot. You were caught in the nesting urge, that powerful primal drive experienced by all mammals. It has been with Man since the beginning of time. You were preparing for your child in your own Cro-Magnon way—no disrespect meant to the Cro-Magnons." Mercifully, it all made sense. Finally, panting from the effort, I can stop beating myself up for what turned out to be a nesting drive.

Young and idealistic, Jane and I were going to do everything *right*. Certainly, much better than our parents did. Jane attended La Leche meetings like a nun attending mass, and we opted for natural childbirth, at home no less, using a midwife. How perfect were we? Long and arduous, the delivery did not proceed according to plan. The midwife announced we had to go the hospital. We piled into her car, she and Jane in the back seat while I drove. Her car was junk; she had engine problems. It stalled every time I came to a stop. I irritably asked myself when I stalled out once again, "What had the midwife been thinking? Why didn't we take my car?" Then understanding slammed into me, "Because her car's backseat is bigger; she can deliver the baby there if she needs to." I drove faster.

We arrived at Sinai Hospital. I dropped Jane and the midwife off and parked the car. Upon my return, I asked the receptionist where to go. She explained but insisted I must wait until they called for me. I was not doing that; I simply couldn't— the clarion call of impending birth was ringing through my soul. I explained that to the receptionist as the elevator door began to close behind me. She seemed dazed by my explanation. Maybe she didn't know what a clarion call was or maybe it was that these words were being delivered by an unshaven man with unkempt hair, eyes lolling in his head from a combination of exhaustion and adrenalin. I'll never know; the door to the elevator shut as she was dialing security.

I found Jane and the midwife in a supply room—all the delivery rooms were occupied. Within minutes, Chandler emerged from the womb. Apparently, he didn't care where he was. He just wanted out. Wet, tiny, helpless, and one hundred percent dependent on Jane and *me*. Whoa, *Me!*

I held him in my arms for the first time, and a burning ball of white-hot fierceness swelled within my chest, instantly incinerating all the nagging questions and self-doubts. I still didn't know how I'd get it done, how I'd take care of this tiny monkey, but I now knew one thing with absolute certainty: I would. In the same moments that Chandler moved from fetus to infant, I moved from boy to man.

Four years later, Keeley was born. Guess what? We were doing natural childbirth again. Why not? It turned out so well the first time. But this time, we did it in a hospital. During delivery, I announced to Jane that the baby looked exactly like Chandler, then had to revamp my pronouncement as Keeley fully exited her mother. It was déjà vu but less intense for now I knew more what to expect.

As a proud all-knowing father and therapist, with at least one course in early childhood development under my belt, I spent months preparing Chandler for the arrival of his sibling. We frequently talked about the baby or, more accurately, I spoke to him. I drew pictures illustrating the baby ensconced in his mom's swollen belly. I talked about his being a big boy and the best big brother ever. And so on and so on—and then some more so ons.

Finally, the momentous day arrived; Chandler met Keeley for the first time. I, the proud and oh so wise Father watched over them, a paternal knowing smile on my face. In my finest *Father Knows Best* voice, I asked, "Chan, would you like to hold Keeley?" He assured me he would. Holding her, looking down in what I was certain was an explicitly loving way, I intuited that he was hesitating to speak, shy in the presence of this tiny Goddess. Encouragingly, I prompted him, feeling the bounty of love in this *Golden Moment* that enveloped us, "Is there anything you would like to say to Keeley?" He nodded affirmatively, once again confirming the keenness of my perceptions. I thought *How lucky Chandler and Keeley are to have me as a dad. What a good job I've done preparing the way, easing Chandler into this change in family life.* In the glow of the moment, I watched Chandler holding Keeley—maybe a little too tightly—in his arms and staring intensely into her eyes. He then spoke in an earnest voice that permitted no misinterpretation: "I hate you. I hate you. I hate you."

I was speechless. In the years to come, I would find that Chandler has a knack for leaving me speechless. I thought *Wow! That went well.* And then tell myself, "At least it was real." The reality was heightened a few minutes later when Chandler proceeded to pee on the floor in every room of the house. His message was clear—Chandler has always been a good communicator. Where I had once felt driven to nest, Chandler was driven to mark his territory—so much for those classes in early childhood development.

Three years later, Caitlin was born. This time, we were not going to go the natural route. The first two pregnancies were breech births and very painful. This time, Jane wanted medications, and plenty of them, the more, the better: somewhere along the way, the purity of our birthing drive had bleached away. The only problem was someone screwed up, and Jane didn't get the medications when needed. Then it was too late; the birth was upon us. Once again, Jane gave birth au natural. Caitlin emerged with lots of dark hair helmeting her alabaster skin. Struck to the core by her her lovliness I exclaim, "Jane, she's so beautiful!"

Chandler had now grown to the point where he cared little about another intruder into the family. Keeley, on the other hand, felt blessed, having a live doll to play with, and play they did. A fond memory is of Keeley and Cait, with a group of girlfriends, playing hair salon under the shade tree on a summer's afternoon. Keeley was chattering while working on Cait's hair.

Cait, now age four or five, chubby little face set in a serious rendering of her role, stoically sat through it all, playing customer to the fullest. All the girls were gabbing as they played with each other's hair, their unselfconscious chatter reminiscent of the excited chirping of birds and females bonding. I was thrilled by the aliveness of it all, so much so that I set up a video camera on a tripod and just let it run. I have no idea where that tape is now, but I don't need it. I see it all in my mind's eye as fresh as the day it happened.

Probably the smartest thing I ever did as a dad was to build a pool in our backyard. Crazily, I cut down a sixty-foot-tall tree by myself, scaling it repeatedly to trim its branches then taking it down eight-foot lengths at a time, tying each section off with rope to prevent it from falling the wrong way: Paul Bunyan has nothing on me.

A dangerous venture, more so when done alone. Stupid, really, but at that time, life was good, safe and assured, and I still did not know about asking for help. I paid a heavy equipment operator who lived down the street to dig a hole and spent weeks shaping it with a shovel into a facsimile of a pool. I built a retaining wall, then called a pool installation company to complete the job. In this way, I could afford a pool.

As a family, we spent the best times in and around that pool. I taught Caitlin to swim underwater at age eight months, and the kids and I swam for hours each week, playing Marco Polo. It was fantastic. They appeared to fly as they swam in the depths of the crystal water, seemingly suspended in air like angelic cherubs, their golden hair shimmering as sunbeams painted the pool. I loved swimming with the kids—their happy faces, their unblemished delight. At moments, this filled me with such joy that I *was* joy.

We barbecued with neighbors and friends as laughter spilled into the air. Those were the best of times, some of the best of my life.

I will write more about fatherhood in a later chapter, but this was the beginning, the early years. Throughout what is to come in the next chapters—my work as a therapist—these children were always there, growing, changing, needing me in ways I couldn't possibly have imagined, and only partially understood.

CHAPTER 15

GETTING SCHOOLED

I was pursuing my plan to get a Ph.D. in psychology, grinding out a living as an auto-body man. I was trying to follow in Juan's footsteps in service of making more money to help support us while taking a couple of courses a semester in the master's program in psychology at Loyola. At the rate I was going, I had estimated that I could obtain a doctoral degree in a mere eleven years.

In the meantime, these blue-collar jobs taught me an important truth: there are many forms of intelligence and auto-body restoration and engine repair are nowhere to be found among mine.

I started out trying to create a business like Juan's—servicing Volkswagens at peoples' homes. I failed miserably. Not only did I not know how to price things but I discovered first hand that all Volkswagens are not the same. For instance, unbeknownst to me the firing order of the cylinders changed in different production years. So, I found myself in someone's driveway, having messed up totally the tuning of their car and not able to figure out why. Talk about embarrassing. Then I tried my hand as an auto-body guy, charged with welding the front and back undamaged ends of two wrecks together to form a functioning third car for sale to unsuspecting customers. Morals aside, without training, I couldn't begin to accomplish that task. I was let go after several grueling months. At the same time, I had been taking a course in auto mechanics, thinking I could earn better money while working towards my degree. Because of being able to list this schooling on my application, I found new employment right away at a Toyota dealership. With unnerving acuity of perception, they recognized my innate talents and assigned me to such daunting challenges as changing oil and pasting on racing stripes.

I was there only three days before the accident that you've already heard about happened. Nevertheless, that had been long enough to be instructed to ignore the "change transmission oil" part on the order sheets. No dummy to deviousness, I deduced the dealership was charging for this service without performing it. It would be impossible for customers to check on the work without putting the car on a lift. Once again, I was reminded how commonplace conniving and deceiving are amongst we human beings. It's clear Jesus wasn't risking anything when he told the crowd, "He that is without sin among you, let him first cast a stone."

Biblical quotes aside, the car accident had a silver lining: A twelve-thousand-dollar insurance settlement after paying the doctors, the lawyer, and the plastic surgeon. I was now able to attend school full-time and did well; I had finally found my form of intelligence.

I have one awkward story from that period, one that sums up its era, the infamous 1970s. One of my professors invited Jane and me to dinner at his house. Jane, feeling ill, bowed out, so I went alone. I knocked on the door. The tall and lean middle-aged professor, hair slicked back as if still wet from a shower, answered. But what is this? He is in his bathrobe. I greeted him personably, but he didn't respond. Face washed of emotions, he simply turned and without saying a word, walked away through the living room, disappearing through a door on the other side. I was left outside, still on the front stoop. "What the heck?" What was I supposed to do? I felt off-kilter. Hesitantly, I interpreted the open door as an invitation to let myself in.

The first thing I noticed was there was no smell of cooking, nor any evidence of a dinner party in the making. Did I have the wrong evening? I didn't think so. The professor hadn't seemed surprised to see me, although his welcome left much to be desired. I thought, *this is weird*, but I chased further thoughts away as they began to scamper about disquietingly. I told my thoughts: *Stop it. He's merely getting dressed. He's embarrassed for running late and being caught with only his bathrobe on.* Thus reassured, I stood patiently, like any good soldier waiting for the return of his commanding officer.

But minutes passed, and there was still no sign of him. Nor, for that matter, was there any sound; the house was completely quiet. Time seemed to dawdle in inverse relationship to my mounting uncertainty. My thoughts returned, skittering here and there while I began to feel more and more like a fool just standing there. Finally, recognizing I was in danger of being a moron, I had enough! I walked to the door through which the professor had vanished.

Whoa! It was a bedroom, and there was the bed, and there was the professor supine on the bed, facing me, eyes veiled, communicating nothing. I had flashes of Little Red Riding Hood and The Big Bad Wolf. Thankfully, he was still in his robe. Extraneously, I noticed a bronze bracelet ringing one arm: Very chic. He spoke not, just continued to look at me with round, unblinking eyes. Were these the better to see me? What was he doing? What the hell was going on? Then… the penny dropped. Oh. Shit! He wanted to get it on with me. Perversely, almost comically, I laughed at myself, when I realized that part of me felt insulted. I wondered, *Is this his idea of seduction or foreplay? Aren't I worth more than this? Am I merely seen as a sexual object?* Then I moved to other thoughts. *I'm heterosexual, and I'm married; I would not be open to this even if the professor were an attractive woman.*

I left such musings and returned to the moment and my senses: I turned and walked out of the house. Driving home, I realized that from beginning to end, the professor had never uttered a sound.

Since my return to Baltimore, I had learned something about myself: I was bull-headed. I had a strong work ethic and incredible persistence. Once I had a plan, for better or for worse, I saw it through. I'd follow my passions no matter where they lay, whatever the obstacles or disappointments. Sometimes, I could not see any way forward. Then I would just keep plugging along and pecking away until something unforeseen and unforeseeable changed, allowing me, sooner or later, to break through to whatever was beyond. Like a sailor, I always kept tacking and jibing towards my goal.

Every sailor must navigate and anticipate the obstacles that might lie ahead, be they powerful currents or fierce winds. As I doggedly pursued the master's degree in psychology in the Ivory Tower of academia, I had a thought: What if I don't like working with the mentally ill? I chided myself, *Wow! What a time to ask this.* My love of theory was one thing, but practice might be quite another. I loved theory. I could play with it all day. My question was, what if I loved theory but hated the practice of psychology? What if all the sacrifices Jane and I had made were for naught? That frightened me. What would I do then? And failing Jane, after all I had put her through, terrified me. It was one thing for me to follow my heart, quite another to do damage to others in the process. That simply would not be fair. With trepidation, I set out to answer the question. I drove to Sheppard and Enoch Pratt Hospital (SEPH), at the time a world famous psychiatric hospital in Towson, Maryland, a suburb of Baltimore, to ask about volunteering.

PART III

IF ONLY I HAD EARS TO LISTEN—

HATCHING 102

Finally, I felt like I was breaking out of my shell or at least knew where I wanted to create the opening. All along it had been calling to me in the form of my interests and yearnings. If only I had had the ears to listen.

CHAPTER 16

ASYLUM

I drove onto the grounds of Sheppard-Pratt Hospital that fateful October morning in 1974, age twenty-four, not knowing what to expect. What I found was far from the prison-like facility I had feared. As I passed through the stone gatehouse, following the winding country lane across a stone bridge spanning a trickling brook, a sense of peace settled over me.

Further along, a pedestrian bridge, hand-hewn from yellow wood, carried walkers across a small valley toward a gazebo that hung like a pendant on a gold chain. Slate-roofed stone and brick buildings designed by architects who had traveled Europe to glean the most humanistic designs of the day—the late 1800s—rose impressively on the top of a hill. Hundreds of different species of trees and shrubs adorned the expansive lawns, and cathedral light streamed through the treetops towering magnificently overhead. In the near distance were a softball field, a hothouse, and a glass-enclosed swimming pool, adding modernity to the scene.

Inside the main building, I encountered airy, high-ceilinged rooms replete with over-sized windows, embellished with stained glass. Color-infused sunlight flowed throughout, washing the rooms with pastel light.

Looking out through the windows, I watched staff and patients stroll the grounds or sit on the Adirondack chairs strewn across the lawn in well-spaced groupings of two or three. They offered a welcoming invitation to conversation and reflection. The sound of bird calls and bees buzzing caressed my ears through open windows.

I was captivated, transported in time, imagining well-dressed patients and staff mingling on the lawn enjoying high tea on a Sunday afternoon as had been the tradition in times past.

Grace and wisdom seem to emanate from this place, hinting of things seen and thought about in ways not common in the world rushing about just beyond its borders. I would come to learn that the totality that was Sheppard-Pratt of that era embodied the best meanings of the words asylum and sanctuary, offering needed respite from a harried world, with time and space to reflect and to form meaningful relationships. But on that day, even with as little as I knew, it was clear to me—Sheppard-Pratt was designed with one goal in mind: the care and healing of the human psyche.

What I did not know then, as I arrived for my interview for a volunteer position, was that I was catching the waning light of the Golden Era of American psychiatry and compassion. The oxymoron "managed care" had yet to be uttered. President Reagan had yet to empty out the state hospitals. Homelessness and starvation had yet to be forced on the mentally ill.

I sat eager and apprehensive before the Director of Volunteers. She was saying, "These are psychiatric patients on a short-term locked-door unit. They might stay anywhere from two weeks to three months." As her voice flowed, the sound of her words receded from me as I thought about what she had just said. *Why are the doors locked? This did not sound reassuring to me. Were the patients crazy,*

I mean really crazy? Violent crazy? And, what does crazy look like and how does it act? Is it as portrayed in the movies? Wild-eyed, raggedy-haired people, dressed in sack-like gray clothing, who will rise in unison to attack me? My body hummed with the uncertainty cast by these unasked and unanswered questions. I dared not ask them. I would not risk being refused a position because I appeared anxious. Instead, I reassured myself: *The hospital knows what it's doing. Doesn't it?*

My first day of volunteering I was escorted to the short-term adult inpatient unit. My escort rung the buzzer and moments later, a nurse looked out through a small, reinforced glass window and let me in. Like a swimmer entering the border of a frigid lake, I tentatively stepped inside, noting the sound of the heavy door closing behind me, its solid lock clunking shut with a sound of finality. I looked around like a badger sniffing the air for signs of danger. People were sitting either quietly alone or chatting with one another. Some looked depressed, others look distressed, some seemed perfectly fine, and nowhere was there a sense of danger or emergency.

The nursing staff warmly welcomed me. They explained I was to sit and talk with patients, escort them off the hall to wherever they needed to go, and otherwise to help in any way I was willing.

My first task I'll always remember: a geriatric federal judge suffering from dementia and the loss of bowel control. I held his arm and took him into a bathroom with shower and tub. He dumbly stood next to it, having no idea what to do, brown-stained pajama bottoms hanging limply from his bony hips. His stink threatened to chase me from the room, and I had to fight the urge to gag. I thought, *How incredible is this? A man of such intellect and accomplishment rendered so low, now unable to think or to remember in any coherent fashion. Just standing here, painted by his waste.* I talked to him softly, telling him what I was going to do before I did it. I gently pulled down his pajamas and rinsed him off with a shower nozzle, relieved as his shit released its hold upon him.

Then I bathed him, all the while talking quietly, realizing it didn't matter what I said, only how I said it. I shaved him, combed his hair and dressed him nicely in slacks and shirt. Later, I watched as his family visited. I felt rewarded that they all had this time together where he looked more like himself and with a vestige of his dignity intact: I had done a good thing.

I soon discovered that these patients were like you and me. The main difference: they were overcome by psychological issues or deficits rendering them unable to manage their lives, at least for a while. I could relate to this. I knew something of being alone in the world, of being overwhelmed, confused and disoriented. I knew something about needing time and space to recoup and discover new purposes and goals for living.

I was also interested in the patients' stories, how they came to be here, and what kept them from moving on. To me these tales were fascinating, prompting my thinking about issues that related to my life, unknowingly beginning a tradition of interrelating the personal and the professional, them and me. I couldn't think of a more productive or interesting way to spend a day.

Upon occasion, I was allowed to sit in on treatment team interviews of patients. I cherished these learning opportunities, wishing they would come more often. One such time, the service chief, Meyer Liebman, M.D., was interviewing a young man awaiting trial, who had admitted to physically abusing his girlfriend. Afterward, Dr. Liebman shared his interpretations, noting not only what the patient had said but also how he had said it. He highlighted incongruities between words, tones, rhythms, pitch, kinesthetic energy, facial expressions and body language, coming to the conclusion that although the patient was a voluntary admission, he was really there to seek favor with the courts *and* one other, far less obvious, thing—to become more skilled at controlling women. As Dr. Liebman supported his thinking with various observations, I listened intently, realizing how little

I knew. At twenty-four years of age, I had never considered the possibility that someone would try to use treatment to become a more skilled sociopath—that some people in treatment weren't seeking to get better.

In my way, I had always been a thinker, but these were thinkers' thinkers. I had found a home, a place where nothing was taboo to think about, relevancy determined only by whether something might deepen understanding. Understanding would often take a while to arrive but, for the most part, arrive it did, clarity emerging where once only confusion had reigned.

I had a sense of having come home. It was as if in recognizing what was going on around me, I was also feeling recognized. I don't know how else to say it—I was getting myself back from this place. It wasn't an experience that I had knowingly sought; I hadn't known of its existence. I had fallen into it, and it fell into me. Something within burst into flame, like a spark laid to dry grass leading to a fire that would eventually roar.

CHAPTER 17

INPATIENT TO OUTPATIENT

Three months later, in January 1975, I was offered my first job as a therapist at Sheppard-Pratt's Comprehensive Drug Abuse Treatment Program (COMDAP). I was excited, certain I was going to make a difference in the world. My naiveté and idealism were staggering—yet all this time I had thought I was such a hard ass. On the walls of my office hung optimistic and encouraging posters, implying that working together and with good will, all problems would be overcome. I was so over the top, functioning as if I were a camp counselor.

Picture me, strumming blithely away on a ukulele while staff and patients sat around a crackling campfire, the flicker of firelight illuminating hopeful faces as sparks leaped toward the stars. The smell of roasting marshmallows perfumed the air; singing and laughter fill the night. Kumbaya! Kumbaya! It's great! You're great! I'm great! Everyone's great! And, we're all so special. I was also out of my mind.

Now, imagine I come to my senses and realize that the boy and girl scouts are street-wise, hardened heroin addicts. Many of the men have done prison time. Many of the women have sold their bodies for drugs. How lucky they must feel that I've arrived to save them! The only thing I was missing was a silver bullet. Let me hear it one more time: Kumbaya! Don't we all feel better now?

Looking back on those times, I'm struck by the compassion these people had for me. They never mocked me, nor made a face. Even the medical director, Bill Abramson, MD, one of the most scornful and scathing individuals to ever walk the planet, largely resisted the opportunity to belittle me. He would enter my office each week to provide supervision, take my chair (he loved these power games), briefly cast a smirk at the posters, but never say a thing. Later, he invited me to his home to give me his now grown children's old toys for Chandler. It was evident they had been stored with care. It was an emotional moment for him and me, somehow representing the passing of a torch and the ending of an era, uncharacteristically tender and warm. I sensed he was grieving the letting go of those times, the aura of which lingered on those well-kept toys. It wasn't me taking care of all those people; it was all those people taking care of me. I had been adopted and didn't know it.

The following year there were cutbacks: My position was reduced to half-time. Fortunately, the administrator, Carl Thistle, arranged to keep me on as a part-time researcher of a potential replacement drug for methadone. My job was to track down the heroin addicts who participated in the program and arrange to interview them in their homes to evaluate how they were doing.

The typical interview would go something like this: I knock on the door. A woman answers, narrow face carved with lines of hard living. I ask if Johnny's home. Suspiciously, she asks, "What do you want him for?" I don't know who she is, so I can't say; I would be breaching Johnny's privacy. So I tell her, "It's personal." She looks at me a moment with a jaded eye then, comes to a decision, shouting over her shoulder, "Johnny, someone here wants you." A scruffy guy, T-shirt and jeans draped on a skinny body, comes barefoot to the door scratching his head and rudely demands, "What do you want?"

The woman, who looked twice Johnny's age, hadn't moved. I guess she's his mother. but I still don't want to breach his privacy. I say, "It's confidential." He pauses a moment considering, then says to the woman, "Sarah, go get me a beer, will ya?" She looks resentful but goes on her errand. I tell Johnny, "I'm the guy here to interview you for the drug-treatment research." His demeanor changes, visibly relaxing. He opens the door and invites me in. Contrary to expectations, the house is neat and clean. We sit in the living room, and Sarah brings Johnny a beer. Johnny offers me one; I decline. Johnny explains to Sarah who I am, and Sarah relaxes as well. It's now becoming clear that Sarah is Johnny's girlfriend. Sarah leaves the room. Johnny assures me he is doing fine, maintaining employment and has no complaints about the drug l-alpha-acetyl-methadol except that he misses the quasi-high he could get out of methadone.

And so the interviewing went, typically mundane by the end but often with many undercurrents at the beginning. After dozens of these interviews, I felt graced by these people allowing me into their homes and their lives. In some way, I felt I was one of them, again discovering that there is little difference between people. Indeed, these addicts were you and me. Many held good jobs, their employers and colleagues never suspecting their addiction.

There were exceptions. One guy wouldn't allow me into his home. "No, man. We talk out here," which made me wonder if he had something to hide. When I told him that his urinalysis proved positive for heroin and that he was being discharged from the program, he became enraged and got in my face, yelling, "I'm going to kill you, you punk. You think you're a big deal, but you're not. I'm going to take you down to size, and you won't know when it's coming. I'll find out where you live." It appeared to take every ounce of his self-restraint not to attack me then and there. He had already calculated that assaulting me in broad daylight, directly in front of his home, would jam him up. I took the threat seriously. I alerted COMDAP and warned Jane and my neighbors to be on the alert.

Another moment that stood out from my two years at COMDAP occurred on a snowy Friday winter evening. A couple with three female children in tow appeared out of nowhere at the open door of my office. I was the last one there; clinic hours were over, and I was getting ready to leave for the weekend. The mother, an attractive blond with an open face, held a toddler in her arms. The other girls looked to be four and six. The mother, looking at me with beseeching eyes, explained they needed methadone and a place to stay. The husband nodded anxiously in agreement.

I was desperate too. What could I do? We're closed; everyone's gone home. Didn't they know you can't just walk in and get methadone? Nonetheless, I couldn't let these people return to the snowy night. I explain all this to them but assure them I'll find a shelter that will take them. Curiously, they decline. They know everything about the shelter, far more than me, and have absolutely no interest in going there. In a corner of my mind, I marvel that they don't seem that concerned. If it were me, I would be in an absolute panic. Hell, I was in a panic, and it wasn't me. But they were calmly resolute, promising to return the following Monday, and then walked back into the cutting embrace of the winter night. I went home worried. I should have done better. I should have done something.

Monday morning, the family returned, completely unfazed. They had found someone to take them in. I then realized that what for me would have been a panic-stricken experience of not having a warm place to stay was for them part of the norm of a rootless lifestyle—nothing to get excited about. Later, as my naiveté and idealism were worn down by the grindstone of experience, I considered the possibility that the parents had been playing me to get methadone and had always had a place to stay. Was it unkind of me to think that? Maybe. Or maybe it was just a sign I was growing up.

In 1977, I was selected from eighty applicants for the position of Program Coordinator of SEPH'S Evening Treatment Program, the evening part of the Day/Evening hospital. Here, patients received treatment but lived at home. The evening program was for patients who worked during the day but needed social support in the evening.

In all truth, it was a dull and lifeless affair, people just sitting around. Worse, it was contagious. Soon enough, I too was sitting around, dull and lifeless, smiling the smile one has when their shoes are too tight as I went through the same boring and predictable routine each night, night after tortuous night. Finally, to quote Popeye, "That's all I can stands, cuz I can't stands n'more," not one more night.

I didn't see how this program was helping or inspiring anyone, except perhaps to feel like losers. Accordingly, the psychiatrist assigned to the program, Steve Saunders, and I began taking patients out into the community to restaurants and exhibits. I even successfully made a case to the Outpatient Treatment Committee to allow patients and staff to have one drink, like a glass of wine, at a restaurant. My thought was that these were working adults and should be treated as such. We also invited people of varying talents, yoga instructors, and art teachers, to share their knowledge with the group. We went on excursions, watching sculptors make clay rise from between their hands into vases as the potting wheel turned. A scene that later lent itself to a metaphor of relationship, the difference being that in a relationship there are two potters at the wheel.

In a period of weeks, the evenings were transformed from a passively resigned march to lifelessness to stimulating and vibrant adult get-togethers with people interacting and laughing with one another.

In the early days of these changes, I struggled with trying to balance professionalism with pleasure. To me, the idea was to help these people access the healing powers of stimulation and enjoyment in human connection, but this went against the more traditional and conservative notions of the therapist and patient relationship. I was learning as I went, making it up along the way. And one thing I learned was that when Steve and I enjoyed ourselves, so did everyone else. Conversely, if we were holding back, hiding behind our professional veneers, then the life would be sapped from the group. We opted for life. We had a very good time.

There was one problem, however. From the outset, I did not get along with the program administrator, whom I shall call Ms. Glum to protect the guilty. I don't know if she just didn't like me or perceived me as a threat to her position. Possibly both. In any event, she had been on my case for months concerning the patient census; there were simply not enough patients to adequately cover the cost of the program. Frankly, I didn't see this as my problem. Mine was a clinical position, not public relations or advertising. She was the administrator.

Ms. Glum didn't see it that way. She held me responsible for the census, yet had no answer as to what I could do about it. One day, I was at the nursing station when the phone rang. It was Ms. Glum calling from her office. In a taut and contempt-laden voice, she reamed me out once again about the low census, concluding her demeaning rant by demanding in a contemptuous tone, "What should I do with you?!" Unknowingly, she had reminded me of my father's denigrating attitude and my role as one of his "little niggers." That was a mistake.

I take full responsibility. My McCormack Clan craziness poked out its ugly head. I responded in a deadpan voice, dripping with equal parts challenge and disdain, "I think you should draw and quarter me and feed me to the wolves." This response had arisen spontaneously given that I was reading a work of fiction set in England in the 1300s when this form of punishment was commonplace. My statement met with total silence and, I assume, bewilderment. Holding the phone to my ear, I imagined Ms. Glum trying to make sense of my words so out of step with anything she could have foreseen. Her silence went on and on, followed by a click. She had hung up.

My flippancy was not to go unpunished. Several months later, Ms. Glum called me into her office at the end of the day to impart *sad* news: "Charlie, I'm so sorry to inform you that we have to let you go. Because of the low-census, we can no longer afford your position. Please accept this meeting as your two-week notice." Frankly, she didn't seem all that sorry. However, she also didn't look all that happy. I'd say her look was along the lines of that found on the face of a toreador carefully placing barbs into the bull, to weaken him before the final sword thrust. She wasn't going to celebrate until the bull was dead. Then I could easily imagine Ms. Glum dancing the Funky Chicken, running naked, hair frenzied, through the hallways of the treatment center well after closing laughing maniacally. It's a picture I hurried to get out of my mind.

Stunned by this unanticipated turn of events, I left for home feeling a mix of fear and excitement. Fear in that I had a family to support and no job, excitement in that I was faced with a wide-open future. The only clue that I was more discombobulated than I knew occurred when I could not find my car in the small parking lot. I just could not focus. I looked everywhere, several times, before discovering it hiding in plain sight directly in front of the door to the clinic.

A week later I received a call from the Outpatient Committee that oversaw the functioning of the Day/Evening Hospital. The chair, a psychiatrist named Dr. Robertson, MD (if memory serves), invited me to an exit interview. As the tiniest cog in the Sheppard-Pratt machine, I was genuinely surprised. What could they possibly want to know from me?

When I arrived for the meeting, I learned that we were waiting for a final member to arrive: Ms. Glum. Shit! I didn't know she was on the committee. After the passage of a few minutes, Dr. Robertson elected to start the meeting without her. "Charlie, we're so sorry to hear that you're leaving us. We invited you in for any thoughts or ideas you might have about the evening program." The phrasing of his comment confused me, suggesting that he saw me as choosing to leave rather than being bum-rushed out the door. I decided to probe. "Thank you, Dr. Robertson. I too am very sorry. It's unfortunate that the budget cuts necessitated the elimination of my position." Now it was his face that held a puzzled expression, along with those of the other committee members. That's when I knew, as Sherlock-Holmes would say, "The game was afoot."

Dr. Robertson explained that Ms. Glum had told them I was leaving because of conflicts between work and school schedules. Wow, what a moment! I was in awe of Ms. Glum. She rose ten notches on my appreciation scale. She had done a Machiavelli– straight-out lied to both the committee and me in a brazen attempt to get rid of me. I was impressed. Amazingly, she would have pulled it off if not for the fortuitous invitation to an exit interview that, it was now clear, she, as well, had not foreseen.

At this point, Ms. Glum arrived and was confronted by Dr. Robertson. She handled the confrontation by sitting stiffly, stone still and silent as a wooden Indian. The silence went on and on, and slowly understanding dawned on the rest of us: Ms. Glum was *not* going to speak. With this epiphany, Dr. Robertson, unsettled, turned to me, "Charlie, I apologize to you for any anguish that this has caused you or your family. I sincerely hope that you will choose to stay on." I assured him that I would like nothing better and took this as my cue to leave. I resisted all child-like urges to taunt "Na, na, na" to Ms. Glum as I walked out the door. I had no further problems with Ms. Glum. I could not have been happier.

Pretty crazy, but as you know, there always seems to be plenty of crazy on the merry-go-round of life. It is, in fact, a crazy world. Why wouldn't it be? It's full of people, each messy in their way and having his or her lessons to learn.

CHAPTER 18

RULE 1—SHIT HAPPENS

The night lay like a shroud upon me as I passed through the dimly lit streets of the projects when the shout erupted from behind, immediately answered by yipping sounds reminiscent of jackals excitedly tracking their prey. As I looked over my shoulder, my heart turned to ice. Fifty feet behind, a gang of black youths was giving chase, shouting excitedly like Zulu warriors, as they closed in on their quarry—*me*. Briefly mesmerized, I could only watch as the Warriors maneuvered this way and that, effortlessly hurdling the obstacles in their path, as each gauged the best angle of pursuit. Excitement writ large on their faces, each vied to be the first to count coup and divest me of my transportation, if not rearrange my facial features. Heart thumping, quickly understanding my role as the hare to their hounds, I broke out of my trance with stunning clarity. I realized I must quickly counter the moves they were making, or I'd be cut off, my fate left in their clawing hands. After several minutes of a wildly chaotic and dangerous game of move and counter-move, I broke clear of them, giving my war cry as I jolted from terror to exhilaration: I had won, at least this night.

What made this experience exceptionally unnerving can only be understood if you have ever driven a moped. If so, you know mopeds are deservedly renowned for their lack of get up and go—there is a reason they come with pedals. They should be called slopeds. Indeed, it is not an exaggeration to suggest that they accelerate like sand through an hourglass. Clearly, this was not ideal transportation if you were being chased. Where was my Dad's GTO when I needed it? There was only one effective solution: once top-end speed is reached, never, ever, slow down.

So there I was night after night, commuting home from the University of Maryland, located in one of the worse parts of downtown Baltimore. Like a grain of salt in a land of pepper, I barreled through stop signs and stoplights, around and between traffic, and cut corners to avoid slowing down, all with little regard for what might be in front of me, given full knowledge of what was following behind. Though the Warriors never caught me, there were many close calls. Ironically, the most significant came when I wasn't being chased at all.

That night I had left the pursuing gang far behind and felt free to stop for a red light given the better lighting, heavier traffic and random police patrols at the corner of North and Charles. Still, I kept a vigilant eye—this area of town was also infamous for its crime. So, there I sat, waiting patiently for the light to turn green, enjoying the gentle breeze of warm air caressing my skin and the smell of cooking hamburgers wafting over from the White Castle restaurant on the corner, when out its door stepped a shark.

I knew he was a shark right away. A guy, maybe in his thirties, garish red baseball cap planted askew on his head, instantly scanning his environment. His eyes passed over me unseeing before they jerked back in an almost comedic double take. As I immediately recognized him for what he was, he immediately recognized me for what I was: prey. Fear tightened my chest as he strolled confidently towards me. As I watched his approach, the sights and sounds of the city recede; my attention now fully focused on the incoming danger. The shark said, "Was' dat you ridin'?" as if we were long lost buddies in casual conversation, only his hard, scarred face and cold eyes giving the lie. Time was on my side; a squad car could roll by at any moment, so I did my best to put off the confrontation. I also pretended that we were just shooting the shit. "It's called a moped. They use them a lot in other parts of the world." He pretended interest as he walked around the moped, head tilted quizzically, and then with brotherly camaraderie said, "Get off da bike. I tries it out," as if he were going to take it on a trial ride, then return it to me. Instinctively understanding that any trace of fear or indecision would only encourage him, I calmly responded, "That isn't going to happen." He looked at me silently and unmoving, eyes emotionlessly assessing. He waited for me to fold under the strength of his dead-eyed stare.

He obviously didn't know that I could take a beating with the best of them. Several heartbeats more and he realized I wasn't getting off the bike. Coldly, he asked, "What if I jus shoot you in da hed and takes' it?" A strange feeling came over me at that moment. As I write these words, I realize the same thing had happened when I last faced a life-threatening situation: the major laparotomy. Rather than anxiety, I felt a profound calm, a sense of acceptance and resolve settle upon me: I wasn't getting off the bike. I responded quietly, without whine or challenge, "You got'ta do what you got'ta do. I got'ta do what I got'ta do."

He stood silently, assessing me once again, as if plumbing the depths of my resolve, surprise and curiosity flickering behind his eyes. Then, he laughed and said, "You aw-rite. I jus kiddin'," turned and walked away. Several weeks later, my moped was stolen off my front porch; I think by the son of my next-door neighbor. Somehow, I survived without it. Until I had to, I didn't know I could.

Such are the workings of life, as capricious and difficult to forecast as the weather. Though my life sometimes seemed—and seems—on track, I often felt (and feel) apprehension, knowing that things can fall apart in a heartbeat. The ups and downs of my childhood would be reason enough for me to feel this, but I also know, as we all do, that life is fickle in ways beyond anyone's ability to foresee or control. The false firing by Ms. Glum falls into that category, as well as my being saved by the unexpected exit interview with the Outpatient Treatment Committee. Such things happen with enough regularity to give rise to the old saw, Men plan, God laughs. This awareness fuels the uneasiness that many feel day to day, especially when things are going well.

One such event is what landed me on that moped, careening through the poorly lit projects of Baltimore's inner city on those dark evenings. I had been pursuing admission to a doctoral program in psychology, confident and assured that given my grades, graduate record exam scores, and work experience, I would be a desirable candidate for at least one school. To ensure this—do you hear God laughing? —I had applied to about twenty schools and then sat back to wait patiently for the acceptances to start rolling in. But over a period of several months, my confidence gradually eroded as, instead, rejections trickled in. My first reaction was surprise, but I wasn't overly concerned. These programs were very competitive, and I wasn't going to be accepted by all of them. But surprise gave way to dejection as the rejections continued to mount. The worst part was that I couldn't make sense of the situation and, therefore, came to invent a reason in keeping with my default story line. I decided these schools had seen through the veneer I projected to the world, and uncannily, recognized me for the wannabe I was. I could think of no other explanation. Then one day, I received a letter of rejection that, for the first time, gave a reason. It stated I didn't qualify for admission because I had only six credits in psychology.

I was dumbstruck. I had a master's degree in psychology, a total of thirty-six credits. And then realization dawned—Loyola had sent out partial transcripts, perhaps as a result of my nomadic moves from day school to night school and back again, as well as from part-time to full-time student. Whatever the cause, such is the way of life. I'm not one of those people who believe everything happens for a reason. Frankly, I wish I were; that belief would be comforting. However, I have never been able to subscribe to what feels like a platitude, reasoning that if you flip a coin a thousand times, there will be occasions when tails come up ten times in a row. I find it hard to believe that is part of some Grand Plan. Indeed, it's related to something far less comforting—statistics. In other words, shit happens. Thus, for me, the thwarting of my ambition to pursue a doctorate in psychology was a significant and unexpected blow, once again proving: Forget fair.

Loyola's oversight had cost me an academic year. I was left thinking, *What do I do now?* I couldn't imagine putting my agenda on hold for another year. Given my paucity of resources, I didn't think I could afford the considerable time and expense of reapplying nor further delay in earning a more substantial income. Accordingly, I accepted reality and tacked once again. My ambition to become a licensed psychologist was not to be, but the far more bedrock desire to become a psychotherapist was still within my reach. While at Sheppard-Pratt, I had learned that unlike the master's degree in psychology (which at that time did not enable licensing as a therapist), a master's in social work offered a license to practice psychotherapy, like psychiatrists and psychologists, albeit with less prestige and pay.

That is how, in 1978, at the age of twenty-eight, I entered the two-year master's program at the University of Maryland School of Social Work on a full-time basis while also continuing to work full-time for Sheppard-Pratt Hospital. I would put in eighty-plus-hour workweeks for the next two years, including summers, a hardship for me but even harder for Jane, who was burdened with taking total care of the kids in my absence. However, I was completely mission focused, determined to get my license as quickly as possible so the hard times could be behind us, and we could finally afford a better life.

I graduated with a master's in social work on January 13, 1980, my thirtieth birthday. Within several months I would be a licensed psychotherapist, thereby accomplishing my goal even if not in the way I had planned. As it does to everyone, life had presented obstacles. And, like most people, I had learned to adapt, move and counter-move, sometimes going backward to get ahead, but never losing sight of my goal.

CHAPTER 19

POWER?

M aster of Social Work degree safely in hand along with more than three years as the Program Coordinator of Sheppard-Pratt's Evening Treatment Program, I felt the need to expand my horizons. Specifically, I wanted to do more clinical work. Amazingly, a family therapist in the Day Program had an equivalent desire to move into a more administrative post. The timing was perfect. Ta-da: I magically transformed into a family therapist with the business cards to prove it.

My career as a family therapist started off with a thud. As I walked down the hall toward my office, I anticipated meeting with the family of a newly admitted patient. As I neared, I observed a good number of people milling around my door. I thought *Wow, this is a big family. It's heartwarming that they all came out in such support.* Beaming in the glow of their family love, I greeted them warmly, and we all squeezed uncomfortably into my closet-sized office.

Sitting knee-to-knee, I began the interview and, after several minutes, found myself becoming more, rather than less, confused about who was who, and what each person's relationship was to the other and the patient. Nevertheless, I doggedly pursued my agenda, fighting ever-harder to make sense of things. But the more I dug, the deeper the hole; I just couldn't make sense of how the patient had two fathers, two mothers, and two wives. Finally, professional veneer worn thin, I confessed my confusion. Soon, the problem became apparent: I wasn't meeting with one family but two—I had inadvertently double-booked the hour. Fortunately, everyone had a sense of humor and, aside from my red-faced embarrassment, escaped without harm.

As the weeks passed, I grew into my role as family therapist, becoming ever more knowledgeable about how little I knew. Daily, I was discovering the uncomfortable truth that graduate programs, most generalist in nature, cover a wide variety of topics but specialize in none. The nine credit hours I had completed in the theory and practice of family therapy had not prepared me for the shifting complexities presented by a single family, much less many different families over the course of weeks, months and years. I was learning that every family has its set of issues and prevailing dynamics, and presents them in myriad ways. But the most amazing thing, one which defied logic, was that each would fight to keep their dysfunctional behaviors, and each would pose a unique and ever-mutating challenge to all efforts to effect change.

Acutely feeling my deficits, I signed up for a workshop conducted by Bill Goldsmith, DSW (pseudonym), a faculty member of the famous Philadelphia Child Guidance Center, on the theory and practice of structural family therapy. The workshop was well-attended and abuzz with conversation as we waited for Dr. Goldsmith's arrival; he was ten minutes late and counting. Finally, rushing in, hair unkempt, he entered the auditorium. In harried fashion, awkwardly struggling with a jumble of files that threatened to spill from his arms at every jagged step, he fumbled his way to the stage. Already the poster-child for overwhelmed and incompetent, he proceeded to trip on the stairs and launch the files across the floor. The audience gasped, and nearby attendees jumped to the rescue.

I felt sorry for him. I could identify with embarrassing beginnings and the feeling of hurried and harried. I also felt sorry for myself. I had been so looking forward to this workshop, but it did not appear that Dr. Goldsmith was up to the challenge. I anticipated the worst: a tedious few hours and a waste of both my money and my precious time.

Dr. Goldsmith, files clutched anew in his arms, completed his unceremonious journey to the podium. There he became a different person. He proceeded to use his bumbling and dramatic entrance, and the assemblies' rescuing response to illustrate how the group was rewarding dysfunctional behavior. He pointed out rightly that it was his job to be on time, organized and prepared, yet here he was, none of those things, and we were showering him with concern and care. With this challenge, he had enlivened the audience and grabbed our attention.

From there, Bill used storytelling and video clips to illuminate the theory of structural family therapy. His ideas were new and heady stuff. I might even say empowering since that was the buzzword of workshops of that era. He certainly had me hooked, excited by the promise of mastery and competence that had eluded me till now. That was a titillating promise, the Golden Fleece stimulating another quest, standing as it did in such stark relief to the uncertainty and floundering of my day-to-day professional life.

Upon my return to Sheppard-Pratt, I set out to implement a plan to acquire such training. I couldn't afford the time or money to travel to Philadelphia, so I began thinking about how I could bring the program to me. Sheppard-Pratt agreed to provide a meeting room, video recording equipment, and a one-way vision room. The participants would pay for Dr. Goldsmith, who was very receptive to the idea. Thus situated, the training group began every other week meetings in 1981 that would continue for three years.

It was an exhilarating time comprised of learning theory, applying theory to practice, analyzing videotapes of sessions, receiving live supervision from Bill via phone from behind the one-way vision mirror, and having Bill join me in the treatment room to demonstrate how a master therapist would do things. I learned the importance of observing sequences of interactions that unfolded like a dance with recurring steps within each family. I learned how to create paradoxical interventions and family crises designed to disorganize the family so that the dynamics would become more visible and the family more amenable to grab on to new forms of organization. The theory was that the families, tricked into consciousness, would be more amenable to taking on new and healthier family structures. I made use of field theory, questioning the relationship between cause and effect. I learned about sub-groups and shifting alliances and the tendency for family members to exchange roles—playing musical chairs on the Titanic—providing the illusion of change while maintaining the very same dysfunctional relationship patterns. By this time, it was well known that when the "identified patient" in a family started to improve, another family member would often begin presenting symptoms, assuming the role that had so recently been vacated. Such shifting of functions, managed by an unskilled therapist, would result in the focus of attention careening from one family member to another, as the dysfunctional family structure remained untouched.

Over time, I developed a growing expertise. Bill validated me as a skilled therapist, admiring to the group my willingness to "go where even angels fear to tread," and predicted that I would publish professionally. But the biggest thing I learned over those three years was this: structural family therapy was not for me.

I would tell Bill, "It's manipulative." Bill would brush this concern aside, arguing that all therapy was, falsely equating influence with manipulation. I would counter, "Influence isn't orchestrated or disguised, and no trickery is involved."

In the structural approach, there was no valuing of the importance of understanding someone, his heart or soul, his motivations. Nor was there any valuing of an authentic relationship between therapist and patient. The therapist did things intentionally—from his superior wisdom—to act upon the patient or family. I didn't like the feel of that; it smacked of presumption and arrogance, two attitudes that seemed to go hand in hand with the pursuit of "empowerment" by a therapist, so highly touted in the workshops of that era.

The last problem I had and the most critical was: it didn't work. Sure, in the short-term, patients and families would change their behaviors, but significant regressions would follow early success. I saw two reasons for this. First, the therapist had lost credibility with the patient and family because the manipulative nature and the lack of authentic connection were felt, even if not named. Second, that change was built on something exterior, behavior, rather than something interior, the way people saw, thought and felt about things.

The theory relied on the premise that if you can change a patient or family's behavior, the psyche (which structuralists did not grant the existence of) would follow. It sounded good; it just didn't work. Patients weren't getting better in an enduring way. And, to me, this only made sense: If people continued to see things the same way, the likelihood of any change in behavior persisting across time was minimal, relying as it would on will rather than want.

The embers of my growing questioning of the merits of structural family therapy were only fanned into flame when I changed jobs in 1982 and was introduced into another, far more complex approach, and far more thoughtful.

I was yearning to learn something new. Something was missing in my understanding of mental illness and human relationships, and how to treat them. Not knowing what else to do, I decided to plunge deeper into the human condition. I applied for a job as a clinical social worker on Long-Term Adult Psychiatric Inpatient Unit B-2.

CHAPTER 20

OUT-PATIENT TO IN-PATIENT TO
IM-PATIENT

What had I gotten into? At the not so tender age of thirty-three, I found myself working on a long-term, locked-door inpatient unit, housing twenty severely ill people. These folks were suffering from a word-salad of major psychiatric disorders manifested at their most extreme: major depression, bipolar disorder with psychotic features, multiple personality disorder, eating disorder, borderline personality disorder, and schizophrenia. Many were suicidal, some homicidal. There was a woman who self-enucleated an eyeball, taking the biblical injunction "If thine eye offends thee, pluck it out, and cast it from thee" quite literally. Another lady leapt from the top of a parking garage and lived to suffer the ongoing pain of her now broken body and festering regret. Yet, another woman, drowned her three children to save them from the Devil. Imagine that. How does one help this woman who, once she overcame her psychosis with the benefit of medications, had to somehow come to grips with the horror of what she had done?

These are tales of human tragedy with a capital T and the kind of tremendous suffering commonplace on unit B-2. Let me assure you; it was not the kind of suffering touched by empowered therapists or behavioral therapy. What therapist would be arrogant enough to assume the all-knowing mantle of power in the face of these grisly life-and-death dramas? What reward would be so great that we could offer that would change the wish to die or a psychotic desire to kill?

Sheppard-Pratt was world famous for treating the troubled of the troubled, the last stop for patients who had experienced multiple unsuccessful inpatient treatment stays elsewhere. Patients came from all over the world: Asia, Europe, and Latin America, as well as the United States and Canada.

When I arrived on B-2, I discovered that the staff equated social work with handing out benefits checks and functioning as a family liaison and discharge planner, none of which appealed to me. To add to my sense of disenfranchisement, the unit was psychoanalytically oriented to its core—the theoretical orientation founded by Sigmund Freud, which, far from the behavioral emphasis of structural family therapy, concerned itself with the workings of the human psyche and forces not visible to the naked eye. I had little knowledge of psychoanalytic theory and practice or ability to use its language. I was starting from scratch once again and feared I had made a huge career mistake.

Attending my first treatment team meeting, I looked around the conference room. At the head of the team sat Maria Klement, M.D., B-2's service chief. Austrian, her English heavily accented, her bearing queenly in the best sense of the term, she sat tall and austere, thinning hair coiffed, back ramrod straight—regal without effort or pretense. She was one of those rare people whose poise would never falter, come tumultuous sea or mutinous crew. In the years ahead, she always managed to remain above the fray and maintain perspective, never becoming reactive or raising her voice. Her hand was ever steady on the rudder of the treatment team.

The chairs surrounding her, forming the necklace to her focal stone, were occupied by gems in their own right. Clarence Schulz, M.D., senior training psychoanalyst for the Baltimore/Washington Psychoanalytic Training Program and author of the book *Case Studies in Schizophrenia*; two psychiatrists, one from Mexico and one from Wales; and a psychiatric resident, incredibly from both Harvard and Yale, who would author several books in the coming years. Finally, a post-doctoral fellow in psychology whose husband was the medical director of Chestnut Lodge, an even more famous psychiatric hospital located outside nearby Washington, D.C.

Yeah! Was there any wonder I was uncomfortable with these Ivy Leaguers? I had none of their education nor their polish. I had nothing in common with them; I didn't even own a suit. I wanted to shout, "Pass the Grey Poupon!" just to create the illusion I belonged.

But that wasn't the end of it. Augmenting this lineup of psychotherapists were a potpourri of nurses, art therapists, dance therapists, occupational therapists, and general mental health staff with decades of hands-on experience and hard-earned wisdom. Viewed through the eyes of a guy who had barely made it out of high school, was kicked out of college, had a less than stellar career in business, followed by an even more trying tour as an auto-mechanic and auto-body man, this was an entirely different world than that to which I was accustomed. I simply didn't fit. Resisting the urge to push my imaginary baseball cap back on my head and scratch my armpits, I escaped from that first meeting unscathed by any requirement to participate—I knew I was swimming in deep waters and sensed they were far deeper than I knew.

My saving grace was that I knew how to persevere alone in a foreign place where I knew neither the culture nor the language.

I knew how to nod my head in what I hoped was a convincing parody of wisdom and avoid saying "Wee" at all costs. I knew how to manage my fear of figuratively getting kicked to the floor or slapped in the face if I said something inadvertently wrong or outright stupid. I knew to keep my mouth shut as I dug in to listen, and listen, and listen, in hopes of learning what these folks had to impart.

In the ensuing weeks, I was surprised by something that should not have been a surprise at all. Despite the academic accomplishments, worldly successes, and venerated, if not exalted positions of the treatment staff, each and every one of them, with the exceptions of the elder statesmen Doctors Klement and Schulz, were rendered human by the need to vie for position in some imaginary pecking order. Indeed, as I came to know them, they were not dissimilar from those Alabama boys outside the Montgomery movie theater all those years ago. The psychiatrists had cherished egos and would posture intellectually like roosters. Add to this the heated arguments that would break out among professional sub-groups, and the result was an atmosphere more riven by emotional agenda than one might ever expect among such a seasoned and polished group of mental health practitioners.

The major source of the tension was the inherent conflicts between the various professional sub-groups. While the psychiatrists dwelled in the ether of psychoanalytic theory, the nurses, facing the reality of dealing with twenty ever-demanding and often combative patients, ground their teeth in suppressed rage, their need for action often frustrated by the psychiatrists' emphasis on theorizing and reflection.

Although the conflicts resulting from these various pressures could readily lead to vitriolic interchanges, I would learn that these moments of aggression fit within a broader tapestry of deep relationships and genuine caring that only accrues between those who have been in battle together. In the months and years to come, I would learn that we were all in the trenches, and no one escaped unbloodied—including me.

Within several months of joining the unit, my frustration was profound. All the treatment team seemed to do was talk, talk, talk. The emphasis was on thinking about thoughts, feelings, and underlying motivations with little focus on doing anything. The inaction was driving me crazy. I kept wondering, *How are we helping? Why aren't we doing something?* I was forever teetering on the cusp of leaving.

What held me back was that I sensed these people understood *something* profound. I couldn't put my finger on what it was, but I knew it was there. I couldn't leave no matter how much of a misfit I felt nor how frustrated I became; my curiosity wouldn't let me. I had to discover what that *something* was. I wanted it for myself.

Beset by questions rather than answers, I started going to the Medical Library every free moment. I read books over lunch, in my office, between meetings, and at home. For the next five years, I read and read and read, immersing myself in the psychoanalytic literature. I paid particular attention to writings on *primitive mental states*, the state of mind to which we all regress given sufficient stress. What I read was often erudite and so intellectualized that it left me cold. But from most of what I read, I was able to sift tidbits of insight that furthered my understanding of the human psyche. And, every once in a while, like sluicing for gold, I came across some nugget that shined a bright light of understanding on what previously had been in darkness. I found this seemingly random occurrence both thrilling and addictive. It kept me reading.

I came to understand that primitive mental states are in fact childhood ways of feeling and thinking, that all of us can relate to, the two-year-old's obstinacy or dramatic loss of control exhibited in an adult being only one example. In other words, re-gressed mental states aren't crazy in themselves, they are part of healthy human development, both yours and mine. People don't regress to something they never were; they regress to something they had been: a former, less developed, state of mental/emo-tional functioning.

A light bulb went on: the difference between those we might call mentally healthy and those less so is not that great. While all individuals regress from time to time, the psychologically vul-nerable will regress far more often or even dwell in these less developed mental states. Even more fascinating to me was the idea that we don't revert haphazardly but return to the devel-opmental state we were at when things first started to go awry. In this sense, each treatment case became a mystery, not unlike those encountered by Sherlock Holmes. Unfortunately, knowing the time or the cause of the problem didn't fix it; that was a far more complex task.

I can imagine some of you taking issue with all this. You might say, "I don't know what you're talking about. I have nev-er experienced regression." But I would respectfully say, "Toro Caca." Have you never been reactive? Have you never yelled out of control at your kids or your spouse, your brother or your sister? Have you never experienced the breakup of a relationship or loss of a loved one like a blow to the stomach that left you feeling like you didn't want to live? Have you never peeked at a Jerry Springer show, or been to the dark places inside yourself? For that matter, have you never shouted at or imagined inflicting terrible things on the turtle-speed drivers who insist on staying in the passing lane? Personally, I've lost count of how many rocket-propelled grenades I've sent up the tailpipes of these inconsiderate daw-dlers. That's what I'm talking about, all that reactivity, absent self-observation, hesitation, or self-reflection. These are the hall-marks of regressed behaviors be they only for a moment or for longer periods of time. When they persist in an adult, we have evidence of a truncated development and mental illness.

I could go on with examples from the everyday life of so-called ordinary people—that is, you and me (okay, maybe just you)—who are normal-neurotics. We suffer guilt (unlike the sociopath or the narcissist), function well, and yet still run up and down the scale of psychiatric intensities. Not only do we all visibly regress in times of high stress, but we suffer tiny regressions daily. Why? Because we're not machines. We're living, sentient, organic entities, cursed and blessed with astounding sensitivities. We're continually responding in ways large and small, most out of conscious awareness, to the moment-to-moment fluctuations of the innumerable happenings in our minds as they co-mingle or co-mangle with objective external reality. Coming to these realizations shattered my previously held and reassuring conviction that the psychiatrically troubled were distinctly different. And if they weren't? Maybe I also wasn't as healthy as I liked to assume I was, yet secretly feared I wasn't. What was I not seeing in myself?

Over the years, I've learned the importance of acknowledging my own less than socially acceptable thoughts and feelings. Consequently, this has helped me to relate better not only to my patients but to all people. My patients feel recognized, understood and accepted because they are. They know because they can feel it. I look over at them, not up or down at them, as fellow travelers in this obstacle course called life. A course that leaves none of us unscathed. Indeed, I see many of my patients as possessing extraordinary integrity and courage in their willingness to examine their lives. This *will to vulnerability* stands in stark contrast to that of others who are not even aware or interested in examing themselves; who dismiss the very notion of problems or weaknesses of any kind, much preferring their polished story-lines over any honest examination of themselves or their relationships.

This fear of examining the low-light reel of ourselves is an issue for everyone, including therapists. In fact, I believe that the primary problem many therapists have in treating more extreme pathologies lies in the therapist's resistance to re-visiting, re-living, remembering, and sometimes re-experiencing the rawness of their own primitive mental states. It's understandable that no one would want to brush up against such feelings. All I'm saying is that a therapist, particularly one dedicated to treating major psychopathology, must be willing.

But this is also true for anyone who aspires to deepen their relationships to themselves and their others. Empathy, a crucial component of any healthy relationship, entails the capacity to identify with the other, that is to recognize oneself in the other and the other in oneself. Real empathy does not allow for cherry-picking. Where I reject or deny a dark or salacious aspect of myself, I will inevitably be denying in myself these less than attractive aspects of my patients, friends, and family. And, the terrible truth is, where empathy is lacking help, love or care is unlikely to follow.

Over the years, I slowly took to heart psychoanalytic thinking. As opposed to the behaviorally oriented surface approaches, it spoke to my soul; It made sense of things, not only *what* people were doing but *why* they were doing it. Importantly for me, psychoanalytic theory also provided a method for shedding a light of understanding on my not-yet-understood feelings.

I now understood that the We and the They (staff and patients; normal and pathologic) was a false dichotomy. At the end of the day, we all place somewhere across the human spectrum, not at one pole or the other. Consequently, there is only a Us, most people struggling to make their way as best they can, others not so much. Sometimes one's way simply isn't good enough. For progress to occur, be it in our lives or that of our others, a path must be found to renew development: to mature, evolve and deepen our understanding of ourselves and our others—otherwise we just run in place, continuing to revolve rather than evolve.

Typically, continuing development ensues from the capacity to tolerate each other's regressions, while simultaneously working hard to make sense of them. When this process occurs again and again, we find ourselves hatching to a space and place beyond that we often might not have been able to imagine beforehand.

However, such processes go against our survival instinct. They require a willingness to tolerate feeling vulnerable, risking blame and shame, and the process takes courage and time. Finally, it also requires integrity, the willingness to honestly face ourselves and confront our hypocrisies and gaps in reason and logic.

Struggling with these ideas, I asked Dr. Schulz if he would provide supervision. I further asked him for a referral to a psychoanalytically oriented therapist. My single criteria: that the therapist is a mature human being. I had met some therapists who were well trained, most better than I, but who lacked the human quality of relatedness. I did not trust such people to be helpful. For me, relationship is key. The therapists I wanted to avoid, knew the theory but functioned defensively, in intellectualized ways, somewhat like scientists treating the patient like an organism in a petri dish. Dr. Schulz's response was confirming, "Ah! The short list."

What I came to realize over my ten years of working on B-2 was that my learning had begun before I had entered its hallowed halls. It had started the first day I had driven onto the campus and had drunk in the sight of the beautiful lawns dotted with ancient trees and well-spaced Adirondack chairs. It had been furthered in the large airy rooms full of light and color, ensconced in the protective battlements of those aging buildings. They had been whispering their secrets all along if only

I had had the ears to listen. What was important? History, setting, time and space, and the safety to consider one's thoughts
and feel one's feelings with someone who can relate to them and
think about them with you.

Inside those buildings, I learned the incalculable importance
of having someone to talk to who is honestly interested. Someone
who is not frightened or appalled but rather willing and able to
enter those dark places. To let you know that not only are you not
alone, but you're also not even all that unusual. To help *you* make
sense of *yourself.*

I do not know if you have had the experience of having another person clearly interested in and capable of attending carefully to your words. If not, you might consider remedying that.
Psychotherapy makes you realize that your thoughts and feelings
are valuable in ways beyond your imagination. As the therapist
asks about a particular word or thought you've uttered or about
the way you've said it that had seemed relatively innocuous to
you, you start to consider your thoughts and feelings in a far
more serious way.

It is as we try to explain ourselves to the therapist that we
come to know ourselves better. Remember when I was teaching
that economics class all those years ago? Only when I tried to explain it did I discover what I did not know I did not know. In just
this way, when we stumble upon our own ill-logic or gaps in our
internal narratives, something intrinsically human happens—we
become the object of our own curiosity.

Think of that! To be curious about yourself, what a beautiful thing. Yet people are almost universally apprehensive about
reflecting upon themselves, particularly with another. Most people reject such an idea out of hand. Why do you think that is?
Might it be fear of what's repressed? Might it be fear of regression? Might it be fear of what the therapist might be thinking?
Might it be that they suspect they are not quite who they think

they are? Might they be afraid of letting someone else in, of being ridiculed, shamed or blamed? What do you think? Can any of this apply to you?

Some of you may dismiss all this as psychobabble. Hey, you're singing to the choir here. I use to be a full-fledged, card-carrying member of your community. But be patient, soon I will illustrate, using myself as an example. If you do not have a clue as to what I am talking about by the end of this tale, then no harm has been done except perhaps that I've wasted your time and a little bit of your money. But to the degree your life is not going well, that you are unhappy with yourself or a relationship, I would urge you to consider the possibility that what I'm talking about is important and applies to you. Indeed, I'll venture that you may discover that the cause of your unhappiness does not rest outside of you, but is largely within yourself.

I know. You don't like that idea. It may even make you angry. But, if you think about it, it's actually good news for the only thing we have any control over is the capacity to change ourselves.

Of course, all this took me years to figure out. It was not written in any one place, but in many places and pieced together over time, lots of time. What may have been obvious to others had not been obvious to me. Each piece was a discovery, both exhilarating and sobering. It was my time now. I felt a growing need to be on the receiving end of the therapist/patient experience, to walk the walk, and not just talk the talk. I entered psycho-analysis.

CHAPTER 21

PSYCHO-ANALYSIS

Given my military brat upbringing, I would never have been open to being a patient if I had not first been a therapist. I simply would not have had the courage to put myself in the hands of another in that way: it was too intimate, too touchy-feely. And, after all, I had not found being in the hands of others to be a particularly safe or rewarding place nor experienced many benefits to acknowledging feelings of vulnerability.

But the truth is, I was driven by a disquiet within myself that I could no longer pretend I did not feel. It was something I had felt most of my life but always explained away. I would say to myself, "That's just the way it is. It's just the way I am. It's just the way things are." But now, as a therapist, continually confronting the issues of others, I was forever being reminded of my own and feeling increasingly like a charlatan. After all, how could I continue to encourage others to confront their unrests while I avoided mine?

I couldn't afford regular psychoanalysis, so I became a training case at the Baltimore Washington Center for Psychoanalysis and Psychotherapy. This necessitated meeting four times weekly with a therapist in training to become an analyst. In the beginning, I had no real goals, other than to deepen my understanding of myself. All I knew was that I would go through a course of psychoanalysis to see where it would take me. Still, I had serious trepidations. A friend had entered analysis several months earlier and told me how, after just a few short minutes lying on the couch, the experience became so intense that he shot bolt upright and could not continue.

Just think about that for a moment. You're lying on a couch talking about yourself with someone sitting out of sight behind you, and the experience becomes so discombobulating that the intensity compels you to sit up as if you just stuck your toe in an electric socket. What would cause that? If we consider my friend's panicked experience, we soon deduce that the only frightening thing in the room was the inner workings of his mind; after all, it's not likely that the analyst was going to pick up a meat cleaver and attack him. So, maybe we army brats need to recalibrate our thinking. Is it possible that included among the most courageous things a human being can do is the act of confronting the workings of one's own mind?

Now, here I was in that circumstance, lying upon the couch, the analyst out of sight behind me, my horizons limited to the ceiling of the room and the wall beyond my outstretched feet. The object of our mutual attention? ...*Me.*

What the hell was I supposed to say? I was not being asked questions or given a clue about what to talk about. And, given the fact the analyst sat out of sight behind me, I couldn't read his facial expressions or body language. It was even difficult to garner cues from his speech such as tone, pitch, pace, rhythm, kinesthetic energy and so on. Why? Because the son-of-a-bitch didn't talk, and when he did, it wasn't in the form of a conversation. No, it was in the form of rare and concise comments, seemingly advanced for my consideration. "Hell," I thought, "if I knew what to think I wouldn't need him."

There was no back and forth. I was left to my own devices and soon became a blathering idiot. What could I possibly talk about four hours a week with a person I couldn't see and who rarely responded? I didn't have much to say or at least not much that I thought was worth saying, after all, on the whole, my life was going okay. It was one thing to focus on others in the role of therapist, for they were separate and usually posing some issue that I found interesting that they wanted to address and it was they who provided the grist for the mill of my thinking. It was quite another to focus on myself with no clear agenda in mind.

My thinking blurred and became confused as I shadow boxed with my internal board of editors, who were critical of my every thought, and rendered me deaf and dumb. It was as if my mind refused to be pinned down in any defined position that would leave me vulnerable to attack in the form of the scathing comments of my internal father or the sarcastic and competitive quips of my inner brothers who in my mind were ready to pounce at every turn. After all, brothers will be brothers.

Given my self-critical babble, I was sure I would be bored to death by the vapidness of my commentary and that the analyst would not be far behind. What could I talk about that would be interesting to *him*, that wouldn't lessen his view of me and bring it into line with my worst critically devaluing thoughts about my-self? A part of me was quite skilled with these, having internal-ized the demeaning, belittling, and mocking treatment by my father. That's what was important, right? Impress the therapist and in that way, stay safe.

As I related to my silent, invisible therapist as if he were a stand-in for my father or siblings, I couldn't imagine anything safe to say. Increasingly desperate, I pushed the pedal to the metal, often saying the most inappropriate or repulsive things that came to mind to prompt my therapist to react. I tried to inspire, cajole, provoke, demand from the analyst some action around which I could organize myself. My initial goal of self-understanding had now become secondary to my need of connection and an external locus around which to organize myself, to stay safe. What did I get back? Typically silence, and in my kinder moments, I filled the void by imagining the analyst as calmly forbearing, patiently waiting for me to stop testing him and get down to work.

Absent the usual external cues to which I had always moored, I had slipped anchor and soon found myself adrift in the swirling currents and eddies of my mind. I wished for something, anything, to focus on, around which to organize myself and to center my world, not unlike the back of that chair in the dining hall of College St. Etienne. The algorithms learned in the formative years of my development, which had organized my understanding of life and how to keep myself safe, strained to wrap themselves around this experience so unlike any I'd previously known. My thinking began to feed upon itself; All that existed were the smoke and mirrors of my imaginings, like a snake eating its tail. I was caught in a wormhole, spiraling backward in time and space toward long-held ways of thinking and feeling, ways I hadn't remembered and wasn't fully cognizant of until catapulted into them by the power of this regressive journey. I was discovering what people learn in a sensory deprivation tank; there is no more frightening place in this world or beyond than our own minds.

What I came to understand as I struggled with the shrieks and urgent whisperings of my psyche was that more than anything else I wanted to be rid of this flagellating self-criticalness. To my consternation, the process of psychoanalysis only amplified my disquiet but in doing so gave it voice. I became emotionally exhausted shadow boxing with myself. And finally, I had had enough. I gave up that hopeless effort of trying to imagine and worry about what my analyst might be thinking and instead started focusing on *my* thoughts and feelings. It was then I gave myself up to the analytic injunction: Say whatever comes to mind without censorship. I had finally fired the censors. My motivation: self-inflicted misery.

That's when I discovered what I had not known before, that the best sessions occurred when I was completely free to associate rather than being driven by a fear-based agenda or funneled by reactivity. In the relatively calm and clearer waters of this more free-flowing state of mind sub-conscious thoughts and feelings were freer to emerge. These denizens of the deep, rising slowly to the surface like manatees, were illuminated in the moonbeams of my analyst's occasional comments. When this occurred, seemingly small, yet fascinating discoveries were made.

On one occasion, struggling in a difficult relationship, I started talking about a dream. In the dream, I had dug a furrow around the foundation of my house, in which I was planting cowboy books by Louis L'Amour. I was aware that I was trying to buttress the house that was clearly a stand-in for my relationship; as I considered this, I realized that L'Amour means "the love" in French. I think the idea of the cowboy books spoke to the desire for a simple life without melodrama, core values of hard work and straightforwardness, all characteristics I discovered sorely lacking in that relationship. I finally realized that not only did I not love her no matter how hard I tried, no matter how many books I planted, but that I didn't even like her.

I had entered psychoanalysis determined to endure the experience no matter what—to see where it or "I" would take me. To my surprise, as profoundly disturbing as it was, the experience was still not as bad as I had feared. After all, I already knew something about isolation, about being alone, about being left with only my thoughts and feelings for company, bereft of human connection.

However, inexplicably, I did begin crying that first session and from every session on for the next six months. Tears just rolled and rolled and I had no idea why I was crying. Only later did I realize that the isolation of psychoanalysis, including the difficulty in connecting with the analyst (at least as analysis was conducted at that time), strummed the taught chords of the uncertainty, anxiety, sadness, loss, all-aloneness and terrible emptiness of my childhood. It was all there, right there, happening *right now.*

What I learned in my four years of psychoanalysis could be summed up in a few sentences. But do not misunderstand; I am not saying psychoanalysis was a waste of time. Far from it, it was a life saver. What I learned was as much emotional as it was intellectual, a developmental achievement rather than merely a cognitive understanding. This growth required the full four years, lying supine on that couch that became home.

As you can surmise, psychoanalysis can be intensely absorbing and regressive for those willing to give themselves up to its undertow, carrying us back into long-forgotten childhood states of heart and mind that in silent whispers influence our lives both in and out of adult awareness. You might well ask, "What's the point of all this?" The point is it's an opportunity to change the experience of yourself forever. I'll spare you slogging through all the psychological swamp mud that it took for me to get there. Instead, I'll jump right over to the firm ground of what I learned.

Gradually, recognizing the pain and insanity arising from my continuing dependence on my analyst's responsiveness, my focus slowly turned to looking within myself for the wellspring of meaning in my life. With this shift, painfully won, I stopped devoting myself to defensiveness and settled into treatment. I began making my thoughts, feelings, and sensations the object of my curiosity and attention, working hard to recognize, observe and reflect upon them for myself. In doing so, I came to appreciate the analyst as someone upon whom I could rely to insert himself into my stream of consciousness *when* he felt he had something to offer, but never to rescue me from myself. Via these struggles, my mind was gradually evolving from a self-suppressive tyrannical governance to a republic with a constitution valuing above all else the freedom of thought and speech. That shift took me about a year.

That may sound like a long time, but it isn't if you consider the nature of it. I had stopped being psychologically dependent. Having undergone this separation, the desire to construct a parental or higher authority in service of the illusion that *He* would take care of me and tell me what to do, or what was what, had been wrung from my system. Instead, I now examined whatever the analyst had to say, but knew I had to decide for myself how it might, or might not, apply to me: I had to be the interpreter of my own meaning. I was on what is called *the road toward autonomy*; I was becoming more independent and more psychologically adult, more free of childlike attachments. Not bad for a single year.

Confronting my fears was a liberating process. Whenever I did, they became more manageable, smaller rather than bigger, and sometimes even dissipated altogether. The result was the unfolding of an internal play-space, where sound thinking could occur in that I was no longer in fear of being slapped down or, even worse, of me slapping myself down for my thoughts and feelings. I came to understand psychotherapy as a revolutionary process. I was breaking out of the constraining shell, the self-fettering tyranny of prejudices and unconscious assumptions, that had ruled freely as a part of the legacy of childhood. Many of these I had learned from the *adults* in my life, the very people who *did* tell me what to think and what was what. I further recognized they, as well as the generations that had preceded them, had never been in a self-examining process like psychotherapy and had imbibed the imparted *truths* of their elders with hardly a hiccup. Thus, ways of being and behaving had been passed down through generations without a second thought, often without a first. As they came to consciousness with the aid of my analyst, I began subjecting these beliefs to scrutiny, in the attempt to carve out a life that made sense to me. Perhaps this is what the great trumpeter and composer Miles Davis meant when he said, "Sometimes you have to play a long time to be able to play music like yourself."

Near the beginning of the third year of psychoanalysis, nestled on that couch that had become a home, I was made aware of an underlying assumption that had been the hub of the way I was living my life and yet had been entirely unknown to me. This awareness came without warning one day when I told my therapist something that seemed completely innocuous to me. I had come upon a recently articulable ambition, one partially tinged by regret in that it recognized the limits of what I could accomplish and, in the vernacular of the army brat, exclaimed: "I want to become the best master sergeant at Sheppard-Pratt Hospital." In the medical model of the hospital at that time, psychiatrists, followed by psychologists, were the officer equivalent, while the best a social worker could hope for was to rise to the top of the non-commissioned ranks.

My analyst, himself a psychiatrist, responded with a deceptively simple and softly posed question, the five words of which spoke to my self-limiting regret and would change my life forever: "Why just a master sergeant?"

PART IV

FOCUSED PECKING—HATCHING 103

Now I was hatching in earnest; we might call it focused pecking. Not only was I breaking out of my shell, but I was also breaking into the world. Originally more a passive object, the equivalent of a leaf being carried along by the currents of life, I was now an active subject, swimming. I could swim against the current or with it. I could even swim to the shore and take a cross-country walk. I was shaping my world as the world was shaping me. It was no longer a one-sided battle. Now we—the world and I—were co-mingling, not co-mangling. I could live with that.

CHAPTER 22

"WHY JUST A MASTER SERGEANT?"

Those words hung in the air and whirled around my brain like ping pong balls in a lottery machine as numerous rationales to sprang to mind. But no matter how I tried, I couldn't push the question away.

It wasn't only the question but the fact that he, a psychiatrist, had asked it. Apparently, *he* could imagine my being more than a master sergeant, so why couldn't I? Maybe this was why he was a psychiatrist, and I was a social worker. I couldn't imagine how rising higher in the professional ranks was an option, but clearly, the possibility occurred to him. My analyst had given me a gift: a future horizon that was expanding and rife with possibilities. I didn't know what the alternatives were, but he certainly had me wondering.

In the prototypic framework of my familial role of being a spectator while Jacques held court at center stage, it had never occurred to me to consider the possibility of being center stage myself: it just was *not* the way of things. What better argument was there than that? In the months to follow, I took the question, "Why just a master sergeant?" seriously, especially since I recognized that I had patterned my existence along just this story line.

Professionally, I had recreated in the treatment team my familial role. Others stood center stage while I lent support and an occasional comment.

But what was my alternative? How was I to compare to people from Vienna, Harvard and Yale and all the medical and doctoral programs the others had attended? How was I to overcome the *medical model* of the psychiatric hospital wherein psychiatrists were the service chiefs and the team leaders, even if the latter were only young residents? The psychologists were also of the officer class, functioning alongside the psychiatrists in the role of individual therapists. Social workers were assigned solely to working with the families, not trusted in the rarified realms of individual psychotherapy. In this hierarchy, mine had been a role that fit me like an old suit of clothes—it felt a part of *me* as if it was *me*. But how could this be? A role isn't something someone is, is it? Isn't a role something one plays or performs?

As I delved deeper, I realized I couldn't attribute my life as a spectator completely to the familial and familiar, I recognized I had motivation for remaining there: fear. Being in the center was like being one of those yellow tin duckies at a county fair shooting gallery, the kind that moves along on a rail while the customer shoots at it with a bb gun. I had discovered long ago that you could only hit them if they are standing up. By extension, I had deduced that I only risked getting shot or slapped down if I drew attention to myself. My dad had taught me that hard-won lesson. Conversely, if I kept a low profile, my chances of remaining unscathed were much better, unless, of course, you count the cost of a self-limited life.

I now understood that to become a new and improved version of me I would have to take the risk of putting myself out there. The essential difference was that I was no longer a little boy growing up in an adult world that could knock me down with impunity. Now, I was a grown man who could stand up for himself.

Beleaguered by such serious thoughts, I groaned aloud as another consideration took hold: I realized I was worried for Jacques. I worried about overthrowing him in the family dynamics. I knew, even if he did not, that he was as dependent on his role as I had been on mine. If I changed my role in the family, what would happen to his? Was there room for both of us?

Certainly, this was a childish thought—the thinking derived from childhood often is—but that didn't make it any less potent. Perhaps it made it even more powerful, connected as it was with the feelings of a much younger, more emotional and sensitive age. My concern for Jacques was palpable, similar to the empathy I felt for him years earlier when I had bested him in a fight, and my mother had derided him for his weakness. As past and present melded in my mind, I only knew one thing—I didn't want to do that to him again.

It took a while, but I worked it out. I was trying to be personally responsible for *my* fulfillment, for *my* life, to keep hatching in service of continuing to become myself. If Jacques came to feel somehow threatened by any evolution I was able to effect (which my adult thinking doubted), then he would have to do more evolving as well—nothing wrong with that.

With those concerns set aside, my last piece of resistance to the idea I could be more than a master sergeant came fully to mind and with nauseating intensity: What if I failed; what if I made a fool of myself? The shame, the humiliation would be terrible. I feared irreparable damage to my sense of self. Didn't it make more sense for me never to try and thus never fail?

These concerns were, in turn, countered by my certain knowledge that if I didn't try, I would be forever disappointed in myself. That awareness would torment me for the rest of my life. Of all possible challenges, *that* was not the one I wanted to refuse. Also,

I couldn't bear the idea of the road not traveled. I had to find out where it would take me or, more accurately, where I would take it. I now understood that my choice stood between the risks of moving forward possibly into a spring-fed life, or staying stuck in a growing pool of stagnation. Furthermore, I knew that stagnation would eventually hook up with its compatriot—despair—as my yesterdays became my tomorrows till the day I died. In that situation, the question "What's the point?" would become trenchant. I now knew that to follow my heart required a key ingredient: the courage to fail.

I took the leap of faith in myself and began speaking up in team meetings, using the mindset developed in psychoanalysis. I focused on expressing my thoughts as they pertained to the clinical cases, rather than wasting time worrying about what other members of the treatment team might think about them or me.

It was gratifying to discover that what I offered was usually taken seriously. One team member remarked in an aside as we were leaving a meeting, "Charlie, you're making people think." I started being invited to the weekly therapists meeting.

Then a day came, near the mid-point of my stay on B-2, when Dr. Schulz advised, "Charlie, it's time for you to stop reading and start writing," echoing the prophecy of Bill Goldsmith several years earlier. I was surprised and flattered. What an amazing thing for a highly-lauded teaching analyst and author to say to someone who did not have any formal education or training in the psychoanalytic orientation.

Thus was planted the seed that would usher in a whole new phase of my career, the likes of which I had never dreamt. In life, as in psychoanalysis, I had discovered that by moving toward rather than away from my fears, I was carving a path outside the strictures of my childhood and beyond that of a master sergeant: I was becoming a man; I was claiming the privilege of living *my* life.

It was all the more exciting because I didn't know where this would lead. What I did know was that it didn't matter. Where it did lead me was to a richer, more fully lived life which upon occasion I wished I had never come to know. But generally, I knew I was much the better for it, even during those times when it brimmed with anguish more than joy.

CHAPTER 23

ANGUISH AND JOY OF A PSYCHOTHERAPIST

B eing a psychotherapist challenges me to the core. Not just the training and education; that's the least of it. It compels me to ask the questions, "Who am I and what am I about?" repeatedly.

Psychotherapy requires the therapist's use of his self. He must attend to his own mental workings—his thoughts, feelings, and sensations—as part of the silent, subconscious communication that goes on in any relationship, including that between patient and therapist. The personal and the professional, the mind, heart, and body, interweave; challenges in one area are inevitably reverberating in the others.

For my purposes, still learning to play the music of my life, this has been a good thing, although often not a fun one. It's painful as I catch the lies I tell myself, recognize my hypocrisies, and confront the incongruities and unevenness of my psyche as it becomes exposed in my personal life or the light of my patients' unremitting gaze. Add to this the fact that patients suffering from major psychopathology and its frequent sidekick, hypervigilance, are often exquisitely attuned and gifted in their ability to read others, and you begin to glimpse how daunting the challenges to the therapist may be. Full understanding arrives when you realize that these people, often prone to find fault in others rather than in themselves, are unhesitant in launching demeaning attacks upon you in the attempt to excuse themselves. In short, as a psychotherapist, I found my personhood and sense of self challenged to the core.

At Sheppard-Pratt, I worked with patients and families addressing seemingly impossible situations, often with life and death ramifications. On any given day, I could find myself physically restraining a patient as she bolted from my office in a bid to escape; confront the specter of a patient holding a broken lightbulb against her throat, threatening to cut her carotid artery; meet with a patient who had leapt from a parking garage and, to her chagrin, survived, now broken in body as well as spirit; or, sitting calmly through a man's agitated rantings while hoping he doesn't attack.

Nevertheless, as dramatic as these occurrences could be, the worst was the psychological assaults. The attacks on my sense of reality and my sense of self in the form of verbal assaults and accusations of depravity in the attempt to blame and shame me for whatever sin they imagined I was making. It's not easy to be charged with sadism, smirking, lust, greed, hate, envy, and neglect, to be called "small-dicked" or "lower than whale shit at the bottom of the ocean." It's not easy because, in part, it's all true. I have and had measures of these elements—sins, crimes, flaws, inadequacies, call them what you will—within me. Don't you? The challenge came when they were focused on with the microscopic intensity of the patient's laser vision. Then they were magnified, made bigger than the whole, bigger than the world, seeming to blot out the sun.

You see, it's not just the words, but the melody of scorn and disdain with which they are expressed, all working together to pin me down, freeze me in place like a butterfly in a collection, but without the beauty.

And it's not just the patient talking; it's the patient behaving in ways designed to elicit the very feelings with which I'm accused. One patient repeatedly bumps into me as we walk down the hall together, all the while accusing me of not liking her. A female patient mocks me derisively for lusting after her, while she crosses and uncrosses her legs, flashes her underwear and leans forward so that her blouse falls open. Another patient recently discharged, assures me he has a gun and challenges me not to believe him. He demands, "Do you want me to show it to you? Are you a coward?" Such onslaughts, when endured week in and week out, forge an inextricable mélange of fact and fantasy, fueling my ongoing questioning of myself.

The challenge becomes so widespread that my sense of reality is wrested from me. On balance, I felt annoyed and irritated by the girl who bumped into me as we walked down the hall. Did that mean I didn't like her? I was titillated by the sexy woman who repeatedly flashed me. Did this mean I lusted after her? I was frightened by the guy that threatened me with the idea of a gun. Did this mean I was a coward? Each of these situations and innumerable others over the course of my career forced me to stop, think, and come to my own conclusions. In this way, the self of the psychotherapist is honed.

But the most unsettling of all the experiences was when I felt my sense of reality wrested from me. This occurred most often when caught in the psychological vortex of a delusionally paranoid family. Rife with fears of persecution, they, to a person, would accuse me of saying something I did not think I had said. When I questioned their assertions, they would claim to quote me from a discussion that had occurred minutes earlier, challenging my capacity to remember specifics. They often would change one or two keywords, use sentences out of context, or actively interpret what I did say in persecutory ways. Under the pressure of this accusatory chorus, it became impossible for me to sort out with certainty what was real and what wasn't, even whether I was a good person or a bad one.

In one such instance, the father, was six-foot tall and fiftyish, dressed in jeans and flannel shirt pressed with military precision, covering a lean body seemingly chiseled from granite, his narrow face and hawkish nose set with unblinking eyes of blue stone. He sat ramrod straight, hair pulled tightly back into a ponytail, conveying a predator's hypervigilance and readiness to fend off whatever threat was surely on its way. His waif of a wife, drably dressed, hair lank and brown, personality beaten down, looked fragile, aquiver with anxiety, as she repeatedly snuck peeks at him from the corner of her eyes as if looking for clues on how to avoid or defuse a coming storm. Their two sons, both large-bodied men with round, puffy faces, seemed to follow in their father's aggressive leaning into the world. Their full-figured wives sat in vocal support of their husbands and through them their father-in-law, who was unmistakably the unchallenged head of this family.

Although a family of few words, it felt like a conversation was in constant flow, their anxiously alert postures, and furtive glances, giving meaning to which I was not privy. I was the outsider. Indeed, somehow, from the very beginning, I was the enemy. I did not know how I had arrived at this unhappy status. My every attempt to connect with them only spurred their sense of endangerment as if I was trying to invade rather than to relate. As I took a family history, the father said with a challenge in his voice, "I didn't grieve the death of my mother. I was glad she was gone." Later, I referred to this comment, saying something like, "You were glad your mom was dead."

As if poked with a hot iron, he immediately took bitter and rageful exception to my words, spitting out intensely, "I didn't say that. Those aren't my words. You are putting words in my mouth." The sons and daughters-in-law were quick to rally behind him, adding to the power of the father's sudden and surprising outrage that was beginning to sweep away my sense of reality. All the while, the mother sat silently, her terrified eyes anything but still as they flicked around the room, reminding me of a mouse trying to find a hiding hole. I now knew the feeling. Overwhelmed by this sudden upsurge of virulent protest and challenge, I struggled to recover the father's exact wording, all the while fearing, given the certainty of their convictions, that I had invented my interpretation from whole cloth. Fortunately, in this instance, I could recover his words and repeated his wording to him. "I believe you said, 'I was glad she was gone.' I'm sorry if I somehow misinterpreted this to mean you were glad she was dead. Tell me, how should I have understood it?" At this he paused, thinking back. Apparently unable to challenge the accuracy of my recall and entered a dark and reproachful silence, as if recognizing for the first time the horror of his words, and as if my intent was to stab him with them.

In such circumstances, I strove to remain open to exploring the family's concerns. Indeed, this openness was both my greatest strength and my greatest weakness. While I was left in a state of *Not-Knowing*, tolerating the uncertainty entailed in the willingness to explore and look at things from different perspectives to make sense of their complaints, they were ensconced in the protective battlements of the complete certainty of their beliefs. Thus, mine was the fate of a flickering flame in a tornado. Why is it people who speak with certainty usually seem so right, when they are often so wrong, while those who speak with uncertainty are quickly dismissed? Shouldn't it be the other way around?

What was real? What wasn't? I no longer knew, and this was my recurrent state of mind. I was often in a labyrinth struggling to find my way through. Eventually, tired of these dread-filled moments, I fell upon a common-sense solution: I invited a mental health worker, Rob, to join me in the sessions. Slight of build, solicitous and non-abrasive, Rob was well-liked by patients and staff alike. Non-threatening, he never conveyed the sense that he had his own agenda and would sit thoughtfully with whatever assignment was given to him. This time his job was to listen carefully to what was said so that whenever I felt the need, I could ask him the straightforward but vital question, "Did I say that?" or "Did I misrepresent that?" I must confess great relief when Rob, would typically respond in his careful phrasing that what the family was hearing wasn't what he had heard. Over time, not only did his stabilizing presence help me, but it also helped the family. Somehow, I suspect that because Rob didn't represent power or authority, he was more readily accepted as an arbiter of reality and a valid alternative to the polarizing all-or-nothing, my-way-or-your-way power struggles that arose in his absence.

It was because of such circumstances that I was continually driven to read the work of my psychotherapist ancestors, to consider their understanding in response to the questions, "What is going on?" and "How should I handle it?" Now you can see that this wasn't only a scholarly concern, but a survival need—the survival of my sense of self as a person and as a therapist.

One thing I learned was that mental health entails integration, not elimination, of the conflicting aspects of our psyches. None of us enjoy a seamless, harmonious unity of experience; we comprise an ongoing cadre of conflicting wants and desires: I *can* be greedy, and I *can* be generous. So, which am I? Integrating these polarities leads to the more sophisticated but more viable understanding that I am both and makes possible the capacity to empathize, rather than condemn, these qualities in others.

In individuals whose development has been impeded such integration is difficult. Concrete and literal, they don't possess the mental capacity for dealing with uncertainty, complexity, and nuance, much less for reconciling paradox. Instead of reconciling the conflict within themselves, they deal with it in a straightforward and practical way: they deny it, they attack it. They also may launch vigorous attacks on the denied aspects of themselves, be they greed, jealousy, lust, envy or whatever, whenever they perceive traces of it, real or imagined, in others.

Consequently, rather than integrate, these individuals disintegrate, developing a fractured connection to themselves and others. In this way, they see another person as *good* when that person is meeting their desires and as *bad* when the very same person is frustrating them. They jump from one judgment to the next effortlessly as the experience of the moment defines the present and rewrites the past.

Similarly, a patient may favor one staff member and shun others. Being human and having their share of hubris, the favored staff member may come to feel that he has a uniquely intimate and connected understanding of and with the patient, secretly viewing the rest of the staff as less gifted or less talented. For their part, the disfavored team members may come to feel that the favored staff member has been hoodwinked or is not up to snuff in recognizing the patient's pathology. In this way, the conflicts between the patient's unreconciled parts of herself are inter-personalized and re-created between people in the external world. While the treatment team becomes conflicted as different members represent or carry various parts of the patient's psyche, the patient is relatively unconflicted, remaining in his unipolar view of the world. All the while, the pressure mounts on the valued staff member(s) as the patient clamors for action and the anointed staff member feels the need to be worthy of the patient's high regard.

Now you know how I got into serious trouble. Let me tell you what I did.

Within the first few months of my being on B-2, the treating psychologist and I decided that a home visit for a patient, Joan, was warranted. Joan, in distress, had informed us that her aged mother was of poor health and needed Joan by her side. For our part, we could easily empathize with such a circumstance and quickly concluded that Joan must visit her mother and that time was of the essence. Joan brought the problem to our attention following a phone call with her mother after Friday' team meeting. The next meeting wasn't until Monday. Neither Joan, the psychologist, or I felt we could wait. We were already frustrated with what we felt to be the treatment teams' undue emphasis on reflection at the expense of action and decided to remedy that fault, at least on this occasion. That's how I came to be driving Joan in my car to see her mother without the knowledge of the treatment team.

Along the way, I noticed quiet indicators that this decision had been impulsive. For instance, I kept asking myself the question, "What will I do if Joan tries to open the door and jump out? How would I stop her when I'm driving?" Such belated thinking did not support the notion of a well-thought-through plan. But, such worries aside, nothing happened, and we arrived safely at her mother's senior high-rise apartment.

While I sat quietly to the side in the clean and orderly living room, Joan spoke with her mother. While she spoke, I considered the possibility I had been played. I had already noticed that Joan's mother did not appear to be near death's door, nor anywhere in its vicinity. She was well dressed and groomed, and there were no nurses or medical devices in view. Moreover, she was sharp as a tack and just as cutting. Cold and scornful, holding herself aloof, she showed no sign of warmth or affection, meeting Joan's every attempt at connection with poorly concealed disdain. After some minutes of this porcupine reception, Joan, a look of resignation flitting across her face, asked if she could to go to the bathroom. I was hesitant. I would have to let her out of my sight—another indication that this hadn't been the most well-thought-through family visit.

While Joan was in the bathroom, I tried to converse with her mother, who was impervious to my every effort to relate and equally aloof with me. Soon, I was on pins and needles and ready to pop; none of this had gone the way I had imagined or the way I had wanted. Now, all I wanted was to escape. As I mused upon my situation and what a wasted trip this had been, I began wondering what was taking Joan so much time. As time passed, my concern grew. I asked Joan's mother, "Do you think she's okay?" She responded with more energy than I had yet seen, expressing certainty that Joan was all right, dismissively waving aside any need to worry. But there was something about the way she said this, perhaps the twisting of her lips as if she had sucked on a lime or her astringent smile. Whatever the cause, a thought slammed into my mind—*She wants Joan dead. Joan is going to be a good daughter and comply.* I sprang to my feet and hurried to the bathroom door.

I knocked gently and called Joan's name. Ominously, there was no response. I hoped that she hadn't heard me. Then I prayed that the silence was because she was embarrassed to be doing her business with me just outside the door. I called out again, and, again there was no answer. With growing alarm, I called out a third time, unmistakably loud and clear. More seconds of silence built upon themselves along with my anxiety with the passing seconds. When, finally, Joan responded, hesitantly saying, "Just a minute." There was something about the way she said it: the time that had elapsed before she answered, compounded by the hesitancy with which she spoke. Something wet and ugly snaked its way inside my belly—the unthinkable was about to happen. Alarmed, I shouted, "Joan, open the door right now!" …Silence.

Then, I *knew*. I tried to turn the knob, but the door was locked. Terrified, I rammed the bathroom door with my shoulder. Lock splintering, the door swung open. There, only two feet away in the closet-sized bathroom, stood Joan. She didn't bother to look at me, her focus one of serious intent on her wrist, a razor blade poised just above it. Body infused with adrenalin, everything moving in slow motion, I lunged, shouting, "No!"—knowing I was too late.

My eyes, fully focused on her wrist, took in the razor cleaving its way, flesh parting, then yawning open, as scarlet meat a half-inch deep came into view, blood filling the trench as the razor furrowed its way across Joan's wrist. Frightened, angry, panicked and feeling betrayed by Joan, I grabbed the hand holding the blade and banged it mercilessly against the sink, shouting, "Drop the razor! Drop the razor!" until she finally did. Freed from that threat, I clutched her wounded arm above the gash in an attempt to stem the flow of blood and wrestled her to the floor, yelling sharply to her bitch of a mother, "Call 911. *Do it now!*"

The EMTs arrived minutes later to find me on the floor, my body holding Joan in place as I continued to clench her wounded wrist. I followed the ambulance to the emergency room, knowing two things: "I'll be fired for this" and "I should be."

Joan suffered a partly severed tendon, which affected the use of her fingers. Fortunately, she later regained full functioning. The following Monday *I* was the focus of the ninety-minute team meeting in a way I had never wanted to be and never imagined. The entire episode was reviewed step by painful step, as various staff members asked their questions, some reprimanding me along the way. I had no defense; I was guilty.

All the while, Dr. Klement listened quietly, exhibiting only an enduring quest for understanding: that same attitude that until this point I had come to find so frustrating. She seemed fully cognizant that I was unforgiving toward myself and resigned to my fate. Near the end of the meeting, her cultured Venetian accent and bearing lending its usual thoughtful formality, she softly said, "Charles, perhaps in the future you should reconsider when you feel an urge to operate outside the auspices of the treatment team." Nothing more was ever said.

With those few words, Dr. Klement had informed me that I still had a future on B-2. I was and am forever grateful. I had been castigating myself, making my father's slaps pale in comparison to my self-flagellating measures, and watching wide-eyed as my ruination charged toward me like a raging bull. It was Dr. Klement who had integrated the conflicting aspects of the situation. I had made a grave mistake, but I was completely aware of it, genuinely remorseful, and she knew me to be an earnest person. She wasn't allowing this singular, if epic, mistake to define me but using it to further my understanding of the importance of the clinical process and encourage my development as a wiser person and clinician.

Thankfully, not all of my clinical adventures ended so bleakly. The story of Sarah comes to mind. Slightly round of face, brown hair unkempt and hanging to her shoulders, she was plain in grooming, dress, and appearance, as befit a person with a deeply conservative and religious upbringing. But there was something about the way she carried herself that was feminine and attractive. I liked her immediately. In her early thirties, she entered the hospital in a state of voluntary seclusion and speechlessness: for months she had refused to speak or leave her room in the parental home. A previous inpatient effort had not proved helpful, and the family was desperate. Head perpetually down, hair veiling her face, she spoke to no one. During the day, she would avoid all human contact and hide in the rooms of other patients, making them uneasy. When discovered, she would scurry out without a sound. No one knew what this was about nor what to do.

Faced with this conundrum, I decided to begin meeting with Sarah and her parents to see what I could learn. Carrying the gray hair of their late sixties, trim, with gentle eyes and a soft-spoken manner of relating, the parents were a matching pair and seemed largely in sync with one another without losing their individual identities. Of deep faith, they did not seem given to excesses of any kind. Slightly built, they dressed and carried themselves with modesty. In contrast to their daughter, they would look directly at you when speaking. Importantly, they were willing to try anything to be of help. That's how we all came to be ensconced in Sarah's room, given her refusal to leave it to join us in a family session.

So, there she was, unmoving and feigning sleep as I brought chairs in for the meeting. Without paying attention to Sarah, I began talking with the parents about family life: history, how they met, what life was like with Sarah growing up, and so on while Sarah continued to ignore our presence. About twenty minutes into this pleasant conversation, in which the father typically took the lead but the mother was never far behind; I noticed Sarah starting to move about; I sensed, to my delight, mild agitation, revealing that something about the sessions was getting through to her. A few minutes later, still lying prone on the bed, her face in her pillow, she began making guttural noises, and we all looked at her in askance. After a few minutes more, her head now turned to the side, facing the wall, these sounds became more intelligible. She was muttering sotto voce, "Shut up! I hate you! Liars." These were the first words Sarah had spoken in over a year. I was thrilled. Sarah's mother asked, "What is that you're saying, dear? We can't hear you?"

And, when the words became more distinct, confusion and embarrassment worked their way across the mother's face, while the father simply seemed puzzled and concerned. Such words did not reconcile easily with their religious leanings or self-image. Each, looking from Sarah to the other and then back again, didn't know what to make of what she was saying. The mother leaned forward, her face heartrendingly hopeful, and said, "What do you mean, dear?" Sarah would not respond to her, falling back into silence, only minutes later, unbidden, to repeat her accusations. When I asked to what she was referring, I also was ignored, feeling like a rude interloper rather than a helping professional.

Several weeks passed with this scene repeating itself during our twice-weekly meetings. Sarah ignored her parents' requests for more information as if she knew they knew what she was talking about. Then one day, Sarah upped the ante. She got out of bed and paced around for a few minutes, apparently not likely the status quo and seeking a way to change it. Suddenly, shifting from a state of barely constrained agitation to a full stop, standing still, head tilted as if silently questioning herself for a moment, Sarah made up her mind, and moved toward her parents, like a person carefully testing the strength of the ice upon which she was stepping. In this stutter-step, slow motion, kind of way, she neared them. Then, to my surprise, began swatting at them. But, given all that it had taken to push herself to this point, her swats kept missing because of her reluctance to get too close. After several failed tries, she readjusted her position, moving slightly closer and began slapping them ineffectually on their arms and legs. I would have been alarmed—I was certainly on alert, but her assault was so feminine and restrained that I felt little apprehension, albeit some concern that if Sarah intensified her efforts, her slaps could become painful, if not dangerous to her elderly parents.

Sarah's father partially raised his arms to fend off the hits. I could see his spine stiffen in response to Sarah's attack, but he didn't retaliate. And, her mother seemed torn between concern and a desire to move towards Sarah and the wish to pull self-protectively away. Obviously grateful that something was changing, yet just as openly confused by what Sarah was saying and how she was behaving, the parents allowed Sarah to continue her parody of an assault.

After thirty seconds of observing this puzzling interaction, I intervened, physically coming between Sarah and her parents, gently pushing her back, almost apologetically telling her I couldn't allow her to keep hitting. Sarah, briefly looking at me, dismissed what she saw, and immediately tried to get at them again. As I again intervened one thing became clear: she did not want to touch me. I felt like kryptonite to her Superwoman, leading to a most unusual dance as I repeatedly moved my body to counter each of Sarah's efforts to get to her parents. In this way, we came to dance a silent samba of approach and avoidance.

Over the following sessions, Sarah's attacks on her parents became more like tussles. She would wrestle or slap at them rather than use her fists—not the actions of a person who wanted to do serious harm. What also stood out for me was that her parents did little to defend themselves. They would turn toward her and hold their arms up in the attempt to ward off her slaps but did nothing to pull away or restrain Sarah. They didn't even ask her to stop, not that that would have helped. Still, they needed protection. I could see that Sarah was beginning to escalate her attacks, her slaps becoming more intense. What began to concern me is that I could see an occasional look of pain or alarm on the faces of her parents. Also, although I love to dance, I had to preserve my role as therapist rather than a bodyguard. Accordingly, I once again recruited Rob, the mental health worker, to join me in family sessions.

His new assignment: to protect Sarah's parents from her onslaughts but to only intervene when I signaled. I also emphasized that I wanted him to be as gentle as possible and to use the minimum force necessary. I did not want Sarah to feel subjugated or overpowered in any way. I just wanted her to know we would not allow her to injure her parents. Rob took on the job with interest and sensitivity, and proved to be excellent at it.

The thing is that behavior always communicates. It has a direction; it has an intentionality that may reveal underlying motivations. My challenge was to figure out what Sarah's intention was. What was it that Sarah and her parents were communicating through their behaviors? As the family sessions continued, Sarah sustained her guttural utterances, along with a repetitious use of words like "Liar," "Shut-up," and "I hate you," invariably followed by the physical assault on her parents. I allowed these to continue. Indeed, I loved them, as long as they were in the form of ineffectual slapping, rather than hitting or hurting.

For reasons that eluded me, I intuited that it was important to Sarah for her parents to protect themselves, perhaps in that way to be more fully engaged in the conflict with her—to more fully connect. To this end, I began coaching them, explicitly suggesting they restrain Sarah whenever she began her usual assault. I encouraged them to wrap their arms around her, hold on tight and to sit upon her to conserve their energy. I know none of that sounds like you would expect as a form of treatment in a psychiatric hospital. What can I say—Okay, sometimes I think outside the box, and sometimes that's a good thing.

I only asked Rob to intervene when Sarah would start to get the upper hand. Consequently, Sarah and her parents were having lots of physical contact. The parents would end up pushing Sarah back onto the bed where they would wrap themselves around her arms and legs and hold on tightly. Now, by the end of each session, I would find Sarah panting, exhausted, held in the arms of her parents. The beautiful thing was that Sarah's mother, who usually wrapped herself around Sarah's upper torso to restrain her arms, would often end up with her front to Sarah's back. In this position, as Sarah lay exhausted and panting, her head would loll onto the chest of her mother, who invariably took such opportunities to gently stroke Sarah's hair, the kind of movement a loving mother makes to calm and comfort a child.

As the family sessions continued over weeks and months, Sarah became less physical and more vocal. She was now speaking, sometimes even in sentences. As speech developed, I began sitting individually with her several times weekly to discuss her family and other relationships. Slowly she revealed she had worked for the Peace Corps and become pregnant out of wedlock while in a remote area of Brazil. Hers was a strict religious family, and her parents and her church had responded to her pregnancy by avoiding the topic and being silently critical of her, or so she felt. When she then miscarried, she also felt condemned by God. Shunned by the world, she, in turn, started shunning the world. Via her self-isolating behavior, she was treating the world as she had felt treated by it, shunning the world as she felt it had shunned her. In my small way, I knew something about that.

Now, this was changing. Sarah and I talked about her pregnancy, the father of the child, what had happened to that relationship, the feelings she had about her miscarriage, and the difficult weeks of fear and isolation before returning home from Brazil.

What was changing now? Why was she coming out of her burrow? That was for Sarah to tell when and if she wished, but I had my ideas. To me, the caring and physical touch of her parents, their unwavering willingness to participate week-in and week-out in these challenging sessions, and the purity of their desire to hold and comfort her illustrated so movingly by her mother's tender caresses were getting through. Slowly, as Sarah's rage ebbed, she began accepting their care and rewarded them by haltingly putting her feelings into words, words her parents were now more willing to hear. They had lost their daughter for a time and now understood why. They wanted her back and were not going to make the same mistake again.

Three months later, Sarah was discharged from the hospital. After a short outpatient stint, she moved to California. Several years later I received a letter thanking me for in her words, "not giving up" on her. She had obtained a master's degree in bilingual education and worked with the Hispanic community. She had gone from being totally without spoken language to speaking two and helping others learn how to speak them as well. I cherished her letter. I cherished her. I wrote back, thanking her for not giving up on us.

Isn't it amazing how fulfilling the experience of being able to help someone is? It is just this experience that makes the therapist's calling worth following and worth suffering. Knowing you've been of help enables the therapist to endure the inevitable failures that occur along the way. Unfortunately, of the latter, I have had many and, unfortunately, far darker stories to tell. Please forgive me, but I need to tell them if you are to understand the journey that has been my life and what has helped shape *me.*

CHAPTER 24

SUICIDE

To live a self-examined life, you can't cherry-pick what you look at. And as I've said, I learned to always move toward that which I did not want to talk about, toward whatever shamed, frightened or embarrassed me, to keep moving forward. So, I'll get right to it: I've lost four patients to suicide.

Most people are their own worst enemy. When you apply that maxim to individuals with major psychopathology, you inevitably encounter people on the brink of destroying themselves. Suicide is motivated by many things: self-hate; a psychotic episode; need to escape unbearable pain, fear or depression; rage; a desire to protect others from oneself. These are just a few motivations that readily come to mind.

When, as a psychotherapist, you believe as I do that the development of a real relationship with the patient is the bedrock of the treatment effort, the loss of a patient is a particularly personal experience. I'm left wondering, "Why did she do it? Why didn't he talk to me about it? What was going through her mind? Why didn't I see it coming? What might I have been able to do to prevent it?" Such questions are haunting and never entirely laid to rest.

No matter how much I think I'm prepared, each death takes me by surprise; each the sudden and unexpected ending of a relationship, some very close and of years' duration. At the same time, each death reveals the presence of unspoken thoughts, feelings, and motivations, pointing to a fatal flaw in the treatment relationship. As a psychotherapist, I can run from such considerations, but I can't hide; they follow me, specters hot on my trail.

At a point in my career, I did a series of talks in Charlottesville, VA, on difficult to treat patients. After one such talk, a young therapist came up to me with a group of others and confessed that she had recently lost a patient to suicide and was guilt-ridden. Her colleagues quickly spoke up in reassuring and supportive tones, telling her this was a professional risk and expressing confidence she had done everything she could. She did not appear reassured by these platitudes, nor, in my view, should she have been. She then looked to me for my thoughts, and so I told her: "Accept the possibility that you are guilty. That you could have done something different, something better, something less, something more. Think it through. Give it time, lots of time, because it takes time. If you have a nagging thought, move toward it, not away from it. Consider it. Weigh it. Also, consider what is realistic to expect of yourself. Be as honest as you can. Think it all through. Then come to your own conclusion. My guess is it won't be one thing or another, guilt or innocence, but a combination of both. Learn from it. Use it. Honor your patient by becoming a better person and a better therapist." She looked me squarely in the eye and thanked me: I had made sense to her.

Popular in the mental health field of the 1980s were workshops that touted the "empowerment of the therapist." One explicitly authoritarian title promised *Irresistible Communication*, promoting an introductory workshop to hypnosis. I questioned the notion that making what you say "irresistible" was in any way a good thing.

Such titles spoke to the uncomfortable feeling of powerlessness and vulnerability many therapists feel in treating their patients. Unfortunately, such workshops touting empowerment don't teach much that is useful in the treatment of major psychopathology. How could they? You tell me. What *technique* can you use to persuade a patient who wants to die not to kill herself? Tell her, "Don't do it"? Use reverse psychology? "Please do it." What surface intervention or trick is going to work when the patient is enveloped by a raw and primal drive to die? What so-called *empowerment* of the therapist will succeed? What *irresistible communication* can be effective? For that matter, how in the world is the therapist supposed to feel *empowered* in such a circumstance? No therapist is especially powerful—or at least, the therapist's power is not something they own and can direct with precision, to force understanding on another. No technique will work when someone has only a gossamer thread of a wish to survive that is slipping with all the resistance of silk through their fingers. Something might work—of course, something might work. But what, for which patient, and when, remain mysteries.

Indeed, the therapist should not feel powerful, although the patient might experience him that way. To feel powerful—rather than aware—is to blind oneself in an omnipotent defense. If the therapist wants to connect with the patient, he must recognize his powerlessness without forgetting his skills, feel humbled, vulnerable and a little afraid of the real possibility of an unfolding tragedy—a tragedy that may well be outside his ability to avert and certainly is so without a connection with the patient.

Suicidal people are not gaming. They are not manipulating. They are not seeking attention. They are deadly serious. The only way to influence someone in that psychological situation, and there's no guarantee, is from the inside out. It is precisely in the therapist's feeling of relative helplessness and vulnerability that he may be able to connect with the patient—he communicates that one can feel like this and survive; one can feel like this and not be alone. It is through the therapist's singular devotion to understanding and relating to the patient's suffering, not trying to fix it, that the therapist may best join with the patient. Indeed, there may be valid reasons for the patient's suffering. Very few others including family, friends, and lovers can do this, although they may try; their own needs leap out and interfere with their ability to listen and to relate. They end up cajoling or begging, lecturing or chiding and the patient retreats. Only after the therapist has repeatedly visited the tar pit of the patient's anguish without any demand for change may he have any chance, any chance, to function as a guide, gently nudging the patient toward life and away from death.

The last thing this process is is an intellectual pursuit. It's an affair of the heart as well as the head, and always a fumbling and stumbling effort of the blind leading the blind. If the therapist isn't willing to tolerate the discomfort of *Not-Knowing*, then she should be treating a different patient population. What the patient appreciates is not the therapist's omnipotent attempts to fix things, but his willingness to join her in the labyrinth, to become as confused and as lost as she. Only then can the therapist more fully understand and relate to his patient's plight since he has entered into it with her; only then can he bring his capacities into play to collaborate with the patient in the effort to find a way through.

What the therapist brings to the effort that is much needed is his capacity to think, feel and persevere. It is in his willingness to grope around in the dark, blindfolded, floundering, and yet forever feeling his way. It's like spelunking. The therapist is a guide. He doesn't know *the way*; he's never been in this particular cave before. But he has been in many caves and knows something about finding *a way*. Together, the therapist and the patient are lost at the center of a cave system. The beams of their headlamps only pierce the darkness a few feet beyond. Both are frightened. But the guide knows something about finding a way. He may note the wear on the rock suggesting a trail or sense the flow of air across his skin suggesting the existence of an opening to the world outside. He may crawl forward until the tunnel becomes too tight to permit passage and then push himself back to try a new direction. He may feel panic if the headlamps temporarily go out, plunging them both into total darkness, the sound of their breaths the only indication they are still together. Over and over the guide does this alongside the patient, hoping that sooner or later his persistence will be rewarded by a glimmer of sunlight spilling into the cave in the far distance.

What the patient most appreciates is not the therapist's magically finding a *solution* which he can impart to the patient from his on-high position which only turns out to be a false hope and illusion. Rather, it is the therapist's willingness to visit the cave in the first place, the cave in which the patient finds himself stuck in the dark and alone, that can create the therapeutic bond. Throughout this labyrinthian struggle, the two are talking, sharing experiences, sometimes even laughing. The patient discovers he is not alone, not forsaken, not given up on, not written off, and that in and of itself can make the difference. The therapist's persistence communicates his feeling no matter how grim things seem, life may still be worth living. Certainly, the therapist thinks so. Why else would he be willing to suffer through all this? Even so, it may not be enough.

As I said, I have experienced the suicide of four patients. Two were distressing but not traumatizing. One was a young man suffering from bipolar disorder, whom I treated for about six months. He left treatment against my advice. A few months later,

I received a letter from his mother on funeral stationery. When I first saw the dark brown envelope, I did not know what it was, never having received such a letter before, but I immediately associated a coffin and felt dread. The letter inside explained that her son had been doing well and just received a promotion at work when he unexpectedly killed himself. How do you make sense of that?

Then there was the surgeon who had made an error on the operating table that might have led to the death of an elderly patient. He was being sued; his shame made public. Of Japanese origin, impassive and aloof, he had only begun seeing me at the insistence of his wife. Uncommunicative, no one, including his wife and two sons felt they really knew him. Similarly, he was not cooperative in sessions. He would not let me into his cave. He blocked the entrance and sat impassively, wooden-faced, responding to questions monosyllabically. All he would say is that he had failed; no discussion was allowed. I was willing, but he was not. Within a few weeks, he hung himself. Unable or unwilling to consider alternative ways of looking at things, his prevailing internal story line, rife with themes of failure and dishonor, and demanding atonement, finally ruled the day.

As disturbing as these deaths were, they did not traumatize me, protected by the relative brevity of the course in treatment and my inability to form a relationship with them. But that was not the case with the next two patients who took their lives.

I met Stephanie, on B-2 when she was in her mid-twenties. She was a strikingly beautiful woman. Open-faced, fair of skin, eyes shining blue, wide and unblinking as they stared out upon the world from beneath her beautiful, curly blond hair. She had functioned briefly in a clerical position before her work injury. Though this injury never justified the full depth and breadth of her illness, it did qualify her for disability and insurance coverage from Maryland's Injured Workers Fund.

I worked with Stephanie for almost twenty-five years, through frequent suicide attempts via overdose, and resultant trips to intensive care units and inpatient hospitalization stays. Stephanie was a mental health professional's nightmare, and almost all refused to take her on as a patient. She was high risk and high maintenance, but my history with her was such that I just could not turn my back: For twenty-five years, I was the only constant in her treatment life.

But things had been improving. Over the last two years, Stephanie was growing, becoming increasingly more sober-minded, thoughtful and aware. Her improvement might have had as much to do with aging as with therapy, but whatever the reason, her growing maturity was evident. Any claim to a contribution on my part might be limited to the fact that, as much as possible, I was always there for her, trying to help her work through and make sense of her emotions. Bottom line: she trusted and loved me, and I loved her like a father loves a daughter, even though I was only a few years older. Her trust was something I had earned: from suicidal phone calls emanating from motel rooms—which I was able to trace to her location—through psychotic episodes in which angels were telling her she could fly outside her seventh-story apartment window and inviting her to join them for a walk. Through the years she brought her ghoulish thoughts to me, and I guided her as best I could away from their siren song.

Her progress was evident in a marked decrease in suicidal ideation and acting out. In its place, she was coming into her own and developing a burgeoning sense of self. She had traveled such a long distance from when we first met on B-2. During these early beginnings, she would sit with me several times a week, though never talking about herself or her thoughts or feelings. Rather, she would describe her parent's visits to the unit in literal and concrete ways, without any hint of what any of it might mean to her. On one occasion, during one of the hottest days of the summer, she observed that her mother wore a fur coat and sunglasses and kept both on throughout the visit. For his part, her father buried his head inside a newspaper from which he did not emerge until it was time to leave. They did not converse with each other or with Stephanie. They just sat.

After hearing Stephanie's mosaic-like description of this wooden visit, I imagined them sitting like over-medicated patients on the unit. I waited to see what else Stephanie would say, but nothing followed. After a few moments of mulling over what I heard, I would look up at the ceiling and say, "I wonder if your father was uncomfortable? Was he hiding behind the newspaper or is he typically the way you describe?" The exact questions weren't important to me; my aim was to stir her thinking. But my questions always met with silence and blank expression from Stephanie's blue eyes. At another moment, I might look at the ceiling again and say, "Your mother's sunglasses hide her eyes. Do you think she has a need to wall herself off from the world? Or is it something else?" Or I might speculate, "Wearing that fur coat could be a protective cover." I might even venture to ask, "I wonder what you were feeling during your parent's visit?" But never, ever, got an answer.

For eighteen months this was the principal character of our meetings, Stephanie describing what was going on around her like a spectator, who did not play a part. I know—that's a lot of time. But that's the point I'm making: care doesn't have a time limit. The purpose of my behavior was to stimulate a questioning mind while keeping her safe from any pressure to respond. I knew that the self of such patients has already been hijacked by the impinging demands of others from infancy on. In protective response, the delicate shoots of the early emerging self become truncated. For them to re-emerge and for development to renew, feeling safe is the key. Accordingly, I was determined not to perpetuate her experience of having the demands of others placed upon her. I was intent on creating a safe and welcoming environment that would foster the emergence of the tender roots of the self when she, not I, was ready.

Then, one day, change—seemingly slight but huge in consequences. Stephanie again described a visit by her parents in detail. But then, after a pause, she looked up at the ceiling and said, "I wonder why they did that?" Taken by surprise, I thought she might be poking fun at me but soon set aside this possibility as she fought to squeeze meaning from what she had observed. It was from such fragile beginnings that we started thinking together and did so for the next twenty-five years.

Something lay people typically do not realize is that it is often when the patient is getting better that they are most at risk of suicide. Some theorize that as the depression lifts, the patient has more energy to complete the task. For my part, I think that the road toward health is a precarious one. Some of the danger resides in the awareness of lost opportunities—once one realizes that yes, love and work are possible, the wasted years become bitter in a different way. No longer is the enemy one's particular demons, but time itself. What was lost can never be recouped. On the other hand, something never had can now be gained. Maybe. The recovering person, like the rest of us, gets no guarantees that even with newfound strength the goal—any goal—will be reached. It's a delicate balancing act, hope against the weight of experience; even experience decoded and understood differently is perhaps sometimes more than a person can bear.

Another problem is that mental health progress entails the lowering of defenses that help protect the individual from being overwhelmed. If the reduction of defenses is not carefully balanced with the person's growing capacity to tolerate and process her feelings, the resultant psychological distress can be overwhelming. Still, on the whole, the pace of a patient's insights is set by the patient. We human beings typically only take in what we can handle; we only hear what we can stand to hear, and only slowly take in more as we gain the strength to deal with what is going on in our lives. But this is far from a precisely controlled process, and sometimes events can catch us by surprise. Of course, you know this, we all get abruptly overwhelmed from time to time. However, for these people, amid a temporary regression, the pain, depression or anxiety can be too much to bear.

I think this is what happened to Stephanie. There was a confluence of events that overwhelmed her. I was beginning a one-week vacation and had arranged for treatment coverage during my absence. But Stephanie refused to accept this coverage, insisting she would be okay. Even so, I arranged for it with the female psychiatrist who prescribed Stephanie's medication and been meeting with her every few weeks for the last year. Nevertheless, Stephanie still refused to schedule appointments. At this point, I threw up my hands. I could arrange for coverage, but I could not make her use it.

Besides, I told myself, Stephanie had not been suicidal for several years and had made significant gains. She had become more insightful, particularly about her parents, no longer taking full blame for how rejecting and disappointing they were. Where previously Stephanie had assumed the problems in her relationship with them were all of her making, thus preserving the hope they would be capable of loving her if only she could be more lovable, she now saw them as incapable of love. Recently, she had knitted a sweater for her mother and within the week saw her sister wearing it—Her mother had given Stephanie's gift away. What was new was Stephanie's ability to look at it head on, and recognize her mother's rejecting and callous nature and name it for it was.

Stephanie was also re-examining her relationship with her father. Till this point, she had idealized him. In comparison to her mother, he was the *good* parent. But what she was starting to accept was that he had done nothing to protect her over the years from her mother's verbal and physical abuse. Some would say the most horrible thing a father could do in such circumstances was nothing at all. A passive, hollow man, forever hiding behind his newspaper, he would tell her, "You must find a way to live with your mother."

None of this was new information, but now, in her mid-forties, Stephanie's somewhat idealized view of her parents was stripped away. Her need of their love had been that of a young child, rife with themes of symbiotic bonding. Now, as an adult, that time and that opportunity were long past. As she was emotionally separating from them, and better able to see them as people in their own right, rather than simply as father or mother, she recognized that her dream would never be fulfilled. The loss was not only that of an infant's unmet need arising out of the early mother/child relationship but also now felt in the weight of recognition of all the years of torment spent in pursuit of something that had never been available.

The call from the Maryland State Police came in at 10 pm on Friday night, the first night of my vacation. Stephanie had jumped from the Key Bridge, a towering bridge spanning the turbulent waters of the Patapsco River in Baltimore. After years of near-lethal suicide attempts, Stephanie had chosen a more absolute and irrevocable measure.

Even now, all these years later, I never cross a tall bridge without thinking of her. I wonder *What was going through her heart and mind that night for her to end her life so decisively?* She could have been psychotic as when angels had told her to fly. But I think not. The bridge was a good distance from her apartment. Going there entailed something of a plan. She wanted to make sure this time.

I never think of Stephanie without wondering, "What else could I have done?" And the terrible truth is that there is always something. That night, she had left me a message to call her. I had decided to wait until the next day. This was just one of hundreds of such messages, and it didn't sound like an emergency. I was also angry. I desperately wanted to be on vacation. I had worked so hard to get her a covering therapist, so that I wouldn't have to be on call. Upon hearing her message, I angrily rationalized, "She knows I'm on vacation. The least she can do is wait until tomorrow morning. I'll call her then." With this, I successfully pushed Stephanie from my mind—until 10 pm.

If I had returned her call that night, she might have lived. I might have been of help. Or, I might not have. It might have simply been a goodbye call. Jumping from that bridge had left no chance of revival in an ICU. All I know is that I miss her, and I regret never having gotten the opportunity to know the woman that was unfolding on her way to becoming.

In memory of her, I keep a small metal sculpture she had given me years earlier in the window of my office. It is ocean boardwalk tacky and features various sea creatures. That is all I thought the sculpture was for years after her passing, until one evening the husband of a couple I was treating, a computer programmer, picked it up and studied it, then announced, "It's code." Disbelieving, I said, "What?" He explained, "The sea creatures are shaped to spell out words. See here the sea horse is an S." I was stunned, but once he pointed it out it was easy to see. It said, "Save Our Seas."

I will never know if Stephanie knew there was a message in the sculpture. If so, why didn't she tell me? Maybe it was evident to her, and she thought it would be obvious to me. Or, was she hiding something in plain sight? Either way, how ironic that she gave me something which contained a hidden message that would reference her ending. Stephanie always had me wondering.

My final loss of a patient to suicide was even more brutal. I shall call her Eve. She was a small bony woman, angular of face, with short cut black hair matted to her crown. Married, in her late forties, she was the mother of two teenage boys. They, like their father, were not expressive, but unlike him seemed to drink everything in with their eyes despite their neutral and sometimes sullen expressions. Eve's husband, George, was a tall, bald, lean and distinguished-looking man of few words given to standing aloof and wearing suits. He worked for a corporation and despite his appearance earned a very modest living. As was typical of my patients, Eve had an extensive history of psychiatric hospitalizations, suicidal behaviors, and abusive treatment of her husband and her children. She tended to somaticize her feelings so intensely that she had undergone multiple exploratory surgeries to discover the source of what ailed her. It was said that every organ that could be removed from her body had been, yet no physical problems were found.

I treated Eve and her family on B-2 for approximately six months and then continued with them on an outpatient basis for another year before her death. Her relationship with her husband and her kids had steadily improved. Communication of feelings came more easily, her children became less sullen and more verbal, her anxieties decreased, and she was agreeably more engaged, clearly feeling better about herself and her relationship with her family. George even smiled upon occasion.

Again, I was just beginning a one-week vacation and cooking steaks on the grill for family and friends on a sunny Saturday afternoon in my backyard, the sound of splashing and kids' laughter floating over from the swimming pool, everyone having a great time—until the phone rang.

It was George, Eve's husband. "I'm sorry to disturb you at home and on your vacation, but I have nowhere else to turn." Dread filling my chest; I asked, "What is it?" Without preamble, George told me: "Eve shot herself in the head earlier today. The ambulance has taken her to shock-trauma. There is blood all over the place. I can't handle it. The kids are at the beach, due back this evening. I don't want them to see it. I have no one to help me. Can you please help me?"

I was stunned, temporarily unable to take in what George was saying. I heard the words, but they held no meaning. I had had no concerns about Eve killing herself; things had been going very well. But then his words and their meaning struck home. I imagined a gruesome scene; then I thought about myself.

In all truth, I did not want to help him. No, scratch that, more accurately, I desperately wanted not to help him. Looking at the steaks on the grill, picturing the aftermath of Eve shooting herself in the head, I had the moronic thought *Steaks will never look the same again.* My day had just turned inside out. But what could I do? I couldn't leave this man alone in his home or allow his kids to return to a slaughter house. Reluctantly, I excused myself from the party and drove the few miles and a lifetime away.

To my surprise their home was a rowhouse located in a lower middle class part of the suburbs. George stood waiting for me on the small concrete stoop overlooking his barren postage-stamp yard with his usual flat affect and reserved demeanor, the tremble of his chin and his shaking hands the only indications that he was barely holding together. Eve had been declared dead.

As I approached, I noticed several dark spots on the sidewalk, my mind reeling from the omen they portended. Inside the house, similar drops trailed up the worn wood steps to the second floor and into the bedroom where Eve had shot herself. Blood spattered a wall and part of the ceiling, and mottled gray chunks of brain matter speckled the pool of blood on the tired wooden floor. I fought the urge to throw up and choked down the fear I was feeling. I wondered what horror had driven Eve to do such a thing. Irrationally, I feared its hand would reach out from under the bed and grab me by the ankle.

I then set my mind to the business of helping to organize George and the cleanup effort, physical action helping me to keep emotions at bay, emotions that were suffusing my body and threatening to shatter me. I could not afford to break; I had to help George. He showed me to the mops, sponges, buckets, and detergent and we began the gruesome task. As I labored in a trancelike state, my mind sluggishly moved from one thought to another, settling upon each as if looking for a place to rest but too tired to make much of an effort. I wondered why there had not been more of a police investigation. Knowing Eve, I didn't suspect George of anything, but the police didn't know what I knew. My mind went on, recognizing that a part of me had driven me to join George in this grizzly world as an act of penance for not seeing this coming, for not having somehow prevented it. I felt George might be having similar thoughts toward me—perhaps this is why he asked me to participate, maybe this was an expression of his anger—though nothing of the sort was said. I didn't think to ask why he didn't call a professional crew or make up a reason to tell his kids not to come home. My thinking was "He called. I must respond." I just was there, stumbling from one thought to the next, in a world without horizon beyond the carnage, unable to finish a thought and not wanting to feel a thing.

It was a surreal experience, sweeping Eve's brains into a dustpan and putting them in the trash, the work gory and the symbolism horrid. My thoughts kept coming as I moved from bedroom ceiling to bedroom wall to bedroom floor to landing and wooden steps and out onto the sidewalk. As I moved from each drop of blood to each piece of brain matter, and back and forth to the small narrow kitchen through the cramped dining room, I remembered Eve. From the kitchen, I would go out onto the back porch and the backyard for a breath of much needed fresh air before returning again and again to my labors, like an ox world reduced to the turning post. I kept imagining her in each of these places where she had ruled and lived and all the family history that had transpired within these dreary confines.

I had just met with her three days earlier. She was a person I knew and for whom I cared. I had gone through so much with her and her family in their treatment journey. We had struggled, suffered and laughed together and, I thought, enjoyed the fruits of our labor. Now, inexplicably, here she was, reduced to bits of brain matter and a puddle of blood, turned to waste, being tossed out like the trash, and I was the one doing the tossing, rubber-gloved hands stained with her blood.

My thoughts churning, I kept moving ahead: scrubbing her blood off the wall and ceiling, unable to avoid the random drop of liquid falling from the rag onto my face. Repeatedly wringing out the washcloth, I watched as the water in the bucket gradually turned from blush to crimson with each rinse.

I had given up smoking, but now the need for a cigarette plagued me. I finally gave in, asked George if it was okay, and took a Salem from a pack Eve had left in the kitchen. I went into the backyard, feeling that to smoke inside the house was somehow sacrilegious. As I lit up, I wondered about myself. How could I sit here and smoke one of her cigarettes, in a sense breathe in *her* air, while she lay dead? Something felt wrong about that. Shouldn't I have asked Eve if it was okay that I take one? But my gnawing hunger, my need for relief from the confounding feelings of angst and sadness, was incessant. Guiltily, I continued to smoke.

During this time, George had joined me, and we spoke fitfully. He revealed that Eve had left a suicide note. She had written that she felt a pull to regress and did not want to risk a return to being physically or emotionally abusive to her children. Eve felt that if she continued to live it would just be a matter of time. She had decided that under no circumstances were she going to allow that to happen. Eve wrote that she loved them all. She had pinned money she had been saving to the lapel of his best suit, newly cleaned, to cover the funeral expenses, and chosen a funeral dress she had laid alongside the suit. She explained that she did not want her death to be more of a burden than necessary, financial or otherwise. Thus, having cared for her family, she shot herself in the head with the idea she was protecting them. As he spoke, tears coursed my face. Indeed, my eyes well with tears as I write these words and remember that time—the terror had been of herself.

Of course, it was now clear that Eve had been planning her suicide for some time. This presented the likelihood that her more recent emotional stability and contentedness had arisen from her decision to kill herself. I'll never know. I'll only regret that she did not feel she could share her concerns with me. But of course, to have done so would have put her plan at risk. She couldn't take the chance of losing control by my having her hospitalized.

For several years following Eve's death, I suffered symptoms of post-traumatic stress disorder but told no one. I could not get the images out of my mind. The chunks of brain matter, the blush-colored water turning ever darker. These pictures had burned their way into my retina and my brain, just as the memory of the blood-tainted drops of water dripping from the ceiling onto my face had burned its way into my skin. I would snap in and out of another dimension of reality. While I was sitting in a restaurant with friends, the food would suddenly remind me of Eve's brain matter or a ruby-colored glass of wine of her blood. A word spoken in conversation would prompt an association to something she had said, and I would be hurtling back in time, totally lost, oblivious to the moment. While my dinner companions chatted on in companionable relationship, I would be alive in a parallel universe of blood and horror.

To describe it as remembering does not do it justice. It was a reliving, past made present, an altered state of consciousness, a near hallucinatory experience. Of course, I would not reveal my troubled state. What would be the point? It would only destroy the mood of my companions. So, I remained alone with it, and it remained alone with me. Perhaps this was also my form of atonement, to never forget, not wholly dissimilar from that of my Japanese patient atoning for his perceived failure. Whatever the manifold reasons or motivations, such experiences would remain with me for several years, coming episodically like the changes in weather, albeit less predictable, until, ever so gradually, they dissipated and finally dwindled away. Now, these years later, I can remember without reliving.

Of course, I questioned myself, "What could I have done?" This self-examination stood in stark contrast to that of the treating psychiatrist, Eve's individual therapist. To my way of thinking, he was glib, commenting in the all-knowing and distance-creating way some people have. "It was inevitable given her psychiatric history," he said—as if that explained anything. He was not inclined toward personal audit or introspection, toward tolerating the pain of a more genuine connection or pursuing any chance that he might learn something from doing a more rigorous and self-challenging post-mortem.

I couldn't do that. I just couldn't. However, unlike my experience with Stephanie, I could not think of anything I could have done to prevent Eve's death. Her presentation had been seamless and confirmed another maxim: The imminently suicidal patient doesn't talk about it. They don't want to be stopped. Eve's unexpected death was yet another humbling and troubling reminder that none of us ever fully knows the mind of another.

I once heard that the words for love, care, and cure all share the same Latin root. I have cause to doubt this, but I like the idea of it. Caring about someone is an essential part of the therapist's ability to be of help. This is not to suggest that care alone is enough; it really, really, really, isn't. Indeed, bleeding-heart therapists without analytic acumen are the most dangerous of all therapists, given to suborning the therapy in service of their own maternal, paternal, or ego-boosting story lines. Still, care is absolutely necessary, and its presence or absence felt, even if never spoken, in the care-full interactions of psychotherapy. Care conveys love and an inherent valuing of the patient, who often, left to her own devices, feels bereft of both.

These deaths can not be undone. No matter how much good I've done as a therapist over the course of my career, these are unmitigated failures of the therapist-patient relationship that stay with me. Certainly, part of the responsibility belongs to the patient, but part belongs to me. The blame can never be apportioned—this much hers, this much mine—because first, we never really know why something happens, and second, death cuts off all questions. That is the horror. I can never ask, and she can never tell. The possibility that I might have done something different, something better, something more, something less is forever present.

This may sound grim. Indeed, it is a weight. But I would not have it any other way. If I can't feel deeply about something this important, how can I possibly have a meaningful life?

CHAPTER 25

THE GOTHS ARE AT THE GATES

Helping patients who often seem beyond help requires sanctuary and asylum, components necessary to healing the human psyche. With this is in mind, by the mid-1980s, you'll recognize that something terrible was going on. Corporations, trying to lower health care costs, hired companies to make this happen. With shameless audacity, they called themselves *managed care companies* when all they were concerned with was eliminating care. To ensure their prosperity, they had to reduce costs, and they did so without mercy or morality.

In fact, they were absolute bastards. Their tactics? Make the provision of treatment so burdensome that you can no longer provide it. How? Through endless audits of each patient's medical records, through demanding repeated phone conversations with therapists and hospital staff, using up their time and putting them in the position of having to *prove* that inpatient treatment was the only option and an effective one. Soon we were all reduced to *treating the medical record* rather than the patient, dotting I's, crossing T's, and documenting anything and everything, trying desperately to enable the patient to remain in care.

Action is the enemy of contemplation, and we had all been turned into action junkies, constantly forced to react to the electric prodding of the managed care companies. Time and space for reflection were a fading value, rapidly becoming a thing of the past. No matter how hard we tried, in the end, it didn't matter. The managed care auditors had their pre-determined judgments in deciding who needed treatment and who didn't. I, like everyone else, was gradually worn down.

Infuriatingly, these life-changing determinations were made by these agents of managed care companies, licensed mental health professionals all, without ever meeting the patient. Imagine that; What a great form of human evaluation. These wizards of psychotherapy, who themselves had been unable to make a living as therapists, mystically arrived at their assessments. They didn't need to interview the patient, that would be cost ineffective and what would be the point of that? They could read the medical record, the treatment plans, the goals, and question therapists on the phone like attorneys taking depositions, bureaucrats preening in their sense of newfound power as they picked at words and read from cheat sheets, like telephone sales people, on how to respond to the therapist's pushbacks.

I guess it's easier to risk the destruction of someone's life when there isn't a human face attached. But the hubris did not end here. The truly mind-boggling and amazingly unethical thing was that when these managed care companies finally drove the patient from inpatient treatment, having touted the viability of outpatient options, they would then renew their assaults, but this time on the outpatient treatment. Immediately they would begin asking, "Are you sure the patient needs treatment?" as if we had never spoken about this before. "Is he a danger to himself or others? What evidence do you have over the last month that the patient has benefited from his four hours of contact with you?" And so it went. Hospital stays beyond several weeks became rare.

Outpatient therapy sessions were approved on a once a week basis, for four weeks at a time.

Now, it was the outpatient therapists' turn to treat the chart, to submit extensive treatment plans, as if you could plot out the human mind, push some buttons, and everything should work.

In these ways, treatment was undermined, and its failure assured. These moral mutants had eliminated any notion of sanctuary or asylum, inpatient or out. No one could settle into the treatment experience. Even on those occasions where sessions were repeatedly authorized, it didn't matter because you knew that that could be pulled away with little notice; no one could ever relax and gain the feeling of sanctuary and asylum so necessary to working on ourselves.

Similarly, the therapist's capacity to provide treatment was hindered—no one wanted to open a can of worms that they might not be around to help the patient close. And how does one work from a relationship when you can't secure one? The managed care companies had managed all right. They had managed to eviscerate the most necessary component of psychotherapy: a safe, secure and reliable place in which to think one's thoughts and feel one's feelings. They had destroyed the cornerstone of psychotherapy: sanctuary and asylum.

If a patient had to be hospitalized again and again due to the threat of or attempt to suicide, the patients, the families, and the therapists were subjected to repeated trauma. No worries, that wasn't the managed care company's problem, was it? And if the patient suicided? Yep, you guessed it: "That kind of thing happens. After all, they are psychiatric patients." Nowhere and no how did the managed care companies or their mignons hold themselves liable. And they had another out. Like Pontius Pilot, they washed their hands of any responsibility, informing inpatient and outpatient therapists alike that regardless of the managed care companies' decisions, it was the therapists who in the final analysis had to provide whatever treatment was necessary regardless of whether they were paid.

The managed care companies' tactics were endless. They recruited therapists to participate in insurance networks using length of treatment as the qualifying criteria. Those therapists who rapidly terminated patients received referrals; those that saw patients for longer didn't. The self-serving logic of that was that those who discharged quickly were obviously more effective. Ummmm? Of course, the actions of those `effective' therapists had nothing to do with the profit motive and the desire for referrals. Thus, a whole new standard of practice was created. You can imagine how it called out to the best and brightest among us to join insurance networks.

I couldn't stand it. I hated those bastards. One reviewer stridently insisted that I allow a patient to take a day pass with her family off the grounds of the hospital. When the patient returned from this four-hour outing unharmed, the same reviewer insisted this was proof that hospitalization was no longer required. Let's move that great thinker to the head of the class. Because a patient managed to survive off campus in the constant company and attention of family members for four hours did not mean she would be okay getting treatment or even be safe on an outpatient basis when family members went back to their lives and were unable to provide the constant attention available in the hospital.

When I asked the reviewer—with genuine curiosity—"Off the record, as a clinician, are you okay with doing this? Does this make any sense to you?", she rationalized her behavior. "That's not the point. I'm merely following the rules here [at the managed care company]." When I countered, "That sounds dangerously close to Nazi prison guards saying they were only following orders," she hung up on me. A day later, I received a call from the office of the president of the hospital rebuking me for my treatment of the reviewer. The managed care company had complained. I asked, "What did I get wrong?" He responded, "Comparing her to a Nazi. She was very upset." I said, "Again, what part did I get wrong?" Exasperated, he repeated, "She was upset!" as if I would understand him better if he shouted or that her being upset was a clinching argument. I responded, "Good. She should be. Maybe I helped her out."

On another occasion, when the treatment team was discussing discharging a patient because of managed care pressure, I simply couldn't stand it any longer. I burst out of my seat, shouting, "This is bullshit!" and stormed out of the room.

I was feeling the destructiveness of what was going on so intensely I finally had to wonder, "What was going on with me?"

I was near out of my mind with this crap, crawling out of my skin. Looking back on it now, I see it. The problem was I was a part of it. I remembered how my fear of confronting the wrong of racism had diminished me and turned me into a coward, years earlier in that Montgomery, Alabama movie theater. I remembered how diminished I felt when I failed to bear witness with that mixed-race couple being harassed by the MPs in Heidelberg, Germany. I felt the fury I had at my dad's slapping me around and demeaning me, my hands helplessly clasped behind my back. I felt the rage at the belittling unfairness of it all and of being told what I *had* to do. And, now, I was feeling diminished again, being made a party to something as callous as destroying asylum and sanctuary, denying wounded souls a place where they might rest and recover.

Not only could I not stand that, but I also could not stand myself. I could not keep doing this and maintain self-respect. Now, I had found my voice and the wherewithal to do something in the face of wrongdoing, even if the only thing I could do was to name it for what it was: evil. I wasn't going to go along quietly anymore.

But even in my private practice, I couldn't escape the attacks of the managed care company. Stephanie, the patient who suicided from the bridge, was repeatedly and without warning denied medication coverage. She would only learn of the denial when her medications failed to arrive in the mail. Consequently, she had to go without medications for weeks at a time before her appeal was heard. And, each time, the Injured Workers' Fund would be harshly reprimanded by the magistrate. But with no real punishment to worry about, they would do it all over again, and again, and again. Of course, this managed *caring* left Stephanie in a state of high anticipatory anxiety. How could it be otherwise? She never knew when her medications would stop arriving; she only knew that they would.

The Injured Workers' Fund would do similar things regarding paying for treatment. I would submit multiple treatment plans, and four to eight sessions would be approved, and then my invoices would go unpaid for months. I would appeal their actions and win the petition, and then they would do it all over again.

What got to me, and I hope to you, is that all this horrid behavior says something about us human beings, and it applies to all of us. We can all wax eloquent about the horrors imposed by Hitler in the concentration camps or by Pol Pot in the killing fields of Cambodia, or of the Syrian refugee problem but similar crimes, albeit maybe on a lesser scale, are occurring around us all the time. And it's not just one victimizer; it's thousands. The victimizers can be anybody. In fact, at times, they are you and me. We all suffer moments where we lose our moral compass, are overly influenced by the authorities in our lives or self-interest. Remember the Toyota dealership that doesn't change the transmission oil? Well, who was the oil changer? That was me. Or the auto-body shop bogusly selling cars without alerting buyers that they were reclaimed wrecks? I wasn't capable of welding the two separate ends of the cars together, but what if I had been? What about the TV I stole from the University dorm? That was taking from the University, not from a person, and I rationalized the University could well afford it, but that's self-serving bullshit: it didn't belong to me, and I took it. Many people cheat on their taxes with this very same rationale.

The point is, none of us is immune from greed or envy, or doing what we're told even if it's wrong, but you should be struggling with it. Why? Because doing so is very much in your self-interest. Ultimately, personal happiness and one's sense of well-being depends more on integrity, doing the right thing and owning one's problems, than on personal aggrandizement or material gain. If we don't keep this in mind, we risk losing our very selves. And the ones to really be afraid of? Those who claim to do no wrong—I know far too many of these.

For all that, it became apparent that the days of long-term inpatient care were coming to an end. Grudgingly recognizing this harsh reality, I began to take Dr. Schulz's urging to heart—I started writing my first paper. Career ambition didn't drive me. Rather, I felt a compelling need to get *something* out, and yet I didn't know what that something was. It was percolating within me but not yet formed. My thinking only started to clarify as I began to write, and this would be true for all my writings to come: Writing would become a trusted friend, helping me sort myself out.

What emerged was an attempt to articulate the hard-won lessons of my years providing inpatient treatment. I felt compelled to translate these teachings to an outpatient basis. Above all, I wanted to preserve an understanding of the vital necessity of sanctuary and asylum. I wanted to support an appreciation of its crucial importance to treatment and to outpatient therapists in particular, who now would need to treat seriously troubled patients on an outpatient basis.

Of course, psychoanalytic theory had always addressed the importance of asylum, but I wanted to add my voice, my spin, and how it applied to couples and family therapy. I didn't want to to be that guy that didn't do anything.

Though recognized only dimly at the time, the writing of this paper was also a means to help me say goodbye to what had been my home during the last ten meaningful years of my life, helping those who once had seemed beyond help.

It took me a year to write that paper, titled *The Borderline/ Schizoid Marriage: The Holding Environment as an Essential Treatment Construct,* with Jane instrumental as my editor. I emphasized the why and the how of creating a safe space, asylum if you will, in which each spouse could come to think about their respective experiences and those of their other. It was well received and published in the *Journal of Marriage and Family Therapy.*

What I didn't know, had never considered, was that this publication would change my life, both personally and professionally. While the tide of inpatient psychiatric treatment was going out, something had been building in me; again, my life was about to change. The tide was about to come in and in a big way. I was about to enter another wholly unexpected realm of existence. My only question and it was a real one, "Would I be up to it?"

CHAPTER 26

COMING HOME, AGAIN

Ringing penetrated my sleep-soaked brain. It took a moment for me to understand that it was the phone. I groped in the dark and bobbled it to my ear, croaking out "Hello." A man's voice answered into my mouth; I was speaking into the wrong end of the phone. I fumbled the phone around while struggling to catch up with his words, which kept sliding off my ears. After a few moments, I pieced together that the man was Dr. Bob Winer, affiliated with a school in Washington, D. C. He was saying, "We would like you to present your paper at our annual conference." Still sleep-addled, I wondered, "What paper?"

He then explained that Patricia Alfin, LCSW-C, one of my supervisees, had sent a copy of my published paper to the Washington School of Psychiatry several weeks earlier. Patricia had not mentioned this to me.

The various bits of information suddenly coalesced: *Jesus, this is The Washington School of Psychiatry. They want me to read my paper at their annual conference.* The Washington School of Psychiatry was one of the premiere schools of psychoanalytically informed psychotherapy in the country, offering extensive training to psychiatrists, psychologists, and social workers alike. I had taken a workshop there years earlier and come away impressed. Their faculty was simply outstanding, and the school was world-renowned. Knowing they were out of my league, but extremely flattered, I responded, "Sure, be glad to," trying far too late for an air of nonchalance.

After a number of conversations with Bob over the ensuing weeks, I ended up writing an entirely different paper entitled *"Projective Identification in the Borderline/Schizoid Marriage."* I learned that I would have thirty minutes to present my paper followed by a question and answer period with the audience. The audience would include 420 psychoanalysts, psychiatrists, psychologists and social workers, most from the U.S. but several handfuls from around the world. For the first time, I learned that what I had been writing about was part of a theoretical orientation that had a name: Psychoanalytic Object Relations Theory of the British School. Wow. Who knew? I suddenly felt full of myself; recognition was not something with which I had much experience. My major success thus far had been being named Senior Social Worker of Adult Long-term Inpatient Services at Sheppard-Pratt in 1988. I was now the top master sergeant that I had aspired to be, supervising the clinical work of social workers on seven adult long-term inpatient units.

The unnerving aspect of this challenge was that, unlike me, most of the attendees had heard of the British School of Object Relations Theory, and many had written papers, and some books, on the subject. Some of the guest faculty attending the conference were elder statesmen in the field and internationally known. I recognized their names. I had read their work. In short, most of the participants at this conference were far wiser, more educated and trained than I. Yet, for forty-five minutes, I would be talking to them about this theory of which I had just learned the name. How wild is that?

I had never received any training or formal education in psychoanalysis, much less object relations theory. I was self-taught. My schooling limited to reading books, psychoanalytically informed supervision, and team meetings. Even my psychoanalysis was suspect, given that my analyst was a trainee. Nonetheless, I had naturally gravitated toward this theoretical orientation which emphasized the importance of human relatedness upon the developing psyche without knowing its name. Why? Because I could relate to it, it spoke to my personal experience.

My public speaking experience was limited to one meeting comprised of less than fifteen people at Sheppard-Pratt. Riddled with anxiety, I had hurried through the talk, reading as quickly as I could, sounding like a chipmunk on steroids. That had been a disappointing and embarrassing experience given my recognition that I had left my audience cold. As I mused upon these factors, a growing panic took hold. I began to appreciate the depth of the leap I was taking, a galaxy apart from anything I had previously known.

When Bob had invited me to *read* my paper, it sounded straightforward: I'd get up and *read* the paper. How hard is that? But now, knowing more details, it was a far more daunting undertaking. Reading a paper was one thing, being asked unscripted questions from a thoughtful and intellectually gifted audience was quite another. I imagined it as engaging in an oral defense of my thinking, being challenged by intellects far greater than mine. I did not belong among these intellectuals from Ivy League schools, Oxford, the Tavistock Clinic and the University of Edinburgh to name but a few. Much of my academic career had been a disaster. I didn't even have a firm grasp of English grammar. As the full weight of my exposure to the looming possibility of public shaming took hold, I feared losing my nerve. The week before the conference, sleep became an elusive companion. I worried at my paper, and my paper worried at me.

The first morning of the four-day conference arrived. I drove to the faculty breakfast meeting and met Doctor Winer in person for the first time. He had graduated magna cum laude from Harvard, then went to Yale medical school. I also met Doctor David Scharff, another Harvard graduate and Doctor Jill Scharff, who had attended the University of Aberdeen, in Scotland. They were the director and co-director of the school, and trained at the world famous Tavistock Clinic in London; each had published numerous books on psychoanalytic theory and practice. The other members of the faculty were equally impressive and respected, so knowledgeable and articulate that I felt like a child among adults despite their warm and welcoming demeanor.

That morning I was invited to co-lead a small group with David Scharff. The goal of the group was to help the particpants process the morning's presentations. Having little group experience, no formal education in object relations couples and family theory, and no experience in training others, I was out of my depth and had little to offer.

That afternoon my discomfort was only amplified as I was asked to co-lead another group, this time with Jill Scharff: I suspected they were evaluating me. Though I would later come to know Jill as a caring and supportive person, on this day I found her aggressive with both the group and me. To my mind, it was obvious she was disappointed in the little I had to lend, and I imagined her thinking they had made a mistake in inviting me to be guest faculty at the conference. I was beginning to agree. She even called me out for being too passive. Again, she wasn't alone. I was feeling like a man without clothes, stripped of any pretense of having something to offer among this group of leaders in the field and students, many more psychoanalytically savvy than me. I left the conference that evening, ego tattered and bruised, dejected and worried about what was to come.

At the following morning's faculty meeting, I, along with everyone else, learned that the first day of the conference had gone badly. Not just my performance, but across the board. The small group leaders were reporting extensive and heartfelt negative feedback from the attendees who complained that the conference was neither illuminating nor engaging: they were disappointed and disgruntled.

After hearing similar reports from each group leader, and feeling the conference and the reputation of the school to be in jeopardy, David Scharff sternly stated words somewhat along the following lines, "It's up to the presenters this morning to rectify this situation and save the conference." Upon these words, my spine turned to goo. By my accounting, there were only two speakers that morning, Jill Scharff and *me*. Dismayed, I replayed the words "save the conference" in my head. I wondered *Who are they kidding? I have already demonstrated the vast limits of my knowledge.* Anxiety coursed through my veins, threatening to paralyze me. I fought to calm myself. I reasoned *Dr. Scharff can't be talking to me; he has to be talking to Jill. She is the internationally recognized and universally respected speaker and author of books. I am universally unknown. I have one small journal article to my name: Skimpy really, only eleven pages. It can't get much shorter than that!* Looking over at Jill, I saw that she was utterly calm, entirely unruffled by this challenge. Thus reassured, I imagine myself being pulled along in the wake of her success. I prayed this to be the case. I negotiated with God, "Please let this be so and I promise I will gladly return to the little hamlet of Baltimore, tail between my legs, perhaps shortened, but still there. In Baltimore I will live out the rest of my days in blessed anonymity, forever regretting my ill-advised foray into the big time."

After the faculty meeting, I did not join the group in the auditorium. Struggling with an anxiety that threatened to disable me, I elected to observe Jill's presentation from the balcony where

I could pace unobserved to my heart's content. That turned out to be a great decision. It worked well. Alternating between listening to Jill's presentation and pacing in the outer hallway to bleed off my anxiety, I was feeling increasingly calm and ever more confident that I could get through this.

That is, until about mid-way through her talk. At this point, I had just returned from the hallway in time to capture an acerbic interchange between Jill and members of the audience. I watched in nauseating fascination as their interaction grew contentious. I didn't know what had happened. Later, a faculty member told me that Jill had chided the audience, instructing them to lay down their pens and listen up. Jill's aggressiveness, seemingly a carry-over from the small group meeting from the day before, was further alienating and infuriating the audience. My anxiety soared, like a kite whose string has broken. I thought *Oh my god! I'm such an easy and convenient lightening rod to their growing animosity and rage. They'll discern my ignorance of psychoanalytic theory and pick me apart.*

With five minutes to go before I was scheduled to present, I forced my feet to descend the stairs, entered the auditorium and joined the faculty group, scurrying, hunched over like a cowering rodent hoping to avoid a hit to the nearest vacant seat. That's when another faculty member leaned over and whispered in my ear, "I thought you had run for it." Surprised at having my assessment of the situation summed up so succinctly, I laughed: at least I wasn't crazy. My anxiety wasn't distorting my perceptions; animosity had indeed been let loose in the room. Lost in such thoughts, I returned to the present as I became aware of someone calling my name; I was being invited to take the stage.

My time was up. After months, weeks, days, hours, and minutes, the second I had waited for with dread and excitement was upon me. It was surreal. I rose on wet-noodle legs and climbed the stairs to the stage, my head feeling like a bowling ball planted on a stick of over-ripe celery.

There, in a daze from the week's emotional roller coaster ride, I was confronted and immediately vanquished by an amazing mechanism: the podium. It possessed a console worthy of the Starship Enterprise. This thing had buttons for lights, buttons for microphones, pin microphones for lapels, standard microphones attached to the podium, handheld microphones, dimmer switches to set the lights for reading, buttons I assumed were for showing slides and videotapes, buttons for moving the entire apparatus up and down to accommodate the height of each presenter, and buttons and switches the function of which I couldn't even guess. I stared dumbfounded at this technical marvel, not having a clue as to what to do. I looked out and took notice for the first time that there were also multiple video cameras fixed upon tripods, their muzzles unwaveringly sighting in on me, set to record every moment for posterity.

I then became aware that the audience had grown quieter. But, I didn't know what to do. I continued to stand there, feeling inanely proud that I could stand at all, hoping that the tumult going on within me was hidden from view. Finally, an assistant, recognizing my bewilderment, came onto the stage and helped me with everything. Mics went on my lapel, mics adjusted on the holder, the podium raised to just the right level, and the lights were amplified to facilitate reading.

Thankfully, he also poured me a glass of water from a pitcher atop the podium, a feat that, given my trembling hands, I didn't think I could have accomplished myself. I had feared spilling water over the podium, shorting out the whole apparatus and thereby the entire conference. Wouldn't that be a moment in the sun?

Finally, I was ready or at least supposed to be. The audience was now completely quiet, seeming to hold their breath as they sensed the precariousness of my mental state. The hum of social noise was totally absent, replaced by an eerie silence. As I looked out at them they looked in at me. It was a Mexican standoff. I was unmistakably the sole focus of all four hundred and twenty sets of piercing eyes in that coliseum: I now knew how the Christians had felt.

Suddenly, to my horror, I realized that my mouth was dry as chalk, I had to have a sip of water—if I hoped to be able to speak at all. There was no way around it. So, with trepidation, ever so carefully, I extended my trembling hand, which an eternity later reached the glass situated on the raised front part of the podium for all to see: I prayed that I wouldn't knock it over. I ordered my numb fingers to be gentle, but they had lost all sensation. They now felt robotic. One by one I instructed my fingers to wrap themselves around the glass, and when this feat was finally accomplished, I exhaled with relief. I thought *I'm halfway there.* Then cautioned myself *Don't speed up. Take your time. Grip the glass but not so hard as to break it. Now, carefully, lift it to your lips.*

When the glass completed its interminable journey from podium to lips, my hand was shuddering so badly that the water was sloshing about. But that was not the worst of it. As I put the shaking glass to my mouth it ticked against my teeth: that's when all those microphones came into play. The tick, tick, tick of the glass against my teeth faithfully amplified and channeled out into the sonorous auditorium. Tick, tick, tick. Clearly, nothing of what I was to present was to be missed. How wonderful. Tick, tick, tick.

At this juncture, I observed that I had unwittingly accomplished the most amazing thing. I had rendered an audience of over four hundred people *totally* still. Please understand me: *Totally* still. It was a silence unlike any other, not a cough, a sniffle, or the clearing of a throat. The four hundred and twenty people were mesmerized, entranced by what they sensed was the beginning of a ten-car pileup of a presentation. Like rubberneckers the world over they couldn't tear their eyes away.

After tick, tick, ticking myself through several sips of water, I managed to effect the ponderous return journey of the glass to the podium. Then, I could delay no longer. In my usual polished and articulate way, I said to myself, *Fuck it. Be real. Go for it. No climbing back down the ladder* and took the leap.

I began speaking, but not according to the script. Instead of seeking the illusion of safety in the written word and launching right into my paper like that chipmunk of long ago, I paid attention to my need to connect with the audience. I spoke extemporaneously, wanting to refer at least to the crosscurrents of tensions that had been rippling through the auditorium that morning, as well as to my evident anxiety. I said, "I guess this is what's called a pisser."

It took a moment for my words to register; such vocabulary is not a customary part of highbrow conferences. But as they did, scattered laughter hesitantly began breaking out, slowly gaining momentum as more people joined in. I perceived it as a laugh of recognition. They could relate to what I was going through and I could relate to what they had been going through. When the laughter died down, I said, "For some reason, the words 'I guess we're not in Kansas anymore, Toto' keep running through my mind.'" The audience broke out as one into more laughter and, thankfully, it wasn't at me, but with me: it was warm and welcoming.

Now, feeling connected, I began reading. I knew from personal experience that listening to a paper being read could be ghastly. Accordingly, I had written the paper to make it as conversational and as easy to relate to as possible. I had even written in the margins the repeated reminder to speak slowly. During my reading, I stopped several times, looking out at the sea of faces, and asked "Are you with me?" wanting to re-establish that feeling of connection with the audience and to invite questions if there was any confusion. This practice did not hold with the format of the conference, but I was functioning instinctively. The response, given in unison, was a resounding "Yes."

When my talk came to a close, a once in a lifetime thing happened. The audience began applauding, then applauding more and more, the sound washing over me like sonic waves. It went on and on and became the closest thing to a standing ovation in an academic setting I was ever to receive. It was rolling and unrelenting and *glorious*!

I do not take full credit for how well my talk was received. I think it was exactly the tension-filled context in which I and the audience had found ourselves that paved the way. I had not talked down to them, or up to them, or tried to be powerful. Rather, I had shown vulnerability, without apology, and soldiered on. They could see me as one of them. It also helped that I delivered a good paper and interesting story: together we had saved ourselves.

After my talk, there was a break, and I went to the restroom. Standing at the urinal, a guy came up to the adjacent urinal, began his business then looked over at me, introducing himself, and saying, "Man, that was great. Really good job." I felt the habituated response of starting to extend my hand in greeting, but caught myself in time, literally and figuratively.

After that, throughout the day, others approached to say something along the same lines. I felt like a celebrity. I was trying to conceal how puffed up I felt. And then, I just wanted to hide. My face hurt from smiling. My brain felt strained by the effort of making small talk with all these people I did not know. My threshold for social contact exceeded given that for me a little bit of people goes a long way, I was now uncomfortably self-conscious. I just wanted to go home.

At the end of the conference, I was invited to join the faculty of the Washington School of Psychiatry. Later, someone told me that I was the only clinical social worker ever to be asked to do so without first completing their training program. I don't know if this is true or not. In any event, I felt deeply honored, even if not fully deserving. In that I had no desire to attend regular faculty meetings all the way from Baltimore, I became Guest Faculty. In the years that followed, I grew to love these people, so unstinting in their willingness to share their time and expertise with others and with me. They did not do this for the money. There was no money. They did it for the love of their profession and the value they placed on the importance of analytically informed psychotherapy. To me their generosity was incalculable.

In the years to come, Bob Winer and his wife, Bo, welcomed me into their home and would provide emotional support during personally trying times. I felt valued and recognized. With them, I was no longer "The Owl" or "The Egghead." The Ugly Duckling had found a home.

PART V

SWALLOW THE SHADOW—

BREAKING OUT

It was here, that monster that had been chasing me all of my life. What I now realize is that it hadn't been chasing me at all; it had been a passenger on my bus. I had been carrying it the whole time.

CHAPTER 27

LOVE STORIES

You'd think that as a couple's therapist I'd enjoy talking about relationships, and you would be right—that is, everyone's but my own. Talking about my relationships is a tricky business. Aside from being very personal, I cannot invent names or hide the identity of people involved. Also, some material is private and not for public consumption, while other parts are not mine to tell. Even so, to tell my story and my version of the human condition, I must talk about what I can.

I have found and lost several loves. I have been addicted to love. I had also experienced how a relationship can seem to change suddenly when the seeds of its demise had been there all along—the changes not sudden at all. I have discovered how peoples' need of relationship can change over time, how what attracts in one era can deter or even repel in another. I have experienced how you can be with people for years without truly knowing them.

I can also confess a problem of listening. Most of us don't listen well. I'm as guilty as the next person of only hearing what I want to hear and of minimizing, disregarding or actively misinterpreting the rest. Like most people, I have a selective memory and pay selective attention, cherry picking memories that support my preferred, even if unhappy, story lines, and, like most, I'm not even aware of it.

Each of my relationships has taught me something valuable. Strangely, it is always the same lesson just given from different perspectives. The lesson is akin to a multi-faceted diamond displayed on the black velvet of a slowly turning pedestal. I stare at it until I'm confident I appreciate all its dimensions. Then, just when I think "I've got it," the pedestal turns, a new facet of the problem revealed, and I'm challenged to broaden and deepen my understanding. But it always comes back to the same conclusion: I am responsible for my happiness, no one else. That also means I'm responsible for my unhappiness, no one else.

Moreover, I've come to understand that when I hold others accountable for my happiness, I am setting them up for blame for my discontents. Then it is I, not they, who is doing the disservice.

The responsibility of looking after one's happiness is a full-time job. I know this sounds selfish, but it isn't; this is one of the truths I had to learn. Being responsible for my happiness breeds independence and lessens the burden I place on my others. What results is that when two people who take care of themselves come together, they don't feel burdened by each other. They are together for the healthiest of reasons: because they want to be, *not* because they need to be.

It took me decades to figure this out. It sounds basic, but it *really, really* isn't. At least it wasn't for me. For me to internalize this lesson, I had to realize that my over-romanticized notion of love was not loving at all. I'm talking the blinding kind that is so eulogized. When I am in the state of being *blinded by love*, I'm foisting an internally derived imagination, an image-in-action, on my partner. It's a wonderful, enticing image of someone who can meet all my needs and carry me to Shangri-La, with only one caveat: if only she will.

I imbue *her*, the object of my love, with all the power to make me happy and fulfilled. Of course, if I am unhappy in the relationship, it is also because of something *she* is or isn't doing. Why? Because *she* could fill my need *if only* she would. In this way, she moves from a woman who excites my yearnings and fuels my imagination to a withholding or rejecting bitch. Of course, the same works the other way around in any over-romanticized relationship regardless of gender.

What I needed to accept is that whenever I idealize and idolize an Other, I am entering a relationship with my fantastical imaginings, rather than with the other in reality. You know the separate other who inconveniently might have wants and needs of her own that are untimely or incongruent with mine: how dare *she*?

I've ignored the early signs of such conflicts in my fevered construction and devout worship of my *imaginary Other.* I've turned the woman into a healing amulet possessing all the power necessary to cure whatever ails me and to make me happy—if only *she* would. When that construction is burning hot, the whole experience intoxicates with promise. The problem: I've turned the real person into a thing: the perfect *object* of my desires. Many relationships, if not all, can trace their problems to a similar dynamic. Let me put flesh on the bones of the point I'm striving to make.

I had just turned age eleven and learned I was about to move from Hanau to Heidelberg, Germany, to give my dad company. This impending departure unaccountably sparked my sudden obsession with a girl named Mary. Though we had been in class together all year, it was as if she had exploded upon my awareness. On this day, her petite frame came through the doorway of the classroom, books clutched demurely to her chest, her auburn hair shimmering in the light as her nickel-colored eyes looked out serenely upon the world, capturing the morning blue of her dress. She moved fluidly across the floor, gently smiling at others as she glided to her desk, only a slight bounce in her step revealing that she was walking at all. I found myself hoping she would acknowledge my presence and bestow a smile upon me. But that was not to be. I sat, suddenly reduced, fearing she could read my mind, shrinking with embarrassment in my chair as she passed by. As she was situated three rows in front of me and to the left, I could safely look at her profile without risk of being detected, at least by her. Every morning I would run to school in anticipation of being able to steal glimpses of her throughout the day. One day she didn't come to class, and I was desolate. I couldn't help myself. Something had taken me over, something that both titillated and tortured me, that I both wanted to be rid of and to embrace. I had no idea what was happening to me. I had never felt such a thing. But here I was, acutely self-conscious of my average face, with blocky Army-issue glasses sitting overly large and askew upon my nose, lenses as large as picture windows, knowing that for her I did not exist.

Where I had not paid any attention to Mary before, now she was the reason for my every breath. Indeed, it sometimes was hard to breathe. Her cream-colored skin, her movements, the slope of her neck, the tilt of her head, her smile, her serenity, all sent my heart trilling with longing. The more she seemed infused with color and light, the more I was rendered palid in comparison. I envied her the bounty of life and contentment that in my eyes poured from her every gesture. I wondered, would she give some of that to me and how had I never noticed her before?

I so wanted to get her attention but had no idea how. Talking was out of the question. What could I possibly say? All I could imagine was repeatedly intoning the words, "I love you, I love you, I love you, I love you…forever." Plus, even if I had the courage to pay such tribute, I feared the incendiary intensity of my feelings, fanned by her presence, would burst into flame and render me deaf and mute. There must be some other way. Perhaps, I could save her life, push her out of the way of an oncoming car—but no such opportunity arose. Or maybe I could garner her favor by doing something breathtakingly acrobatic or athletic—but no such talents were at hand. Perhaps I could defend her honor if given occasion, gladly declaring my love in this knightly manner—but the occasion did not arise. These perseverative musings only rendered me increasingly anemic and bleached of color in my mind, undeserving of her smile.

I felt unworthy to speak to her or be in her presence. All I wanted to do was serve her in some way, to drink in the warmth of her smile and some sign of affection for me from her eyes, knowing that such a moment would make me complete.

But I could not imagine how to bring this about. And, with each passing day, as my opportunity to find a way was closing, hope was waning within me. Increasingly desperate, as the dark gulf between dream and reality grew, I finally fell upon a way to express my love. I would buy Mary a present. Marshaling my courage, I shyly told my mom that I wanted to get a girl a present. Her wise blue eyes looked back at me, reflecting a whirlpool of tenderness with amusement flickering deep within. Thankfully, she did not delve. She merely suggested we shop for a bracelet. So my mom and I went to a store to look for jewelry. She asked, "Charlie, what do you think Mary might like?" No idea came to mind, but as I perused the bracelets, I spied a piece, made of silver chain threaded through tiny grayish-blue stones, the color of Mary's eyes. It was lovely and delicate: it was Mary. I pointed the piece out to my mother and proudly paid for it from my savings—this was a gift that had to come from me. At home, Mom wrapped the box, and I put it in my book bag, knowing the rest was up to me.

How was I to give it to Mary? I didn't want to do it in public; the risk of embarrassment and humiliation was far too great.

But where else was there? Then I knew the answer. I could follow her home from school and wait until she was walking alone. So, plan in hand, I followed her each day, staying well behind to not be discovered. To my growing dismay, each day she was accompanied by one or more friends. Pitched between rising anticipation and the fall of disappointment, I was caught in the alternating gales of excitement and torment, but continued to power through in anticipation of the golden moment to come, if only it would. Then one day, as fate would have it, the last day of class, I realized she was alone. I struggled to breathe. Just like that, the moment was upon me, and I knew I had to seize it. I ran to catch up with Mary and jumped in front of her, my face flushed and heart in danger of collapsing upon itself. It was at that moment I realized that I had no idea what to say and that I couldn't bring myself to look directly at her. Fearing that I would break apart like a china cup, I could only steal the briefest of peeks. Time froze. Caught in that excruciating moment of indecision, I became a blind man, frantically feeling along the walls of a burning room, trying to find a way out of the growing inferno. Finally, the heat unbearable, in desperation, I blurted, "I want to give you this," thrusting the gift out to her.

Mary, off-balance and disoriented by my sudden and intense arrival, reacted as if mildly concussed, her eyes unfocused and her face delicately contorted in the effort to make sense of the loud arrival of this boy with whom she had never spoken. All the while, she responded instinctively, hesitantly opening her hand to reach for the proffered box. Once this baton had been passed, I waited for a million thunderous heartbeats, then, unable to bear more than a scintilla of the exquisite vulnerability rocketing through me, I did the manly thing—I turned and ran.

In hindsight, I realize that my hit and run tactic had prevented Mary from saying anything. But more importantly, it protected me from her responding in any manner more in line with my fears of rejection than my hopes of love found. I had simply lost my courage and robbed myself of time with Mary and being with her as she opened my gift. Now I would never know what she might have said or had the opportunity to receive that long-dreamed-of smile. But I was safe and felt released from my obsession. I had paid homage to my love, and that was enough. I felt complete, at least for a while.

I never saw Mary again.

Was this love? Certainly. But not of Mary. I did not know Mary. Until I gave her my gift, I had never spoken to her, nor she to me. And, now that I think of it, through my hit and run tactic, she still hadn't and never did. Obviously, my love could not have possibly been for Mary as a person in her own right. Rather, my love was for *my* mental creation of Mary, a Mary that met the wellspring of my every longing. I imbued *my* Mary with the power to fill every void within me and, why wouldn't she? She was *mine.*

Given all this, you might think it a wonder that I have had any relationship that has worked across time and changing circumstances, and for the most part, you would be right. But in all fairness, in these flawed ways of relating, I am not alone. Aside from all the breakups and divorces that ordinary people have, include all those unhappy relationships that people maintain out of habit, fear or insecurity, economic considerations or "for the children." Many of these relationships started out in a state of elation, only to be followed in the days, weeks, months or years by growing discontent, cynicism or even disgust and contempt. Such is what often happens when the dew leaves the rosebud of our initial dreams of fulfillment, specifically when we *know* that the Other could fulfill them—if only she would.

Yes, many people stay together in these unhappy coalitions. Separation and divorce *are* costly, financially and emotionally; breakups *are* painful and disturbing and feel shame-filled with failure. Most of us fear the unknown. Consequently, many of us prefer to stay with someone we don't like rather than venture out into a future we do not know. But even if we do, we are doomed to repeat the past if we continue pursuing a fantastical relationship, rather than one based in reality.

My first wife, Jane, and I journeyed together for twenty years. Those early years, at least for me and I think for Jane, were not blissful, but at least relatively happy ones. In that era of my life, I was as happy as I knew how to be. We had made our three-month trip around the country, I had returned to school, and we had weathered the car accident. I then returned to school, but this time full-time and Jane worked as a teacher. I was proud of her. I think more than she was of herself. She was one of those people who had to be perfect in whatever she did, and the resulting stress was considerable, but there was no talking her away from that standard. Though highly regarded she left that occupation given the pressure of the unrelenting high standards she held for herself. At some point, she took secretarial jobs with a temp agency. In this role, she worked for Meals on Wheels of Maryland. But even there her intelligence shone through. Within two years Jane was named its acting Director.

We had three kids, a house with a pool, and decent jobs. We laughed at the antics of our Pomeranians and our children, enjoying together their toddling achievements as they moved from infancy to elementary school age. We took hundreds of photos and hours of videotape movies. We made love with some regularity (though never enough for me), and argued upon occasion. Jane became a stay at home mom for several years before reluctantly returning to work at my insistence once the children were all in school. She was a devoted mother, always wanting the best for the kids, hence the willingness to undergo the pain of natural childbirth, not once but twice even through the pain of breech deliveries. To my chagrin, she often prepared different meals for each of the kids to meet their culinary desires. Though I totally disagreed with this activity and still do, it spoke to her wish to provide her children with the happy childhood she had never known.

What I did not grasp at the time was the level of Jane's discontent. Many years later she would tell me she was surprised at my insistence she return to work. She had thought we were happy. Indeed, we were, but I was feeling the financial pressures. I didn't see work and happiness being mutually exclusive. She did not feel able to stand up to me. I did not know that. It was unfortunate for both of us. It was not that words were not spoken from time to time, but I was blind to the meaning of them. As I said, Jane was a soft-spoken person. I, however, had come from a loud family, where one got through with obstinacy, and the importance of what was being said stood in direct correlation to the volume of its delivery. I came to be unhappy as well but always assumed this was the way things were in any relationship and that, despite the occasional raising of the word divorce, we would make our way through.

It seemed to me that it was around 1988, following Jane's helping me edit my first published paper, that the worm started to turn for real. During this time, she had shared that she had engaged in some self-cutting in her adolescence. I assumed my paper had re-stimulated the intense feelings of that time. Recently, she corrected that impression. She told me that she knew the relationship would end when I first entered psychoanalysis a year or so earlier. I had attended a conference in which I learned that there was a high rate of divorce among people in analysis and I had mentioned this to her. I don't remember this and probably thought nothing of it except the danger individual therapy could pose if the patient's renderings were swallowed whole by the therapist. I certainly didn't believe that applied to me or us and didn't appreciate the meaning it had carried for Jane. Later, when I entered analysis, Jane wondered to herself, *Why would he put our marriage at risk?* though never voicing this concern. But the fact was our marriage was already entering the rocky beginnings of its demise helped along by Jane's inability to take a stand and express herself with me. Instead, she stayed mostly hidden, unable or unwilling to express herself in a consistent, unwavering and self-affirming way. Her resentment grew, a silent specter chewing away at her love of me.

Over time things went bad. I mean bad in a major way. Unbeknownst to me, Jane's discontent had festered and grown with each passing conflict and fed upon itself. Unable to put things into words, the result was not at all sweet, quiet or gentle, the feminine attributes I so valued in Mary and then in Jane. One evening, as I was trying to talk through what was going on between us, Jane vehemently recited a long catalog of my complaints. If memory serves, I think she had even written them on a piece of paper. To me, this inventory seemed to include every complaint I had ever made during those twenty years. Recited all together and all at once without pause they formed a damning refrain. It felt like a punch to the heart and for the first time made me truly aware of the primal level of her rage toward me arising from the damage I had unwittingly inflicted. I was overwhelmed by her feeling. Frankly, given my deafness of hearing and her quiet way, I hadn't known she had been listening, much less preserving my criticisms, like bodies frozen in a cryogenic tank, only to be brought back to life en masse, imbued with a zombie-like horror. To me it seemed clear: all the things we had not sorted through between us during the years, she had been dialoguing with in the privacy of her mind. The result was that she found me sorely wanting. There I was, undeniably guilty, with no occasion to appeal in any meaningful way. There I was, selfish, self-absorbed, self-centered, attacking, belittling, and shaming. I was also uncaring and tyrannically controlling, pushing her to live her life in my way. Somehow, to my own revulsion, I had taken on for Jane all the attributes my father had had for me. I couldn't think of anything more awful. Dumbstruck by the intensity of feeling with which this damning portrayal was drawn, *I* didn't even want to be with me. I felt ugly and repellent to the depths of my soul.

She tried, and I tried, but there was no possibility of repair. Yet, we continued to struggle, to try to make things work. I believe Jane was in torment, in part with her inability to love me—I think she felt terribly bad about that—and the possibility of divorce. All of this made all the worse by her unrelenting self-criticalness, the voice of her mother damning her in her own mind. I imagine on some level, she felt it was all her fault.

Caught in this web of conflicting desires and strictures, she began acting out, trying to expel her feelings. She gave herself over to excess drinking. She would purportedly go for runs but end up being brought home by strangers upon whose yards she had passed out. Her psychiatrist would call me when discovering her in a drunken state with our young kids in tow in the waiting room, unable to use the session or safely drive home. Whipped about in the maelstrom of her self-attacking thoughts and feelings, she fought for control through bouts of anorexia along with purging, and soothing relief via delicate self-cutting that was so extensive the scabs on her wrists formed leathery bands. Desperate to escape her unrelenting misery she made suicide attempts, which led to multiple emergency hospitalizations.

It was terrible. I worried for her, for myself, mostly for the kids. From them, I received worried calls when they noticed blood stains on the cuffs of Jane's blouse or when she returned home carrying a brown bag they feared contained alcohol. I was angry. I couldn't understand how she could behave so self and other destructively, when I knew—thought I knew—she had more strength, love, and resources than some of the clients I have described.

But this period, as frightening and dangerous as it was, was not all bad. Jane was engaged in an epic struggle to claim her own life and to become herself. She was breaking out of her quiet and of being in my shadow, a need so compelling that it erupted with ferocity as if she were clawing her way from the cold depths of a mountain lake to the surface for air.

A large part of my suffering was caused by the realization that I was toxic to Jane, a woman I loved. To her, my very presence was absolute poison. I don't think there is anything more heartbreaking than to ever so slowly, over months and years, come to understand that you are toxic to a person you care about, and there is nothing you can do about it. It is like being roasted over an open fire, skin bubbling, on a slowly turning spit.

But in hindsight these problems had not arisen as suddenly as it seemed; rather they had only come to a head. And, looking back, I am sure that there was nothing I could have done. The only way I might (or might not) have met Jane's needs was to change who I was. I wasn't willing to perform that self-mutilation. And in truth, I believe the same was true for Jane. In a strange way, I was proud of her. She needed to destroy me in her mind without killing me in reality. She needed to break out from my oppressive shadow to find her way. It was in this sense I *was* toxic to Jane. And, indeed it was partly true. I had come to dislike many things about her way, but at the same time, she had come to dislike many things about mine. We had each changed. What had been a good fit in the past was now only an anvil, weighing each of us down and threatening to crush us under its weight.

The story of Jane and myself is unusual and dramatic in some ways, but not uncommon in others. We were married for eighteen years and lived together for two. I helped her leave her family, as she helped me leave mine. We moved in together within three weeks of first meeting. We each loved being in relationship to an other who held us in high regard. Our needs meshed for a long while. Both of us were from emotionally violent backgrounds and suffered self-esteem and self-confidence issues. I had needed someone who would support me in my journey, a need Jane met perfectly, having, at that time, no competing agenda of her own—at least not one ever stated.

She passively went along with most of my wishes, such as the trip to Mexico and then to Baltimore to begin anew. She went along with my working and going to school full-time, even though this shifted the burden of childcare almost completely upon her without respite. She had yet to find her voice, at least one strong enough for me to hear. Reciprocally, I think I met her need to have someone lead the way and at least maintain the illusion of knowing what he was doing. I was the verbal and outgoing one at parties. She was shy and uncomfortable, often wanting to leave early or occasionally falling asleep in a spare room. Over time, I felt burdened by her consistent need to leave, as she must have felt controlled by my need to stay. We began taking two cars. It seemed like a brilliant idea. I didn't appreciate the symbolism. Even if I had, I doubt I would have changed it. And so we rolled, each in our own direction, so slowly that it was not apparent, like a steady rain leaching nutrients from the soil of our relationship.

As my career moved forward, I was invited to more faculty dinner parties. Jane felt she had little in common with these people and was uncomfortable in their presence. I felt the same, but where Jane saw these gatherings as something to avoid, I saw them as fascinating. They broadened my horizons. It was not unlike the experience of traveling in a foreign country or to walking through that colored shanty town all those years ago; it was just far more welcoming.

Where our respective needs had meshed in our early years, our needs of the middle years were pushing us apart. Jane expressed hers in the uncomplicated metaphor of wanting a small brick home with a white fence and more children, to me a version of the TV show *Little House on the Prairie.* Jane had a real and vital need for a quiet, non-complicated life, her own sanctuary and asylum, a safe space, in which she could emerge in her soft-spoken way to be herself.

But I did not understand that. At that time, I kept thinking we would adjust to one another's evolving needs, convinced we could breach the divide. I kept telling myself, "All we need to do is hang in. We will find a way; both of us will grow." But even with couple's therapy, that was not to be. Our needs were too divergent and in fatal competition with one another.

But before I fully arrived at this understanding—indeed I think Jane was far ahead of me—I had occasion to function as a single parent for a considerable time. Jane had crossed one boundary too many. She had continued to act out her need of hospitalization, inevitably exposing the kids to more than I could continue to allow. As she later told me, once I drew that line she just had to cross it. When she was hospitalized again via suicidal acting out, I met with her in the psychiatric ward and told her I wanted a separation. We wept passionately together, the rending one of the most painful experiences in each of our lives that had already known their measure of pain. So many years traveled together, so many shared experiences, and now it was all coming to an end. Something neither of us would have ever intentionally scripted.

And what about the children we loved? They would no longer have an intact family. None of us would wake up ever again to celebrate a Christmas morning together nor a Thanksgiving dinner. Jane and I wouldn't watch our children grow in the same house, nor would we grow old together. The future lay open, like a blank gray sky stretching into infinity. Jane and I were both bereft.

The feeling of having lost the love of my wife, the growing understanding that she experienced me as toxic to her, the challenge of trying to run a household and meet the needs of my kids, who were angry and heartbroken, was excruciating. Add to this the complete absence of family support systems in the area, the financial pressures of maintaining a household on a social worker's pay, the cost of various therapies for family members, and the continuing needs of my patients and my hospital responsibilities, and the pressure was immense and unrelenting. Depression, anxiety and emotional and physical exhaustion became my constant companions: I lost forty pounds.

Absurdly, the thing that almost did me in for good was a tiny creature—head lice. I received a call in the middle of the day at work to get the kids from school. The school was experiencing an epidemic of the little critters, and my children had them. I had to cancel appointments abruptly and miss important meetings; I didn't want my kids stuck shamefacedly in the principal's office. I took the kids to the pediatrician. She prescribed shampoo. I did the drill: I washed their little heads and ran a fine-toothed comb through their silken hair; I laundered the sheets and vacuumed the house. Then, I proudly took the kids to school the following morning having done it all on my own. Then... the school called back: the kids still had head lice.

This series repeated itself for four or five days running. By this time, stressed to the max, guilty for neglecting my patients, mortified at my inability to rid the kids of head lice—knowing that Jane would have done a much better job—I returned to the pediatrician. She gave me something more powerful, guaranteeing it would work. I was furious—why hadn't she given me the good stuff in the first place?—but said nothing. Instead, I blew up at the poor vice-principal of the middle school following yet another call. It was not his fault; I just snapped. It was just one call too many.

During this grueling time, I learned to ask for help. Having always fended for myself, I often didn't realize when I needed it. But reality broke through the walls of my obliviousness for no matter how hard I tried, I could not be in different places at the same time. What I marveled at was how people I barely knew and sometimes hardly liked were so ready to help, often spontaneously offering what I had not recognized I needed. I received offers to help out with the kids, and already cooked meals were brought by. It was humbling and heartwarming, reminding me that I wasn't completely alone unless I made myself so.

Outside of work, after grocery shopping, cleaning house, cooking dinner and cleaning up, intervening between bickering children, and nurturing them to the best of my compromised ability, I would retreat to the safety of my room and collapse on the bed depleted, feeling completely alone, overwhelmed and inadequate. That all alone, all alone feeling and terrible emptiness I had experienced so long ago at Collège St. Etienne was with me again. Somehow, I had managed to return to that nightmare without end, now made worse by my knowledge that my children were sharing in a similar experience, the loss of their mother and the home they had known, and I was helpless to keep them from it: I walked around in a world of broken shadows, teetering on the brink.

All the while, I was treating patients and going about my business as if everything was fine, sometimes crying in my office between appointments. To my surprise, I found myself more rather than less available to my patients. My work was deepening. As they were struggling with their impossible situations, I was struggling with mine. My treatment skills were developing: I could hear more, listen better, empathize deeply and, in general, relate far more fully.

All the while, I would look at everyone else at the malls and the grocery stores, their lives seemingly going on untroubled around me. I would see families, couples, and groups of friends all apparently happy and living perfectly normal lives while mine was in irreparable tatters. I thought *Something must be terribly wrong with me for such destruction to permeate my life and for me to pass it on to my kids.*

I returned to therapy. I had left psychoanalysis in the middle of my marital troubles because it did not provide the active support, counsel, and advice I needed. A colleague referred me to Len Press, LCSW-C, whom I had been distantly aware of as a grandfather of clinical social work in the Baltimore area. From the beginning, where I had felt disconnected from my analyst, I felt connected to him.

Therapy with Len was not psychoanalysis. We faced each other, and he was interactive, not silent and aloof. He offered the connection I needed. He was the human being I had been looking for years earlier. Len was a constant, empathic presence, able to support and lightly confront as necessary. What he gave me was right on target. He helped me contain and make sense of my depression, anxiety, and agitation.

Len explained that the losses and feeling of abandonment I had felt at Collège St. Etienne at age eleven and twelve were reawakened by the loss of Jane and my marriage and by my inability to keep my children from suffering a similar loss regarding their mother. He educated me to how the losses incurred at around age ten to twelve parallel the losses that occur at around age two to three as the young child starts to separate from its parents. The difference between the typical ten to twelve-year-old and myself at that age being that the separation for the former is by choice as the pre-adolescent moves incrementally to a peer group, away from the family to the wider world.

In my case, there had been no incremental transition; it was all *then* nothing. My parents and siblings were torn from me within moments, and there had been no peer group waiting to catch me. At Collège St. Etienne, I was the only American, not being in contact with my brothers, and I didn't speak French. Also, I was put in a classroom of much younger boys to learn the language from the ground up and in the course of the first year moved up two classes as my grasp of the language improved. Nothing and no one was a stable fixture in my life.

I had been totally alone and isolated. This aloneness took root within me and to some extent remains to this day, though it has not visited me for some time. But I fear it's still there, like an ember buried in the ashes that could burst into flame given an ill wind. Now with the loss of Jane, I had returned to that alone, all alone feeling that had no end in sight; I had returned to Collège St. Etienne.

Ron Zuskin helped me through this time. He confronted me, supported me, and compassionately pushed me to recognize that holding on to Jane was destroying us both. Jane's therapist was telling her the same thing, noting that we were like two people in a burning house, neither willing to leave.

When Jane was ready, I told her she could move into the house if she wanted and that I would move out. In this way, she could be with the kids, and the kids could be with her—healing between them could begin as they obtained the mothering they and she had so sorely missed. Some months later, I received a letter from Jane asking for a divorce. To my surprise, she expressed concern I would be angry and feared I would hurt her in some unspecified way. That was an eye opener, serving to cut the final strands for me, revealing far more about how she saw me and her own childhood history than who I was. In reality, all I felt was relief that she had the courage to initiate a divorce, to leave the burning house, thus freeing me from the fear that I was abandoning her.

Despite our differences, we cared for one another. The divorce went smoothly, and through the ensuing years, our shared concern for the kids kept us in contact. Jane attended AA religiously for many years and continued for some time in individual therapy. She also did yoga and attended meditation classes in a Buddhist sanctuary for a while. At the wedding of our son, she took a moment when we were alone together at the table to express her regrets. I was moved by the wisdom and compassion with which she spoke. Through the years we have celebrated our kids' milestone events together as a whole family, inclusive of current spouses and extended family on all sides: wonderful occasions, forever healing across time.

Just the other day we were both at Keeley's house. Jane was rocking Caitlin's one-year-old son Ryan in a chair while I was walking about with Quincy, Keeley's three-month-old, firmly tucked into my arms. Ryan raised his arm alongside and above his head then flipped his hand like a periscope and waved at me. Jane called my attention to it and smiled at me. I smiled back: all was good.

Jane returned to work, formed many valuable friendships, and in retirement has come to devote herself to the care of her six grandchildren, even overruling her considerable travel anxiety to make frequent trips to Atlanta to be with the grandchildren there and to give Chandler and his wife Nina a break from parenthood. Where once for several years she had been relatively absent in the lives of her children, she is now fully present, an integral part of their lives. She's a tribute to the power of resiliency in the human spirit.

Now she is living happily with her husband in a small brick home he grew up in, actively involved in the lives of her grandchildren—just what she has always wanted and by her self-report happier than she has ever been.

Unfortunately for my kids, before we arrived at this point, their parents' shenanigans continued to upset their lives for some time. Both Jane and I began dating other people. For my part, I made about every mistake a person can make. I entered a rebound relationship with a much younger, flirtatious and titillating woman, Lynn, whose broad smile and light gray eyes flashed with all the power of the sun whenever she saw me, illuminating my very being. I was out of my mind, desperate to get away from my fear of forever-aloneness, completely infatuated with her smile, feminine curves and the tight-fitting outfits that she loved to flash. She was my fountain of youth, my way out of years of despair. I imbued Lynn with the power of renewal. It was as if my life was in her hands. Also, for her, I was an elixir, rather than a poison, a feeling I had missed for years. Consequently, she was Jesus to my Lazarus. In other words, I became a cliché. And, even though I knew this on some level, it did not deter me. The promises of magical possibilities reigned supreme. So desperate was I to fix my life, I interpreted youth for renewal, lust for love, and the power of my longings and considerable imagination to imbue Lynn with all the qualities necessary to meet my needs, if only she would.

It did not matter that we had absolutely nothing in common.

I turned her into one of those healing amulets and gave her one to wear just to make it official. I designed the wedding ring to entail the weaving together of seven strands of gold, each strand representing a member of the newly formed family: her two kids, my three kids, her and me. That was my formula—stir, do not shake—and ta-da, a new family was born. Wow! What a great idea!

Lynn was pretty, vivacious and flirtatious. She also knew how to use her assets to her advantage and to buttress her sense of self by manipulating men. She would flirt anywhere at any time. Be it with a bartender or an acquaintance at the beach. Lynn was a great fisher of men, constantly luring them then pushing them away, in her own catch and release program. She was tantalizing but rarely fulfilled the promise. What I had always known but only gradually grown to appreciate once the fever of her hold on me started to abate was that she had no female friends. All the tributaries to her sense of self flowed from male attention.

We were divorced within three years.

After Lynn, I had one other long-term relationship with another petite, quiet and sweet woman with incredible doe eyes, along the prototypical lines of Mary. She was also named Jane. My friends, literary giants all, referred to her as Jane-2. Jane-2 was yet another woman who was hard to get to know. Over the years Jane's keeping her thoughts more or less to herself took its customary toll. I was increasingly unhappy as the relationship failed to deepen. Jane, in response to my unhappiness, then announced that she thought we should live apart, but that she wanted to continue in a relationship with me. Having no interest in this, I still asked, "Would we be monogamous?" She answered, in an oft-handed way, "I guess so"—that sounded like a "No" me. Then, before we separated, I received an anonymous email accusing Jane-2 of having an affair. I can't say I was surprised. She had a history of having an affair when exiting relationships, like a surfer riding a board out of a curl: no downtime for her. She denied the affair in her quiet way, but I had caught her in lies before when she found the truth too shameful. In any event, it did not matter. The relationship had long been over even though I had refused to admit it.

I grieved the ending of this relationship despite having learned once again that there is no loneliness quite as lonely as loneliness *in* a relationship. I was surprised by the depth and breadth of my grief over the ending of my relationship with Jane-2. That is until I realized that I wasn't only grieving the end of my relationship with Jane-2, but the end of all my magical miracle pursuits of a healing other, of which Jane-2 was the most recent incarnation.

I was letting go of my internal image of the idealized and idolized woman that I had constructed. I now knew a fundamental truth: the more broken the relationships of childhood, the more unrealistic the expectations of relationship in adulthood. What I had done was take the instances of bliss felt in my childhood years with my mother, times when I had made her smile and momentarily became the center of her universe, and pieced them together into my mythological Other, capable of making me whole and complete, if only she would. I now realized that my pursuit of what I thought was the repository of all that was good and held the key to my happiness was, in fact, only the cause of its demise. The loss of this long-cherished emblematic Other, the recognition that *she* did not exist, felt cataclysmic as if in the loss of *her,* all hope was gone.

I was parting not just from Jane-2, but from them all, from my mother, from Mary, from Jane, from Lynn, and from Jane-2. I was now a man without a destination. What does one do when there is no golden fleece to be found?

The past might not be dead, but I did have to put it behind me. To do that I had to grow up this part of me. I had to contend with whatever might ensue with the loss of my quest for a healing Other. I now knew that it wasn't the women in my life who were the heart of the problem, the heart of darkness: it was me. It was me who was unerringly attracted to people with whom I could not securely connect, so I could try to win that connection over and over again, thus compulsively trying to undo the undoable losses of childhood. Whenever successful, no matter how briefly, I felt loved and lovable, a bliss unlike any other and utterly addictive. A feeling so powerful that I would pursue it time and again. In this way, I re-enacted the entirety of the original injuries, repeatedly proving to myself my lovability with each *win,* while alternately confirming my innermost fears of unlovability by losing *her* again and again. With each turn of the screw, I was returned to being that eleven-year-old boy in that ancient courtyard, the cold rushing in and slapping my cheek, filling the void left by my mother's turning away instead of holding me in her arms and taking me with her.

Perhaps you've guessed it by now, but for me, weathered by time and experience, a great love story is one that would not make much of a story at all. It would not entail the white-hot, spectacularly short life of a shooting star, as in the histrionic, emotionally unstable relationship of Romeo and Juliet. Nor would it involve the epic endurance of separation and loss conveyed in the movie *Cold Mountain* in which the hero leads the life of a cicada, enduring years and overcoming great perils to finally reunite with his love, copulate once and die.

Why is it that classic love stories so often speak of great suffering? The characters in these stories are invariably struggling with impending separation or loss and typically do not spend much time together, except in their heads. Take the story, *The Bridges of Madison County*. In the movie version, the passions of the characters portrayed by Meryl Streep (Francesca) and Clint Eastwood (Robert) are fueled by frustrated longings for soul-mate connection, with the angst of impending separation and loss tossed in to create the requisite sense of urgency and dramatic tension. Parenthetically, perhaps it was just such a feeling of impending loss that contributed to Mary's suddenly bursting upon my consciousness at the very moment I was about to leave my mother and siblings behind for Heidelberg with my dad. Whatever the case, Francesca and Robert's relationship only lasts a handful of days. Regardless, or perhaps because of this, they *fall in love*. A key element is that because they have known one another for only a few days, they remain perfect in each other's eyes.

Great story, but, if you think about it, as crazy as my own. At least Francesca goes on with her life. She accepts her relationship with her husband despite his limitations, has her friends, raises her children and enjoys her grandchildren. But Robert remains smitten with Francesca for the rest of his life; she is his one and only. This is suggested when one day, years later, Francesca receives a box containing all his earthly remains. Think about that. *Really?* Robert's life is reduced to a few trinkets in a cardboard box left in homage to a woman he barely knew. If the symbolism of that doesn't tell the whole story, what does? Was there no one else on the entire planet whom he could love during all the ensuing years? Had he spent his entire life shorn of a loving relationship. Had the affair with Francesca impoverished him, if not financially, emotionally? I suspect Robert idolized Francesca to a degree that ruled out the possibility of anyone else, tainted as they would be by the yellowing stains of reality, ever being able to compete. You know, those real women who frightened me. The kind that farts, snores, has morning breath, wakes up grumpy, bitches at you, orders you around and complains, but also loves you, hugs you, and creates a home. Until you laughingly or otherwise say, "stop it." Or vice versa. Then the two of you hug, apologize if necessary, smile sheepishly at your foolishness, and do it all over again. Now *that's* a love story!

The truth was I was too damaged to connect romantically with a healthy woman. I mean, my god, what the hell would I do with one of those? They would certainly reject and abandon me, disgusted by my flaws and my neediness. They were frightening. What I could do was repeat the familiar and the familial, no matter how awful that turned out to be. I could engage with dependent women who could express my dependency needs for me while I maintained the appearance of competence and independence. In this well-known story line, I was an expert, forever reliving an epic love story of my own, suffering included. In it, I endured impossible losses and climbed blissful heights in the romanticized pursuit of my childhood longing—a woman who would uncannily fill the void within, if only *she* would. The predictable but long-denied cycle of ecstasy and enmity would ensue, each cycle resulting in less ecstasy and more enmity until I was rendered into a heap of smoldering ashes. But, heroically, like the Phoenix, or perhaps like that little boy glorified by his father for surging up from the midst of the scrum, I would arise, damaged but undeterred in my quest for that quintessential woman. Throughout it all, I would be in the stably unstable relationships of my childhood. In that sense, I would feel at home, albeit a home I now could no longer bear.

The challenge was daunting. What ailed me was not something in the here and now, but in the there and then. Trapped in the amber of my broken needs for attachment, the fragments of which resided at my core and hindered my development, I finally understood, with searing clarity: I'm doomed; my yesterdays will be my todays, and my todays will be my tomorrows, till the day I die. That was such a sobering thought it spurred another—unless I do something about it.

I knew I had nothing to lose. I was done, burnt to a crisp, fragments of clay pottery laying broken and trampled upon the ground by the endlessly recurring misery. I thought *fuck it.* Then corrected that. *No. Fuck me!* I was fed up and angry with myself. I demanded: *How long are you going to continue to do this to yourself? It's not your mother doing this to you. It's not your father doing it to you. They're long dead. It's not your long list of partners doing it to you. It's you!* At that moment, I gave up my dependence on the myth of the healing (m)Other. I turned to face me straight on.

The big question was: how?

CHAPTER 28

MEETING MYSELF

How? That question haunted me.

My mind took me back to a different time: the time of depression brought on by my separation from Jane. I had lost forty pounds without trying and wanted to stay in bed but couldn't, given the needs of work and kids. One day Ron-Z called and suggested we go hiking and rock climbing at a place called Wolf's Head in the Catoctin Mountain Park, near Camp David. I didn't feel like doing that, but I knew I had to do something in the attempt to stave off my doldrums. "A day in nature," says Ron, "just the thing."

It was a warm, humid, sun-soaked day and the hike laborious—up and down hills and through the trees to the cliff. The cliff rose before us, curved like the bow of a ship, about fifty yards wide and thirty feet high. Boulders, like ocean swells, littered its base. The left part of the cliff was more of a steep hill, but as we moved along to its right, it transformed into true vertical, earning its name. At first look, I thought *I guess we climb on the left,* for the vertical end of the cliff looked unscalable to my untrained eye.

Accordingly, Ron and I started clambering up the left side while taking in the tree-lined view of the valley below and the panorama of the range of hills stretching as far as I could see. Within minutes, I grew bored of this activity, once again having discovered that how things look from one perspective can be quite different from another—what I had imagined was more daunting than the reality. What had seemed difficult from afar, swallowed whole by the eyes, was manageable up close and taken step by step. Needing a greater challenge to wrest me from the smog of depression, I gradually moved along the base of the cliff to the right, trying increasingly difficult climbs, until, some thirty minutes later, skin covered in a sheen of perspiration, I stood at the right end of the cliff, head bent back looking up at the true vertical end: The Wolf.

I thought, "I think I can do it," but must have spoken aloud for Ron asked, "Are you sure?" I smiled. "I have no idea, but it will be interesting to try." I was thinking, *thirty feet is not all that high, and if I can clear the first ten, I can clear the rest. The only problem is the boulder-strewn ground at the base of the cliff; there is no safe place to fall.* Ron, exercising common sense, opted to walk around and meet me at the top. I began to climb.

I soon entered a rhythm, telling myself to maintain at least three points of contact at all times while moving the fourth limb, be it arm or leg, to the next point of purchase. Plastered against the cliff wall, cheek to mottled stone, my perspective was reduced to the grain of the rock in front of my eyes. Tilting my head, I scanned upward, looking for signs of another quarter-inch fissure to hook with my fingers and groped blindly below with my foot for any narrow outcropping upon which to wedge the sole of my boot. First one, then another, and on it went. Before I know it: *Oh shit. I'm twenty feet up!* A surge of fear coursing through me. I paused to take in the larger surround. That's when I encountered my second surprise: There was nothing above me to serve as a fingerhold. What started as a niggling concern, minimized by my unreasoning confidence that I would find something, grew ever more acute as my continued examination of the cliff face beyond my fingertips only confirmed that the rock was smooth.

I considered my alternative. Climb back down? No. I wouldn't be able to see where I was going, where the footholds were. Feeling around for a foothold with my free leg would soon drain the other of strength. I would quickly come to a point where I couldn't pull myself back up and precipitate a fall. With this sinking realization, I began examining the cliff face that stretched out above me once again. It appeared just as smooth as it had moments ago; as if I hadn't already learned this lesson many times, I thought to myself *apparently desperately wishing for something doesn't make it so.*

With mounting apprehension, I readjusted the parameters of my search. Instead of looking for a clear handhold, I looked for any blemish on the rock's skin. Eventually, I noticed a faint shadow that might or might not be a ledge, albeit one much smaller than the ones I had used before. The bad news was that this imperfection, suddenly transformed to beauty mark by my endangered situation, was four inches beyond my outstretched hand. Insanely, the solution to my troubles was made clear: I had to leap for it.

Fueled by fear, my mind tormented me: *It could be a ledge, but maybe it's only a shadow. If it is a ledge, it might be too narrow to hold. Or it may be covered with sand-like pebbles of stone that, working like ball bearings, would cause my fingers to slip, pulled by the weight of my body.*

The idea of initiating such a leap, small in inches but large in consequences, hit home. This was not a game. I remember the words of the hospital attendant from years ago: "This is for *real.*" I could be seriously injured, if not killed, by the fall—it was suddenly harder to breathe, and fatigue was beginning to take its toll. My legs were trembling episodically; cramps could follow at any moment. The indisputable fact arrived: I couldn't hold this position forever and certainly not long enough for help to arrive.

At this point, Ron, curious about the silence below, peered over the cliff's edge ten feet above. He anxiously called out, "Charlie, are you all right?" Given what I had been thinking, something about that question struck me as hilariously funny. I don't know where it came from or what it meant, but insanely a full-body laugh erupted from within me accompanied by a burst of words, "I think I just met myself!"

It is then that I had a revelation stripped of all fantasy, imaginings, or worries: I had gotten myself in this situation—no one else—and it was totally up to me to get me out. There was no one else to blame and no one else to fix it: There was only me.

As I pressed my body to the cliff face, I realized something that bordered upon the profound: What felt like the safest position, that of full-body contact with the solid rock, that which felt the most secure, stable and familiar, was the only position that guaranteed I would fall. The cliff had become a metaphor not only for my marriages but my life: The songs of my childhood danced to in my adulthood could be the death of me.

As a leg was seized by another spasm I was reminded: Not only do I have to leap, but I must do it sooner rather than later. The longer I waited, the more fatigued I would become and the less likely to succeed. My focus reduced to the immediacy of the moment as I surrendered to this knowledge. I knew what I had to do. My chattering thoughts and fear would only weaken me, and hesitation would not do. As I accepted this reality, all the doubts and uncertainty fell away. In their wake lay the resolute calm of acceptance. I breathed deeply, gathered my strength, and readied my legs for the push.

I jumped, my fingers scrabbling blindly up the rock wall, clawing their way to the shadow and me to my fate.

Moments later I made it to the cliff top. Ron helped pull me over and with a quizzical look asked, "What were you laughing about? And what was that about meeting yourself?" I smiled and responded truthfully, "I have no idea"—It was all too much for me to take in at the time.

Now, age fifty-five, I was on another cliff face, securely ensconced in the self-destructive patterns of my life. I realized I would have to walk the walk and not just talk the talk. I would have to face that which I feared the most, harkening as it did to a time of unremitting chaos and nihilistic anxiety, of being totally alone in the world. I would have to face being alone, possibly that *all alone, all alone* of times past, and stand up to whatever that experience would beckon from within me. Not only would I have to be alone, but I would also have to embrace it, thereby entering more fully into relationship with myself. I had to face my fear. Just as when I stood on that diving platform in Heidelberg, Germany, my fears had hijacked my life and imprisoned me. And now, just as on that occasion, enough had become enough; immobility had become insufferable and worse than whatever consequences movement might bring.

In the months to come, I came to realize I was never alone; I always had *me*. My kids, ranging in age from their early to late twenties were out of the house, grown and self-responsible. Now, relatively free of obligation, I had time to get to know myself in this new kind of way, not running from my aloneness but embracing it. And what I learned was that self-relationship was like any other relationship. As with any other companion, I could become tired or bored of me. But the boredom would pass, giving way to other spans of time when I would thoroughly enjoy my own company, singing without restraint with that voice that got me kicked out of choir as I relished cooking the meal I was making for myself.

The progress I had made in developing a deeper and kinder relationship to myself was brought home to me when I went out with the Z-Man and his girlfriend to celebrate the Chinese New Year. To my chagrin, at the restaurant, they got into an intense argument. You know—one of those fights where what they were fighting about isn't really what they were fighting about.

As the evening closed and they drove me home, they argued all the way. Trapped in the back seat of the car, I didn't listen to the words; I had been there before in my own relationships. But, I couldn't block out their angry and bitter intensities, which strummed the chords of memories of my own punishing history of unhappy moments in relationships. Finally, the question I knew was coming arrived. From the front, the Z-Man asked, as if just remembering I was there, "Charlie, what do you think?" I said what I had been thinking and feeling, that I could never have imagined feeling before: "I think I'm glad to be the one person in this car who is going home *alone.*"

Despite my abandonment anxieties, I had finally learned a valuable lesson: no matter how lonely, lonely might be, there was nothing lonelier than feeling alone in a relationship.

But my problem wasn't fully resolved. I still wanted a relationship, just a healthy one. The problem was me. I now understood that I was attracted to women who weren't right for me. That isn't to say they weren't good people; they just weren't good for me. Modifying the word radar, I began using the word Gal-dar to describe that acutely attuned and unconscious system of attraction that went off with all the fanfare of a video arcade machine whenever I was around an attractive woman. The thing I knew was that the Gal-dar part of by brain, located in the deepest recesses, was before and beyond words, and impervious to reason or logic.

But, I saw a solution. Just as Delta Force members learn via training to stifle their fight-flight responses and keep a cool head under fire, I might not be able to change the signals from my Gal-dar, but I *could* change how I interpreted them and how I opted to respond. In the past, my electric attraction towards a woman served as a green light, a go-signal, spurring me on to pedal-to-the-metal pursuits. At these times, feeling myself knocking at the door to the Garden of Eden, I totally ignored the fact that I was oblivious to the snake. Trust me; there is always a snake, not only yours but theirs. After all, we're talking about inevitably flawed human beings. The only question is, can you deal with it in a constructive way?

Where such intimacy leads to good results, I can continue to move forward in the relationship. But, where it meets with bad results, I needed to be open to that understanding right away. I call it traveling with both headlights on or eyes wide open. The left eye looks out through a lens of hoping and wishing; the right eye should look out more dispassionately, taking into account the hard data of reality. The two working together lead to the best chance of a mutually enriching relationship in fact.

Now, I understood that the onset of such electric currents was not a green light, a go signal. Rather it was yellow caution light, indicating potential danger, if not an outright flashing neon blue and red emergency light. I came to understand it as the equivalent of the Sirens in Greek mythology: beautiful women, standing on rocky shoals, luring sailors to their deaths. Rather than making me want to give myself up to the mating call of my attractions, the siren song now clanged in my head with much the same urgency one hears in old submarine warfare movies as the captain urgently shouts, "Dive! Dive! Dive!"

I understood that the woman who was triggering my Gal-dar was unknowingly tapping into my pathologic need for the heal-ing and fulfilling other. I further realized that if she succumbed to my pursuit, I was probably tapping into hers. That understanding, combined with my ability to remember the pain that resulted when I failed to heed these warnings, took the steam out of any ideas of headlong pursuit. In fact, over the ensuing months, as I stopped feeding The Wolf of my siren attractions, the Siren Song dissipated, not completely, but significantly.

I had learned something important: because I had a desire did not mean that it was good for me or that I had to act on it. I had learned that being alone could, in fact, be better, far better, than the eventual torment of being with an Other with whom I could not connect.

I also now knew that to have any hope of securely connecting with another I had to become more secure within myself. I had to accept my ultimate aloneness and individuality in the world; I had to stay on the road toward independence, to never be willing to lose myself again by giving myself up to the thrall of another.

My experiences in relationship led to an axiom that on the surface seems counter-intuitive: healthy relationships are comprised of two relatively autonomous individuals, each of whom can leave it. The leaving would be painful, but they would and could do it. While these people are willing to work on improving a relationship, they are not prepared to stay in it "no matter what." In this way, they refuse to be disrespected or taken for granted in any ongoing way. Having such a personal standard leads to mutual respect rather than mutual contempt, and to inter-enriching and creative co-mingling between the partners rather than the co-mangling unilateral pursuits of control and possessiveness.

Of course, such calculations are not digitally calibrated. Being of both the mind and the heart, they are imprecise, dancing between attraction and the illusion it brings on the one hand and awareness of the potentially rocky shallows of the reality on the other. This is a to-and-fro process between moments of fully absorbing engagement with the other, untrammeled by the distancing effects of self or other analysis, alternating with other moments when I take the time to fully consider my experience that has arisen from that relationship.

As Carol Ann Maltas has written, I was more cognizant of entering a tripartite process of illusion, disillusion, and re-illusion. As my initial image of the Other is disappointed in reality, I can follow it up by a re-illusioning of the Other. However, this re-illusioning in health is moderated by reality and not given to its previous aery heights. In this way, across time and circumstance, the relationship becomes more and more based in reality, even if never fully arriving. Isn't that a concept: loving someone in reality—now that's exciting! The axiom that follows is that feeling without thinking is just as crazy as thinking without feeling. To row the boat successfully you must use both oars.

If I had known and applied these learnings early in life, I might have been able to enjoy the relationship with both Lynn and Jane-2, without ever having gone full in. They would have been more transitional. But given that to me each of them felt like water to a man lost in the desert and dying of thirst, such considerations weren't possible. Each of them had to be what I needed them to be regardless of who they actually were. For example, both Jane-2's excessive quiet and lack of self-expressivity and Lynn's titillating and flirtatious behavior that forever stoked the fires of passion but lacked quenching fulfillment frustrated the wish for secure attachment. Nevertheless, in my state of illusioning them to be what I wanted them to be, this data was ignored, until under the weight of its pervasive presence I could deny it no longer. Then, when things didn't change, dis-illusion-ment became de-illusionment, along with its traveling companion, cynicism—and the relationship was done.

I hope I've been clear that much of what I've been through in my adult relationships has been self-inflicted. I do not think that in this I am the exception, but the rule. Of course, things happen to us that no one can foresee. Even so, if you can accept that you are the author of your life, it may help you avoid some of the mistakes I've made... but, again, I doubt it. I think we human beings make whatever mistakes we *need* to make until we resolve the issues that birth them in the first place. In my case, the need was of what the self-psychologist Stolorow called a self-object. Without getting too specific, the term self-object relates not to a person but to a way of experiencing a person that endows that person with the ability to maintain, restore, or consolidate the organization of the perceiver's self—essentially what I've been calling my healing amulet. Without it, I feared falling apart, just like a toddler with the loss of his blankie. In adulthood, I was experiencing the women in my life much this way.

What can help in learning from your experiences is owning responsibility for them, recognizing that some relationships that went wrong were not mistakes at all, while others may have been. For instance, the marriage to Jane was never a mistake; not leaving it earlier was. In my view, we met each other's needs for years and then we did not.

Whatever happens, *do not* blame the other; they are simply doing what they feel driven to do, just like me, just like you. If you accept responsibility, then at least you know you have something to learn and are at the helm of your life.

At the end of the day, it is always worth asking, "Why have I needed this in my life?" "This" being the source of your disquiet. When analyzing your relationship, you will almost certainly discover that evidence of the source of your unhappiness was there all along. *You* chose to ignore it. *You* opted to downplay it. Ask yourself, "Why?" and consider the implications of any and every possible answer. The most difficult part to see will be your contribution, for it will arise out of the most deep-seated parts of you, those early primitive childhood needs that reside in the murky depths of your psyche. But this is the most important thing to discern for it will tell you the life lesson you still have to learn.

I no longer need to find an absent mother to try to bring to life as if in doing so I prove my worth or lovability. And I no longer need an Other as a self-object, to calm or soothe me, and serve as the foundation for my existence. I no longer need a perfect relationship and, in truth, I no longer need a relationship at all, but I do want one. If the relationship is a connecting one, I am far happier sharing my life with another than when alone. Having a real and substantial feminine energy in my life adds to it immeasurably, and helps complete me, but that's different than needing someone no matter the cost like a choking man struggling for air.

I am responsible for most of the problems that have been etched into my life. This is not to say I believe I am God-like and accountable for everything. I know things have been done to me that were outside my control, but I am responsible for how I deal with them, how I take them in, the conclusions I draw. *I* am responsible for continuing to steer my life using my feelings and the compass of my fulfillment and personal meaning. After all, it is *my* life we are talking about, not the life of my parents, my friends, my lovers or my kids. And, at the end of the day, I alone am responsible for writing its story.

CHAPTER 29

WRITING MYSELF

I can't tell the story of my life without mentioning my love-hate relationship with writing. The love part is that it has been a huge part of my life and a reliable companion. The hate part is that it has been a huge part of my life and a struggle. For me, writing inevitably entails a mentally laborious effort comparable in the physical world to hooking a plow to a flea-bitten mule to take on a rocky West Virginia field.

The worst part and the best part of writing for me are one and the same. When I start writing, I usually have a topic, but never know what I'm going to say or how I'm going to say it. It is only as the letters scroll across the computer screen and words and sentences begin to form that I discover that for the first time and, even then, it's only the first version. Typically, I don't like what the words say, or how they say it, but I've learned to trust that they *always* point toward something. It's my job to form this *something* into furrows of understanding. The payoff is that if I persist, I am usually able to put together a sentence that express-es something approaching what I was thinking and feeling but hadn't until that moment fully known. It's then the crop blooms, and I take in the joy and the discomfort of self-discovery.

Because of the commitment and effort that writing entails, I almost always start writing angrily. Parts of me rebel, demanding, "Why are you doing this to me? I'd rather be out and about." Another part retorts, "Because I need to get something out, and I don't know what it is. It will keep gnawing at me until I do." Of course, such conflicts are exacerbated when I am *given* a topic to write about rather than responding to something clamoring internally for release. On these occasions, driven by obligation rather than desire, at least starting out, I only feel a requirement to comply, and by this time you understand my unsettled relationship with compliance. However, sooner rather than later, I come to make everything I write my own for it is only in doing so that I am able to write something well and squeeze out the resulting sense of satisfaction that makes the effort worthwhile.

Following the publication of my first paper in 1989, all of my writing emanated from writing talks delivered at the Washington School of Psychiatry or elsewhere. One day, around 1991, David Scharff, M.D., the Director of the Washington School of Psychiatry at that time, was building a library of psychoanalytic books and approached me about writing one. However, this was at the same time I was suffering depression from the collapse of my marriage with Jane—I just didn't feel I had the focus or the energy. David persisted, noting that I already had the book half written—it was there in the various talks I had given—and offered that when he was going through a similar personal difficulty, writing a book had helped him through it. He ended his pitch by remarking that it only took him a year. *My God*, I thought, *a year isn't much.*

But what I was to discover is that I was no David Scharff. I couldn't get started; I just didn't have it in me. But he had succeeded in planting a seed in my mind, and it had taken root, growing and gaining purchase even when I was not paying attention. One day, months later, without planning, I just sat down and started writing in an on-and-off kind of way, struggling between ambition on the one hand and depression on the other.

That seed had been growing within me, and I now needed to get something out. I recognized that the book would be an elaboration of that first article written several years earlier, conveying the importance of sanctuary and asylum, and the why and the how of creating it in outpatient therapy in the treatment of major psychopathology. The one thing I knew was that I needed the book to be personally meaningful; something that was near experience rather than intellectually distancing. Consequently, my writing entailed re-visiting many difficult clinical cases—but this time reliving them through a lens deepened by personal suffering and understanding. Because I wanted the book to be near experience, I toiled to write it in a way that would induce in the reader some measure of the experience, the emotions, of working with personality disordered people and their attacks upon the person of the therapist; in this case me. I wanted the reader to experience the desire, the hope, the despair, the anxiety, the confusion, the doubt, the frustration and the occasional golden moments of intimate connection as would any therapist aspiring to work with this patient population. It was not an easy book to write, nor is it an easy book to read but, as my editor Margaret Diehl, who loves the psychological exclaims, "But, oh so worthwhile!" Because of the personal nature of the writing, it was very demanding and, after a chapter or two, I would have to take a break: From writing, from thinking, from feeling, from remembering. Then, weeks or months later, once my psyche had renewed itself again, I would return to it, each time pushing a little further ahead.

In this way, the book became a constant companion. Even when I wasn't physically writing on the computer keyboard, it was always on and in my mind. And, as any companion, it took on many characteristics ranging from a dark cloud of obligation to a source of illumination and gratification. It became my Mount Everest, the yin and yang, the dark and the light of my life—an arduous climb with occasional moments of satisfaction whenever a higher plateau, the end of a chapter, was reached. Many times I wanted to quit, but couldn't; I never wanted to be that guy that talked about writing a book but never did: I never wanted to be that guy that quit.

A mere seven years later I was done.

As a boy who struggled mightily with writing and continues to do so to this day, I would never have guessed that writing would become such an integral part of my life. Nor would I have dreamt that I would be published. But, as with that first article, *something* just takes me over, and then I have to get that *something* out. It is in writing that I find out what that something is, and that is how it has remained. I always discover when I write, and that is how my love of writing continues to be reborn again and again.

Of course, writing entails thinking, composition, the arranging of words and thoughts together in a desirable order. Writers compose and writing leads to composure, as it brings order to chaos and helps make sense of things. For me, writing became a vital tool for communicating with myself, of making the subconscious conscious. It provided a medium for me to get things out onto paper, to sort them through, and then to take them back in again, in a better understood and thereby more manageable way. It was my personal version of my mother's nightly meditative walks.

If there is one regret I have in life, it's not beginning to write sooner. I've come to the art late and only wish I had more time to hone my skills. Now, I will never be the writer I might have been. Still, to do what I could to enhance my writing and to be with like-minded people, I joined the New Directions: Writing With A Psychoanalytic Edge program in Washington, D.C. This three-year program, founded by my friend Bob Winer and using

Bo Winer as a workshop leader, proved a saving grace every bit as much as the Washington School of Psychiatry had years earlier. There I renewed my acquaintance with many friends, made new ones, and to this day continue to benefit from their gracious encouragement and support. Some of what I wrote there has made its way into this book.

It was a great ride, one rife with accomplishments and satisfactions, or at least as much as I needed. And all that mattered a great deal on one level, but on another, not so much. Like the protagonist in the myth of Percival, I had gone out and slain many dragons professionally but continued to ask myself the question, "Is this all there is?" Something was missing, and I knew it. Worse, if I looked hard, I knew what it was. It was *something* inside, and I had found the words for it: Happiness, contentment, fulfillment. I just didn't know how to achieve it. So, with this topic in mind, I started writing some more.

CHAPTER 30

THE ONLY DANCE THERE IS

One morning Dad said, "Charlie, come with me, I want you to see something." We descended to the lake shore, Dad carrying a tin cookie can half-full with dried corn kernels. A morning fog, three feet thick, blanketed the surface of the lake as the rising sun cast its uppermost wisps in a golden halo. As we stood upon the shore, he began shaking the can, creating noise like rain on a tin roof. I stood quietly, puzzled as to what he was trying to show me. Then I heard something, and as I strained to hear, recognized the powerful rhythmic whooshing of air, that was growing ever louder as whatever it was, hidden in the haze, came our way. A frisson traversed my spine and bloomed in the back of the neck, body alerting me to potential danger, something with which my mind had yet to catch up. Then, thirty feet away, a flock of geese in full-flight burst into view out of the fog. Frighteningly, they were coming directly at us like pre-historic beasts with a singularity of purpose. Frozen in place, I thought *they have no time to stop* then, when my mind registered that it was already too late, they all as one spread their wings, somehow breaking their careening flight to settle with great splashing onto the water, turned to froth by their wings, just four feet away. Only then did I realize that I had stopped breathing. As Dad grinning cast the corn kernels upon the shore and fed them, their reward for the show they had just given, my heart calmed.

Of course, neither the neighbors nor my mother appreciated his luring these poop factories into their yards, but, as usual, the feelings of others were like the writing on the Rosetta Stone to my dad. They just didn't register. Nonetheless, I loved that moment, the pure power and wonder of it had called to my primal nature and Dad had shared that with me.

I was touring Florence, Italy, a few years ago with my wife Janet and visited the US military cemetery located there. Beautiful, reminiscent of Arlington National Cemetery outside of Washington D.C., and similar to one I had visited with my dad when touring Italy years earlier. Perhaps it was even the same one. Awe-inspiring, its thousands of white gravestones, standing perfectly aligned like pearls on the green felt of the manicured grass, graced the rolling hills. As I walked alone among the monuments and those thousands upon thousands of graves, I wondered who these people had been? What were their stories were, the lives lived, the families left behind, the parents long dead, given that these men and women, young for the most part, had died seventy-plus years earlier. I doubted that there was anyone alive to remember these people? Were the meanings of their lives reduced to standing eternal guard as one of these gravestones, awesome to behold in their regimented multitude but their individual stories lost forever?

I must have meandered among the graves for half an hour musing upon such questions when a daub of color caught my eye. There in the distance, among all those thousands of graves, I spied a single bouquet of fresh flowers as if in answer to my unvoiced questions. Intrigued, I made my way to that grave, the flowers resting on the grass, carefully arranged by the stone, and became lost in reverie. It was the grave of a young man, a private, killed in his early twenties. Captured by the unknown story behind the flowers I began to speculate. Who could have left them, given that this man would have been approximately ninety years old if he had lived? Someone had recently visited him and paid homage in a very personal and loving way. Who could it have been? Was it a girlfriend or a wife, nearing the end of her own life, still carrying the flame of her love for him? Was it a brother or sister, who had missed him terribly and still held him alive in memory? Or, was it a child, now near seventy years old herself, paying tribute to a father she had barely known—or not known at all? Those flowers, resting on that grave in the sun, were a poignant reminder, made all the more so by the likelihood that whoever left them would, in a matter of years, also be gone: then there would be no flowers at all. Gone. Forever.

It is in this way, as I focus on the memories of times lived with my parents that the nostalgia slips in like the morning dew, both sad and gently caressing, of stories lived and of stories told that would eventually, under the erosion of time, be lost forever with no one there to leave a bouquet of memory.

As I reflect back upon my life, all the varied experiences and people I've known, I find myself recovering more memories about my parents. Memories that first emerge as insubstantial as ghosts, best seen when not looked at directly but from the corner of my eye. I realized I had been so angry at my dad for his terrible behavior that it took me a long time to also acknowledge the good things he had brought into my life. As I continued to reminisce, without forcing the effort, these memories came more fully into focus, and then I realized why I had needed to keep them as ghosts: despite all that was said and done, I missed him and those wild and wondrous moments that arose from time to time.

Now that I had discharged the effluent of my outrage over much that had happened, memories of the times of laughter and touching sentiment were able to make their way to the fore, as they no longer stood in mutually exclusive and battling relationship to the bad times.

I remembered the day as a toddler that Dad took Jacques and I fishing in a small rowboat for the first time. Jacques and I sat there, our lines hanging limply off the side, dragonflies buzzing along the surface of the water, as Dad fished, casting again and again. Sitting there I felt an unexpected tug on the line and spoke up in my little boy voice, tongue unable to wrap itself completely around the words, "Daddy, I caught a fith." It took me a few tries to get his attention, but when I did, he looked doubtful yet surrendered to the need to check, exclaiming, "I'll be damned, you sure did," his words filling me with pride. He would repeat this story occasionally through the years, laughing, and each time I would feel that swell of pride like a peacock displaying its feathers, yet refuse to give him the gift of showing my pleasure.

Dad did one fatherly task very well: he introduced his kids to the external world, what the psychoanalyst Winnicott called the excitement of the streets. According to Winnicott, this paternal activity introduces the child to the broader world and all the risks and uncertainties that that includes. In this way, the father helps the child move out of the nest and separate from the mother—a vital aspect to becoming one's own person. Of course, these days, mothers are often the ones escorting the children out into the world, but still, there are gender differences, mothers typically maintaining a greater protectiveness than that found in fathers.

It was Dad who repeatedly carried us into various parts of Europe, staying in a range of places, from campgrounds to hotels. He took us to Paris, Versailles, the Eiffel Tower, the Mona Lisa at the Louvre. He also took us on a tour of the Netherlands, visiting the Madurodam, the amusement park that boasts a miniature city that we could walk about like giants. We drove mile after mile through fields abloom with tulips and passed charming windmills. We awoke to breakfasts of meats and cheeses, butter and jellies and bread of all kinds. We traversed the snow-capped Alps, our car laboring up the steep inclines while we looked out with interest at the toy-like villages, miniaturized by distance, that dotted shadowed valleys and sun-lit towering mountainsides alike. We camped at Lake Garda, Italy, ensconced in our family-sized tent that Dad taught us how to erect out of a confusing mélange of canvas and aluminum rods. There we rode a large powerboat, bouncing across the swells, laughing with exhilaration as the spray of windblown water anointed our faces. To our amazement, we spied a Spanish galleon and wondered what it was doing here on a lake. Dad explained that Lake Garda was the place where B-grade pirate movies were made.

It was Dad who led us on an amazingly well-informed and fascinating tour of Italy. Given that he was a compulsive history buff and always reading on the subject, he brought the ancient buildings and cities to life, taking us hundreds and thousands of years back in time with his stories as we crossed the straight lines of Roman roads carved into the soil and viaducts descending the hills.

It was not only the cities that he knew but the countryside as well, for it was in Italy that he had fought in WW-II. Dad told us of Mussolini and how he got the trains to run on time and how an angry mob hung him at the end of the war. He took us along the route of his military campaign, from one end of Italy to the other, retracing the steps he had first made some twenty years earlier as a young artillery officer. He often stopped at different places to recount a memory of what had happened there. Upon one curving mountain road, a sniper's bullet just missed him as he drove in a jeep. On a hilltop, he had fallen into a latrine when German artillery rounds began probing their position, one exploding nearby. And, from a hillside overlooking an open field bracketed by dense woods, he recreated the incredulity he and his compatriots had felt when a German infantry battalion emerged from the trees below, marching unknowingly to their carnage. Dad described the suspense as they waited, fearing discovery, until the Germans were in the very center of the field, farthest from the safety of the woods on either side, before opening fire and annihilating them.

Most amazingly, we stopped at a hilltop manor that Dad said was the home of a girlfriend he had made at the time. We knocked on the door, and an attractive, dignified middle-aged woman answered. Dad introduced himself, and with surprised delight, she gave him a warm hug and kiss on the cheek. Dad introduced Mom and the rest of us, and the adults visited together while we played in the front yard of her manor.

I marveled at Dad's capacity to navigate across Europe and through the densely packed streets of the Italian cities with a map alone, a respect that grew only more profound as I repeatedly lost my way, even with the benefit of GPS, some forty-five years later. We visited the Vatican and the Colosseum in Rome, and Dad told his stories of the principal characters of the time and the events that had happened there. He explained the symbolism of the sculptures found in various squares and within the many fountains that dotted the city. He purchased indulgences in Rome for each of us that guaranteed we could bypass the trials of Purgatory and gain direct access to heaven upon our deaths.

He did the same in the United States. We toured many of the places I would go to years later in my trip with Jane and to which I subsequently took my kids: The Grand Canyon, the Painted Desert, the Petrified Forest. We rode ponies in Colorado and stood near bison. All this we owed to Dad, and now, finally, I can find my way to thank him, as tears evoked by the richness of these memories flood my eyes.

Still, there was that element about Dad that everything had to be about Dad. And sometimes even those events were noteworthy. I was about age fourteen, and we were living in Annandale, Va. One evening, just before Christmas, I heard the doorbell ring and went to answer it. But there was no one there. What was there, propped against the door frame, was a five-foot-long, ten-inch-wide and five-inch-deep, piece of luggage covered in shiny brown leather, sporting a ribbon and a note. Curiosity ignited, I brought the box in and excitedly shouted my discovery. Soon, the family was gathered in the foyer, and Mutti opened the note. The card was not signed but was addressed to Dad, expressing gratitude for some unspecified service he had generously performed. We then opened the box to discover one of the most beautiful rifles, with scope, that I had ever seen. Clearly, a very expensive gift. Mutti, astounded, was overcome with emotion and spent minutes lauding Dad for the goodness of whatever he had done. Dad, unusually, was standing on the periphery of the group, modestly insisting he had no idea what had warranted such a gift but clearly pleased by the adulation.

But something was nagging at me. The case seemed familiar. I struggled to remember where I might have seen it before. And then I did. I had seen one just like it in the basement rec room several days earlier and had forgotten all about it. I was amazed. What were the chances that Dad would come into a matching set of such beautiful rifles? Aloud, I marveled about the serendipity of life, awestruck by the miracle. At this point, Jacques began shushing me, which left me confused. What was I saying that was wrong? In looking back, I think it was the shushing tone that caught mother's attention. It alerted her that something was afoot. While I stood there in confusion, she started questioning, and the truth came out. The anonymous and praise-giving gift-giver was Dad himself. Mother, having been completely taken in, felt the fool, an experience she did not tolerate well. Feeling hard used and manipulated, embarrassed by the extent of her adulation of Dad that had now been turned on its head, she was indignant. That moment of Christmas fun and excitement had turned into something ugly that would cast a pall on the house for several days to come.

But that was Dad. He knew no other way. This was well illustrated one summer evening, while the sun was still well above the horizon at the lake house. Mark, in his early thirties, was fishing from the shore when Dad brought out a lawn chair and sat near him, watching. I stood nearby, waiting for dinner and enjoying the evening air. After a few minutes, Dad began barking advice. "Mark, go ten feet to your left and cast twenty feet out." Mark would comply. When that location failed to produce a fish, Dad would bark, "Mark, cast five feet to the right of that spot and five feet in." And so it went, Mark holding the rod and casting to Dad's repeated recommendations. At this time, Mutti came onto the upstairs deck, and called out, "John, it's time for dinner." Dad, still seated, his back to Mom, immediately raised his right arm in the universal hand gesture signaling stop, and irritably chided her, "Shush, Madeleine, I'm fishing!" We all loved that story. It said it all.

Then there was golf as "the boys" went out on the links. Dad, Jacques, Edward, and Mark, each bringing their high-end clubs and lessons to boot. I only golfed with them and so only two or three times a year. I didn't feel a need of clubs. While they took the game very seriously, I enjoyed the psychological warfare of it. So, there I would stand, a zip-lock bag filled with balls and tees in hand, standing at the club house, while the others proudly displayed their shiny clubs and, slightly embarrassed by me, tried to give the impression that I wasn't with them. On the course, Jacques would approach the ball and addressing it would say,

"Okay, ball, get ready for a ride." Spontaneously, I took this opportunity to become the voice of the ball and responded, "Okay, asshole," winning a laugh from everyone... but Jacques. Another time, when Jacques was about to hit a ball from the fairway, and everyone would normally maintain a strict quiet, I would await the crucial moment, right in the middle of his deliberate back-swing, the product of thousands of dollars in golf lessons, to start the engine on my golf cart. The noise cut through the silence and disrupted his concentration, throwing his swing off to his red-faced fury—brothers will be brothers.

Dad's gambit was always to alert whoever was teeing off about the dangers to be avoided. "Watch out for the woods on the left and the pond fifty yards out on the right" as if we couldn't see them with our own eyes, effectively raising those dangers in our mind. Our hands holding the club followed our eyes, the ball following not far behind.

Then there were just the nightly things that would occur while visiting. Having drinks while Mutti made dinner, everyone talking in the kitchen. Jacques and Dad loving to tell their jokes, their eyes welling with mirth as we all laughed together.

In all these things: touring, camping, socializing, good food, wine, and spirits, we were all conjoined. So when it came to teaching and exposing us to things by the doing of them, Dad did pretty well.

However, when it came to thoughtful and heartfelt conversations, this was Mom's domain. She was the yin to his yang. She was the one who engaged the nightly discipline of meditation called prayer and the evening walks when she talked with God. When I visited, I would join her for these walks on the hard-packed dirt streets that crisscrossed their way through Lake Monticello as the sun gave way to the moon, and the stars came out to compete with the glow of the fireflies. We walked and we talked, of God, of what was on her mind, of what was going on in my life as the song of the crickets and the chorus of the bullfrogs vied for dominance and threatened to drown out our conversation.

But all the while, throughout the years, despite the concerns she carried, she maintained an active, nurturing and loving presence; in the end, when she had done whatever could be done, she left it all in the hands of her God.

But this had not always been the case. Earlier in life, as the mother of twenty-somethings, Mother would stand strongly against anything that broke her sense of what was right. She took issue with Jacques' wife Christine going out one night with her girlfriends while Jacques was in Vietnam. She sputtered with indignation over what she felt as the impropriety of it. Christine wouldn't listen.

On another occasion, Mom, when visiting Jacques and Christine in Atlanta, took issue with how Christine raised the kids. Christine, insulted, told my parents to leave her house. She and my mother didn't speak for several years before making amends and going on to have a very close relationship. In this way, Mutti learned that others had their own ideas about things and didn't take kindly to her dogmatic viewpoints. The thing to be noted was that mother's focus was always Christine; it was never on Jacques—as usual, he could do no wrong. When I would point this out to Mutti, she would say, "She's the mother; he is staying loyal." That wasn't my idea of fatherhood, but apparently, it was hers and, I think, Jacques'.

The same had been true when Mom confronted Jane about pre-marital sex, making Jane unwelcome in their home during my hospitalization following the car accident, essentially leaving Jane no alternative but to leave. In the years to follow, Mom and Jane would become very close, their love of and respect for one another plain to see. When Jane and I were divorcing, Jane, unbeknownst to me, made the pilgrimage to talk with Mom, to express her regrets. Jane's relationship with her mother had been an abusive one. I knew my mother filled that void for her. That relationship healed to such an extent that at Mom's funeral, Jane and I, standing side by side, watched as one of Mom's brothers went to the open casket and placed a beret on her head. Jane marveled, "She looks so beautiful." Years later Jane told me that it was at this moment, as we were standing together, that she knew there would be forgiveness between us.

I harkened back to the care Mom showed during the difficult times Jane and I were going through, never saying a critical word of either of us and making no judgments.

Mom always worried about the kids and took care of them. She was the ground upon which the family rested and the glue that held it together. Almost always a positive presence, she was in turn respected and admired by all. She did most of the cooking and the cleaning. Sure, she would rail at us boys to clean our rooms and make our beds, but invariably followed behind whenever we did to remake the beds and straighten up the rooms to her own exacting standards.

She was always a presence during family occasions, laughing along delightedly with the rest of us. She could be a character as well, once donning a cowboy skirt and hat, corncob pipe in mouth as she hammed it up for a picture. In her war with the geese, she used a pellet gun to shoot them in the butt in the vain effort to drive them from her yard.

Mom, Madeleine Marie Alberta McCormack (born Turgeon), passed away on February 20, 1997, at age seventy-eight. I had driven all night with the kids in the car to attend her deathbed, only to arrive an hour too late. When my brothers met me at the car and told me of her passing, I burst into tears. A devoutly religious woman, she had grown far more tolerant and spiritual over the years, no longer governed by dogma but having developed her thinking on issues that troubled her vis-à-vis the church. Having developed her own beliefs, she no longer marched in lockstep with church doctrine but continued to attend Mass every Sunday and to kneel at her bed every night for prayers. Her developing spirituality served her well in her living and her dying. She was now a whole person and not burdened by despair or regrets as her life drew to its end.

Many years ago the philosopher Ram Dass wrote a book entitled: *The Only Dance There Is.* In it, he offered that most people have a signature way of going through life and that it is only danced harder as life nears its end. I took this to heart as both a blessing and a warning.

During her last two years, diagnosed with terminal cancer, Mutti had lived her dying in a way beyond compare, with grace, unflinchingly, and without fear. Indeed, to my utter surprise, she made the whole process beautiful. I marveled, *how was that possible?* She had lost all her hair, became emaciated from the radiation and chemotherapy treatments, and given to frequent bouts of nausea and dry heaving. Yet it was unmistakably true. It was the most wonderful of gifts. She was made strong by her faith and a soul-full conviction that she was returning to God. Her only worry? The family she was leaving behind. Her concern was for others. She insisted that she and my father move to Aiken, S.C., so he would be near Mark and Carol Ann when she passed.

She and I spoke about death and dying during my visits. On two separate occasions, she did the most unusual thing. She struggled out of bed in the late evening while I was sitting with my siblings and their spouses around the dining room table. She came over, placed her palms on the table for support, leaned toward me, looked directly into my eyes, glaring fiercely, and emphatically said: "Charlie, have a *good* life! Charlie, have a good life!" Then waited a moment, until I, looking directly back into her eyes, responded, "I will, Mom. I will." Then without another word, she turned and tottered her frail bent body back to bed.

This exact scenario happened not once, but twice, several months apart. My mother, sapped of energy, nauseated from chemotherapy, making that trek from her bed and repeating the very same words in the very same way as if it were all important to her to drive the point home, to drive the point *into* me. It was as if she could see the darkness planted all those years ago and refused to leave me for a second time. She was telling me that she *knew* with absolute conviction that it was within my power to move beyond it—if only I would. It was her blessing and her dying wish for me.

I got the point. Like a radioactive pellet inserted in the middle of a cancerous tumor, the whole notion of "Have a good life," whatever that meant, became a goal for me.

In the end, my mother was at such peace with herself and her dying that her sense of humor and her solidity as a human being never flagged. Indeed, it burned ever brighter as cancer ravaged her body but never grazed her spirit. Near the end, a picture was taken of her and my daughter Keeley sitting together. My mother's head bare, bald crown held erect, as both she and Keeley stared resolutely with their steady blue eyes into the unblinking lens of the camera. Two strong women, the younger channeling the older. I wondered if they knew how spiritually alike they were?

It was soon after this picture was taken that my mother, smiling with amusement, showed me a note she had received from her best friend, Dot, whom we knew as Aunt Dot. The note was a couple of sentences long, and in beautiful cursive, wishing her farewell and concluded with the words, "Bon Voyage." *Christ! I* thought. *Now that's courage and class on the part of both those good and strong women and friends. How does it get any more real than that?* Each of them faced death unflinchingly. My mom's death would be within weeks, Aunt Dot's years later, but neither was afraid to talk about it or face it. For them, death was an accepted part of life, not separate from it.

Mutti was buried at Arlington National Cemetery, the funeral services conducted in North Post Chapel, Fort Myer, Virginia, the very chapel where she and my father had married more than fifty years earlier.

As Ram Dass had foretold, my mother lived her dying the way she had lived her living; she only did it better and better as the years went on. I can't think of any greater gift a parent could give her children: the witnessing of the ability of an individual, of a soul, to evolve until death do them part, never becoming a finished product.

My father also danced his dance and to a predictably different outcome. His health declined drastically over a period of years suffering alcoholism, hardening of the arteries, strokes, and Alzheimer's disease. To my bewilderment, his death was harder for me to digest. It was not that I missed him, at least not that I knew at the time; it was more a sense of being profoundly unsettled. That might seem counterintuitive, given my feelings toward him, but the more I thought about it, the more sense it made.

It's like drinking milk. Lactose issues aside, we can easily digest fresh milk, and it becomes part of us: In a sense, it is in our cells; it is always with us. That's how I felt about my mom, and so my grieving for her was almost non-existent. I miss her, but I also feel that she is always with me. As she took her daily walks, now I take mine, sometimes communing with her.

Certainly, I had felt grief and mourning over the loss of her earlier in my life when she walked away from me in the courtyard of Collège St. Etienne, but much healing had ensued over the years in the form of various demonstrations of her love of me. It wasn't the perfect love I had wished for, and it wasn't always in a love language I could appreciate, but it was a real love, only conveyed with increasing conviction by her unremitting insistence that I have a good life. By the time of her death, I knew that regardless of what had happened or why she had always loved me. With that certain knowledge, she was always with me.

But Dad was a different story. Earlier in my life, in my thirties, I thought I had finally separated from him. This notion arose from two interactions in which I refused to tolerate his treatment of me. The first took place while I was visiting my parents with Jane and the kids. I had gotten up from the dinner table to get seconds when my father barked an order in command voice one would use in ordering a dog to heel, "Charlie! Bring me some more roast beef." I felt belittled and enraged. He had often referred to us in our earlier years as his "little niggers," and now he was talking to me in that denigrating fashion once again. The ugliness of it and the fact that he thought it okay to talk to me this way, much less in front of my kids, was utterly intolerable. I knew that if I acceded to his behavior, my children would have the idea that such treatment was acceptable. Also, it would drive home the point that I, their father, was subservient to his father. I wasn't about to have that. I had been independent of him for years, making my own history, becoming myself. I had to stand up for them and for me.

Nonetheless, a primordial fear ran up my spine; I was still snake bit from his abuse of me and others during my childhood years. But recognizing the stakes, I overrode it, willing to fight the fight on this particular hill. I responded sharply, "No! I'll be happy to bring you more roast beef when you can ask politely." Silence suffused the room. But, as would any good narcissist, he refused. He simply stayed silent. And, like any good narcissist, he never got up to get his roast beef. The family conversation gradually resumed.

The second instance occurred as much of the family, during a quasi-reunion, was gathered around the dinner table in animated conversation. I began to insert myself into the flow, when my father, sitting catty-corner to me, slapped me on the forehead without warning. I instantly realized he felt stymied in his efforts to get a word in edgewise and that I was the handiest outlet for his frustration. But I didn't care. That was his problem. He had to learn to man-up. I would not tolerate that treatment ever again. I immediately slapped him back on his forehead with equal force, then said in a low, tight voice, my eyes fixed upon his, "Dad, don't *ever* hit me again."

I was willing and able to take him down there and then, and he knew it. Dad looked straight at me, then for a weapon, his eyes falling upon his steak knife. He looked at me again then back at the knife as he moved his hand toward it. With genuine disdain, words dripping with the acid of contempt from my mouth, I said, "Really? You're going to kill me?" He looked up from the knife at me, then back at the knife, clearly considering this question. After a long pause, the tension left his body, and he let the moment go. He never hit me again.

Regarding my hatching, this was an important event. I had come to the point of being willing to lose my relationship with my father forever, and by extension, with my mother if necessary, if the cost of staying in relationship involved tolerating abuse. That realization freed me. I now knew I was no longer dependent upon them. I no longer needed them. I wanted my parents in my life but only on the right terms. In this realization, I arrived at psychological adulthood, having learned a lesson that is obvious when you think about it: you can never ask permission to grow up. You just do it.

What I didn't recognize at the time was that putting my Dad in his place in external reality didn't necessarily mean I had gotten rid of his presence in my internal world. There, I was to discover he was lurking behind every corner. There, I was to discover a terrible truth: the more troubled the relationship, the more difficult to let go.

Dad was sour milk: He curdled in my stomach. I swallowed, but could not digest. How could it be otherwise? He had never made amends for anything. I don't think I ever heard him say that he was wrong or that he was sorry. It was clear to me I never held any special place in his heart. I do not think anyone did, at least any more so than a rich man values counting his money. Consequently, his loss was more troublesome. He was gone from my life forever, yet continued to be felt as a remorseless stranger, a gaseous ball of indigestion.

The last time I saw my Dad, he was sitting in the large living room of his nursing home, which bristled with the faint, acrid scent of urine. Jane-2 and I had spent several hours with him, showing him family photographs to stimulate his memory. Occasionally a look, which I took to be one of recognition, would cross his face and then disappear. This process mirrored his attempts to talk; he would begin a sentence only to lose the thread before completing it.

Music from the forties played on a boom box, the walls of the room lined with patients in chairs and wheelchairs, some dressed in suits or frilly dresses from another era. Sometimes a patient would join us on the couch, mistaking me for a son, brother, father or friend. Everyone seemed to look at me with devouring eyes, hungering for contact with whichever partially remembered person my presence had evoked within them.

At one point, a little boy ran into the room chasing a large yellow balloon that he kept bouncing in the air. I worried that his mad-dash presence might result in an injurious collision, but miraculously he avoided this. As he darted about, none of the wizened patients seemed to notice. Their heads continued to hang down; mouths slack-jawed, parchment textured hands continued to lay still upon their laps.

Then magic happened. The boy lost control of the balloon, and just before it landed on the head of one of the female patients, her hand shot up and knocked it back into the air. This event repeated itself five or six times as different residents reacted to the balloon. Before I knew it, the room was alive with active, smiling people. To my delight, my father was one of them. For a moment, he had returned from wherever he had been; instincts had taken over and brought him into the present, out of his mind and into his body.

The boy's father soon entered the room and retrieved him. And as suddenly as it had begun, it stopped, like a ballerina atop a music box that just wound down. All the patients slumped back into their previous states as if nothing had occurred. Perhaps, as far as they knew, nothing had.

At this point, I went to the bathroom. While I was away, Jane-2 asked my father if he knew who I was. He said "No." As I was leaving that day, he asked with desperately beseeching eyes if we could visit again. I said I would, all the while feeling guilty because I did not want to and because I thought this might be the last time I would ever see him.

Several months later the call came. My father had died.

Although we had not been close, I missed those random moments when our time together would suddenly sing with manic aliveness before disappearing again, so like the yellow balloon.

Thus, my parents lived lives together but in polar contrast. My mother's life does suggest the importance of spirituality in some form, of thinking beyond ourselves, of working hard to try to do no harm, of trying to do good, of trying to help others, of taking ownership of our lives and behaviors. My mother did this in a big way over the years and maintained her nightly discipline of walking for a half hour when she would commune with God. Because this contemplative need was firmly rooted within her, she grew through the years. Bearing witness to all this, she taught me by example that there is nothing better for a child to see then a parent continuing to grow into her life and into her death. She taught by example that there might be times along the way you might rest or need a chance to recover but that sooner or later you always get back on your feet. You never give up on yourself.

Where my mother was selfless, my father, believed in little beyond himself. He never took ownership or responsibility for his life or behaviors, often did harm verbally and physically, and never made amends for anything that I witnessed. While my mother grew and learned lessons from life, he withered. In contrast to my mother's beautiful death, which reflected her spiritual growth and aliveness to the world around her, his dying process of years' duration was marked by increasing alcoholism, paranoia, fearfulness and isolation mirroring his self-devouring self-absorption. These two separate paths were not coincidental; each reflected the cumulative outcome of how they lived their lives.

The lessons I learned from the way my parents lived their lives and deaths do not feed my fearfulness. Indeed, they give me hope. My mother's example had proven that if you genuinely work on yourself, think about your life, try to help others, and take responsibility for yourself, then you will continue to grow as a human being and better meet the challenges that the different phases of life inevitably bring your way. If you do not do these things, if you do not take responsibility for your mistakes and learn from them, then you do not develop. You will be left in an ever-weakening position heading toward despair rather than a generative and meaningful life. This had been my dad's fate and my dad's Karma: He died frightened and alone, trapped in his ever-diminishing and depopulated world with the walls closing in.

My dad, John Crisler McCormack, died on September 4th, 2003, at the age of eighty-five. He was buried on a rainy day at Arlington National Cemetery with full honors, casket pulled on a caisson, followed by the honor guard and led by a riderless horse, empty boot facing backward in the stirrup. Mark and several cousins walked in the procession. At the gravesite, a bagpiper played "Amazing Grace," followed by a bugler sounding out the hauntingly beautiful last twenty-four notes of taps. Then, the sharp clap of three rifle volleys rang out in final salute and farewell, silence flowing into the ensuing void and me.

When I review my life, I'm reassured that I'm living it more along the lines of my mother than my father. But, something is still not right. I think I should be happier given all that I have for which to be thankful. And I have a quest. I promised to have a good life. So the question is: What am I missing?

PART VI

RECONCILIATION—HATCHING THINGS IN

Typically, when I think of reconciliation, I think of a couple reconciling after a pronounced conflict. And it's kind of like that, but this time, the couple is within me: I am reconciling with myself, trying to come to terms in a real way with me in my life. I want to play the music of my life as myself. Some could well say, "You already are." But not quite so; I had never arrived at a place of relative contentment. This lets me know I had more to do, more to resolve. Where was that place hiding?

CHAPTER 31

GRAND FATHERHOOD—THE CHILDREN AS THE FATHER OF THE MAN

I wish the story maintained a straight line and that it could come to some quick conclusion. But that is not life, nor the way of things. Life is full of non-linear progressions and different narrative angles that frustrate the desire for simple story lines or answers. Throughout the journey, I have thus far described there have been other equally important stories taking place simultaneously of which I have yet to speak. The thing about language is that you can't say everything all at once. All that would come out would be babble. This said I must now speak about family life, my role as a father, a father-in-law and a grandfather. Might the cause of my continued unease lie there?

The story of my fatherhood begins in the story of my son-hood, in my relationship with my father and my mother. Fortunately, it does not end there. Across the years I've undergone major transformations as a father, and that's just when considering raising kids. It doesn't include the role of fatherhood beyond my children's childhood, when their mates and in-laws come into my life, along with grandchildren, and long-held traditions change.

What is the role of "the father" when kids are grown? I have no clue. I've been making it up as I go along and when in doubt I just try to get out of the way. No worries, though, my kids don't hesitate to *help* me.

Chandler got the worst of the parenting deal. That wasn't because of his parents' troubles—those affected all the kids—but because of me. Healthy, positive father-son interactions were not something with which I had experience. The only thing I knew about father-son relationships was oppression, enslavement, hatred, violence, and the importance of avoiding my father at all costs. My guiding light as a parent: Don't inflict any of that on Chandler. As frail as that beacon was, it was all I had to light the way.

In contrast, where my daughters were concerned, I was blazing a new trail, unhampered by abysmal prototypical experiences of the father-son variety. The relationship with my mother, for all its faults, had been far more connected and fulfilling.

Also, there were the gender and role differences. My girls didn't have to compete with me to find themselves. We complemented one another, while Chandler and I shared male energies and occupied similar territories and we already know how Chandler feels about territory.

Moreover, males and females are put together differently. I know that's not some wildly original formulation, but I'm speaking of the less well-known differences. Did you know that women see more color and see things more all at once, while men tend to be more focused and compartmentalized, and able to detect fast-moving objects more readily? While the male's capacities allow him to be a better hunter, the female's capacities allow her to do everything else, thereby becoming homemakers and the glue to family and tribal life. These gender differences result in different ways of seeing and organizing experience that complement one another.

And then there are the hormonal differences. Where testosterone-laden males tend to relate along a power and competition axis, estrogen-infused females tend to bond. Thus, my daughters' energies and mine tended to complement one another, and we got along fairly easily; their issues would be with their mother. For them, I was regarded as a bastion of safety and reliability—and someone to twist around their little fingers.

With Chandler, it was more complicated; we both felt this. Once, about age eight, he asked me in a timid voice whether I loved the girls more than him. That broke my heart. I took him into my arms and held him tight, wanting to reassure him. But, in truth, I also felt the different flavor of the father-son relationship. To this day, I don't know how much that difference is related to gender or the less than perfect fit between different personalities, and how much it relates to my relationship with my father casting its pall on that with my son.

I do know I strove for tenderness and empathy at moments when my dad would have responded with callousness and brutality. I did not always win, but mostly. Once, when I was coaching his soccer team, he came up to me whining about another boy kicking him in the shins. Busy overseeing all the kids and annoyed with his whining, I gruffly told him, "Kick him back"—not the best fatherly response, nor coaching one for that matter. At another time, during an unusually rancorous episode between him and Keeley, I pushed him against a wall to get him to stop and "listen up!" That was getting a little too close to being like my dad, although my dad would have also smacked me in the face. Again, not the best father-son interactions, nor anything I would ever do with my daughters.

As Chandler grew from little boy to boy-man, we moved from predominantly tender relations to more manly pursuits marked by growing competitiveness. Less-than-tender moments began to emerge from what previously had been warm and cuddly times.

Where once Chan and I could wrestle—tussling, tickling, and laughing together—now we could not. Those interactions had morphed into something more serious.

As Chandler grew older, now able to see the distant horizon of his young manhood, he began trying to assert his dominance, no longer satisfied by me pretending to lose. Occasionally, he would get carried away, arms thrashing around, and deliver an elbow strike into my face full-force. It may or may not have been intentional, but, my reptilian brain would raise its head as quick as an adder's strike. I would usually contain my instinctive response. Instead, my anger would squeeze out around the edges, and I would sharply rebuke him. In this way, something fun turned into something painful and unhappy with increasing frequency. I could not blame Chandler; he was striving to grow up and still sorting fantasy from reality. Caught up in his playful excitement he didn't realize the harm he could do.

I didn't have a clue as to how to handle this other than talking to him about it. However, I did know that the time for such physical interactions was coming to an end. It saddened me, for I loved tussling with him, the hugging and the tickling. But I could not stand the ugliness that stirred inside me during those painful moments that came without warning. I knew this ugliness. It lurked within—my own dark matter. I did not want my son exposed to it, and I did not want to feel it.

From my awareness of my failed parenting moments and those of my parents, I've come to the belief that all parents owe their children an apology. Not one that burdens the child with the obligation to forgive, but one that takes ownership and responsibility for damage done. If you would expect this from your children, why would you expect less from yourself? Every human being is imperfect, deficient in one way or another, cursed by weaknesses, shortcomings and blind spots and consequently, inevitably, does damage even if not of the malicious kind.

Parents are mirrors to their children. The child gazes into the mirror of the parent's eyes in hopes of seeing himself. Some parents reflect the negative to the relative exclusion of the positive, perhaps raising kids with a poor self-image. Other parents may do the opposite, raising fair-haired boys or girls, who sense that their less attractive undersides are being denied by their parents: its own form of rejection. Each parental extreme is a distortion of reality. The child senses this, even if words aren't found for it, leading to a less than secure sense of self.

Parents often make me angry. They don't seem to realize that their children are also a mirror to them. Some parents never look into this mirror and examine themselves, granting themselves papal infallibility even though their kids are screwing up right and left. Others may note their deficiencies but only throw their hands up saying, "I can't help myself," shrugging off the responsibility of doing something about it, shirking their duty to grow. Both styles of parenting are betrayals of the child's trust.

It's my belief that it is in our willingness to confront our shadows, especially when they are casting their pall upon our children, that we engage in our most loving acts.

For me, one instance of a damaging action followed by a simple act of repair comes to mind in my relationship with Chandler. He was age four or five, and I was on a ladder re-attaching a ceiling light after painting the room. I dropped a screw that fell onto the tarp covering the floor and rolled out of sight into a crease. Chandler was in the room watching. I asked him to give me the screw, but despite my best efforts to direct him to it, he could not find it. I felt increasingly frustrated in my attempts to direct him verbally to the right spot because, in fact, I was not doing a good job of it; the right words were eluding me. As I became increasingly frustrated with myself, my irritation unexpectedly burst through, reminiscent of my father's penchant for putting his children down to build himself up. Sharply, I chided, "It's right there! Why don't *you* see it?" as if the fault were Chandler's. I immediately recognized what I had done and felt ashamed. I got down from the ladder, picked Chandler up in my arms and hugged him to me, all the while repeatedly saying, "I'm sorry. That wasn't your fault; that was Daddy's. I wasn't good at telling you where it was." Hopefully, this lessened, any tendency Chandler might have had to internalize the problem as having been of his making, which children translate to having been a problem not of behavior but of their essence.

While these emotions roiled within me, I had an epiphany. The aggravation I had just experienced in trying to communicate must have been as nothing when compared to the abiding annoyance my dad lived with every moment of his life. In the struggle to push his words out, he must have felt flawed, incompetent, and inadequate, thus fueling his need to repeatedly belittle his children. Unfortunately, because of his reliance on narcissistic defenses, the need to deny his vulnerabilities, he could not acknowledge those feelings, either to himself or others. Thus, he could never be at one with himself. He remained forever divided, one part housing the desire for perfection and omnipotent invulnerability, always attacking the other, which housed the feelings of weakness and vulnerability that he so despised. It is in such ways that denial functions. In that Dad did not struggle to come to terms with his feelings, instead choosing to attack them, he could not learn from them nor relate to them in others.

Hence, his vulnerability to psychological breakdown. What he did with his feelings was project them into his children and at times his wife, treating us as if we were worthless, while continually raising himself up by putting us down. My dad helps me appreciate that the ultimate cowardice is the refusal to look at ourselves when there is every reason to do so.

The last thought I have about this incident with Chandler is that I'm fairly sure that it would not have happened with one of my daughters. I would have held them to a different standard, treating them more gently as girls.

Being a parent for me has been a journey of episodic self-discoveries and self-confrontations. Parenting *is* a full-contact sport. Children are a lot like heat-seeking missiles: They keep bumping up against us until they invariably push on whatever weaknesses exist within the parent's personality. It is at just such moments, when the child has managed to get under my skin, that I can learn something about myself. It is at just such moments that the child has given me an opportunity to become a better man.

Though we've had our struggles, my relationship with my daughters was easier. There was only one time I ever felt my relationship threatened with either of them, and that was with Keeley. She was a teenager and had breached some rule of the house and was refusing to comply with the consequences. Our argument turned ugly and escalated to the point where Keeley drew her trump card: she was going to call her mother to come and get her. As Keeley was leaving, I said, "You know, you can't come back until you're willing to pay the consequences for your behavior. You may not agree with a rule, but you can't change it after the fact. We can discuss changing the rule, but you have to comply with the consequences." I was totally committed to this stance. I knew if I didn't hold her to consequences, she would be inclined to pick and choose when she would comply. In essence, I would have no parental authority, and without parental authority, you're not a parent, you're a peer. I knew Keeley still needed a dad. A week later, Keeley called asking to come home. The prodigal daughter had returned: thank God! She met the consequences, *and* we changed the rule.

Another time, Keeley and I conflicted was when she was seventeen, and a twenty-two-year-old man was coming to take her out. I put my foot down when the man arrived, even though it was awkward. Keeley complained that her mother didn't have a problem with it. I sent him away anyway, without Keeley. Years later, Keeley told me how protected she had felt. Trust me; that wasn't clear at the time. With such challenges, I grew into my role as a father to a teenage daughter.

I have two memories of parenting Cait that readily come to mind. She was a different kind of kid, never directly challenging but growing and separating in her own way. One time occurred a week before Christmas. I was living alone. Cait was around age eight and staying overnight. In her sweet, little girl voice she told me she had spent all her money purchasing gifts for everyone else and didn't have any money left to buy a present for me. She wanted reassurance that that was okay.

My instinct was to *parent for the good feel*, to say, "Yes. Absolutely. Don't worry about it," while secretly enjoying her affectionate response confirming that I was the *best dad ever*. I knew that was what she rightly anticipated and what would meet with her approval: I would be the moon and the stars in her sky. This was a chance to be the *Good Dad* in her eyes, a feeling I desperately wanted, given her parents' impending divorce and the guilt I felt about exposing my children to the breakup of the family. But I thought a moment. I knew her siblings were getting me special gifts that year and I didn't want her upstaged. I also wanted her to know she was important and that her gifts mattered because she mattered. She needed to be a participating member of the family. I also worried that as the youngest she had been most at risk with her mother's leaving. I feared Cait was using infantilization as a strategy for getting nurturing attention in the family—one that would not auger well with the need to continue to grow and mature. With these concerns flashing through my mind, I responded, "No, honey. That isn't okay. I would really like a gift from you and, in fact, I would like it to be a very special gift." Crying out, Cait responded, "But Daddy, I don't have any money!" to which I answered, "If you need money, your mom and I can give you work to earn it."

Tears welled in Cait's eyes as she exclaimed accusatorily, "Daddy, I came to you so you would make me feel better, but you've only made me feel worse." I answered, "I get it. I understand. You don't have to get me a present. I'm just answering your question." That year she bought me a long sleeved pullover shirt that I wore for the next decade. I loved that shirt, and I love Cait. That parenting moment took a toll on me because I wasn't sure it was the right thing to do. But right or wrong, it wasn't malicious; it was to help her gain full membership in the family. *Parenting for the good feel* isn't a good thing. I think that one of the greatest difficulties of being a parent is often not being sure we're doing the best thing.

Once, Cait asked me if she could have a piercing. My thought was *If you need to ask, you're not ready for one.* Thinking I was smart, I told her she could only have a tongue piercing, *knowing* that she would *never* do such a thing because of the pain. Several weeks later she returned from a trip to the beach and stuck her tongue out at me to flaunt her silver piercing: in such acts of defiance, caterpillars find wings.

It's long been my belief that the best thing a parent can do is to focus on raising kids not that they love but that they like. When kids are being unlikeable, that is a call for parenting. Another thing I believe about parenting is that parents need to raise children that transcend them, not in monetary terms, but as people. It's my belief that at some point the kids, now adults, have to be able to confront their parents and challenge them where they are falling short in one way or another. When this happens in an adult way, as opposed to a form of teenage rebellion, it marks the arrival of adulthood and peer-to-peer relationship between parent and adult child.

My kids meet these criteria. They share many of my values. They are generous, spirited, resolute, kind and thoughtful. Each has a solid work ethic and clear ideas about parenting that they implement with little hesitation. I don't always agree with their parenting but then what grandparent does when it comes to their own childrens' parenting? What I do recognize is that I have had my time to parent, and this is theirs. Usually, unless sorely pressed by a grandchild's misbehavior, I don't give my opinion unless asked. Typically, it isn't.

Each of my kids has challenged me to grow. When Chandler was in his late twenties, he introduced me to a meaning of love that I had never considered and which I felt to be the purest experience of love that I ever had, aside from the first time I held him in my arms. At the time, I was strongly opposed to his girlfriend who was an extremely damaged woman. Given the nature of my work and expertise, I knew life with her would be a living hell, not only for him but for the rest of the family in that she would be part of every gathering, splintering its easiness with the jagged edges of her perpetual dramas and excessively vulnerable personality. After Chandler had ended the relationship, he confronted me with being too invested in its ending and warned me, at least as I took it, that if I ever did that again, he would no longer have a relationship with me.

It was at that moment that I had the epiphany. I knew with absolute certainty that if it would keep him safe, I would gladly do it all over again, *even* if it meant losing Chandler. That was as powerful a self-less feeling of love as I've ever had. I would sacrifice myself in a heartbeat if it kept him safe. I had never known that feeling before.

Chandler later corrected my interpretation, clarifying that he only meant he would not confide in me about his relationships, not that he would end ours. Here again, I was responding in a way reminiscent of the all or nothing relationship with my dad, and in a way that had never splashed over into my relationship with my daughters.

The amazing thing he was telling me—amazing because I had never had the experience before—was that he could handle his relationships and that he needed me to trust him on that. He was telling me in no uncertain terms that he was a full-grown man, and I needed to let him handle his life.

Please be clear—for this is the wonderful part—he was not *asking* me, he was *telling* me. He wasn't asking permission to grow up; he already had. He wanted a father, but no longer needed a parent. Lesson learned. I was so proud of him and I was proud of myself that I could tolerate his confrontation without defensiveness and proud to have been part of raising such a strong man. Here it was evident; the child had become the father of the man. Hatching of Charlie was proceeding apace.

Keeley also taught me but in her way: by example. An extrovert, she has the unusual characteristic of being able to walk into a room full of strangers and make friends right away. In truth, Chandler's somewhat the same. I don't know how they became this way; perhaps they're simply old souls reincarnated. Nevertheless, I've watched this time and again and still haven't figured out how she does it. She has developed relationships with *my* friends and *my* siblings, making them her own. Having grown up amongst them, they are as much a part of her valued relationships as they are mine, and she lays claim to them. She regularly makes the long drives to visit, taking her husband Jason, Caitlin and Caitlin's fiancée Justin, and all three of their little ones, on a regular basis. Reciprocally, my friends and siblings love these visits. Sometimes, when I've been especially good, I'm even invited along.

Keeley also confronts me in gentle ways that are easy to hear. Just last year she told me that it was important that I get together more regularly with her son, Cormac, if I wished to have a deeper relationship with him. I responded, and indeed Cormac and I have developed a special bond that is a boon to each of us. It is Cormac that I am holding on the cover of this book.

Keeley also doesn't hesitate to call me when she needs help. I'm always glad to be asked and pleased to provide it. When this is going on, I feel connected and contributing to the lives of my kids without fear of being intrusive.

Of my three kids, Caitlin reminds me most of myself. She's more self-absorbed and has had the most trouble in her journey. Not that the others haven't—they have, and each has had to suffer. But Cait's has been more enduring. She is burdened with the most self-doubt and social anxiety, both companions well known to me. And through the years she has managed to keep moving forward in a herky-jerky journey, so reminiscent of my own. Now in her early thirties, she has grown into a very solid human being, one who always has your back, and even stars in web events selling a line of clothes. When she looks at me with those big, no-bullshit eyes, I know I'm in direct communication with the real deal—no veneers to worry about here. She has become her own person and is living her life.

In more recent years, with the birth of her son Ryan, Caitlin proclaims, "Dad, with Ryan's birth, I feel like I have something bigger than myself to live for. He's already made me a better, more mature person." Does that sound familiar?

Several years ago, Cait gave me a teaching. She asked me what I would like for Father's Day. I requested she write me a letter about her thoughts on our relationship through the years. Not a feel-good letter, a real letter, written from the heart and her truth. I didn't get that letter on Father's Day; it had been a big ask. But that Christmas, the house full of company, Cait surprised me. Out of nowhere, she extended an envelope. I had no idea what it was. She told me it was the letter I'd requested. I was briefly confused, not remembering what she was talking about. Then I remembered and immediately filled with the honey of heart-felt appreciation and thanked her. As I started to open the letter, Cait calmly said, "Dad, I wouldn't read that letter right now." I asked, "Why not?" "Because it will make you cry." I thought *That's not likely. I'm a pretty tough guy. I'm surprised Cait doesn't know me better.*

I opened the envelope, and fifteen seconds later I was sobbing with the memories of the joys and the heartaches. It was just the kind of letter I had wanted. What Cait had written was so beautiful and called up so many memories, both happy and sad, that we had lived together. Someone took a picture of her and me hugging at that moment, my eyes swollen and tears streaming down this tough guy's face. Wow. What a memory. I'm moved to tears even now. Guess who didn't know who very well?

I think that a good and meaningful life is strung together by just such moments and that it is vital to be in the business of building them. Never put things off, never wait, never hope for a better time, never avoid conflict when it comes to dealing with people you care about. Such delaying tactics are seductive, following the path of least resistance and avoiding dealing with the initial anxiety, but they are also the path of least contact. They serve to maintain the illusion of harmony via the avoidance of potential conflict and deny the harsh reality that tomorrow is guaranteed to no one.

Be true to yourself and manifest yourself truly—have genuine relationships with all who are important to you, warts and all, if you want a guaranteed way to keep growing.

Your head can't tell your heart what to feel. But it can do two things. It can try to repress what you feel, or you can use it to make sense of what you're feeling. The former strategy is eventually doomed. Just because you are not aware of your feelings doesn't mean they are not having an impact, for they certainly are. When outside of awareness, one's feelings take up residence in the body and come out in other, less direct but powerful ways that leave us feeling confused as to what's going on. Using our heads to make sense of what we're feeling may lead to an initial spike of discomfort, but that's followed by an overall decrease as we make sense of ourselves.

As I look at my feelings, I'm feeling good about how my kids have turned out and about the lives they are living. I'm proud to be their dad. But, still, there is a continuing feeling of unease within me of which I have not yet made sense. None of these relationships has been completely smooth sailing. Each one has entailed conflict and some unease. I don't think that they could have happened any other way in the real world. But I still seem to feel a dread that doesn't stick to anything I have yet spoken of. Where else to look? Ah! What about the in-laws? After all, these *better halves* are not neutral presences. Indeed, they impact upon me. I had thought about parenthood from many angles, but not much from the standpoint of a *father-in-law* with people who grew up in different family cultures and with different family values, and who owed no allegiance to me.

CHAPTER 32

FATHER-OUT-LAW

An unanticipated aspect of fatherhood has been the impact of my kids' significant others on my life. That was something to which I had given little thought. What if they didn't like me or I didn't like them? That would be tough. Till their arrival, I had imagined them as some two-dimensional, cut-out figures playing support roles to those of us center stage: The McCormacks. I hadn't thought about them as living entities, each with a different center to their respective universes, and with opinions, belief systems, cultural biases, idiosyncrasies and unique personalities that may or may not jell with my own.

Add to this the effect on me if they don't treat my children well. Though truth be told, I would be more upset with my adult children if they put up with such a thing. Finally, there is the question of how they would get along as a group. If poorly, the acrid dynamics would taint every family gathering. Put all these things together, and you have the makings of a complex family stew of relationships rife with the potential for drama and struggle. I mean really, in a room of ten people how many do you actually enjoy? Keeley? Probably nine. Me and Cait: three and a half. Chan: six or seven.

Now, years down the road, two of my children have been in relationships for years and are married with kids of their own. Cait is in a serious relationship and soon to be married. Each of their significant others has become an integral part of family life. When we're all gathered together, I look around and am amazed. Everyone enjoys everyone else even though it would be hard to find a more diverse group.

Think about this. It includes a straight-talking German woman who is also a very successful businesswoman, an African-American who reads the Bible each morning, and a bald Muslim whose entire body below the neck—at least the parts I've seen—is covered with tattoos. What the hell is going on here? What happened to the traditional, white on white, white-bread brew? Can a man have no peace?

It's an amazing cast of characters. Let me start with Chandler's wife Nina, a native German. Both Chandler and Nina are very tall. Nina is at least 6 feet, and Chan is 6' 3". When I'm visiting them, I feel like I'm in the Land of The Giants. Also, given how attractive they both are, I feel like a large-nosed, hunched-back troll that just came out from underneath the bridge—by the way, even if I do say so myself, a part I played to perfection in an elementary school play. Nina gave up the presidency of a branch of a German company located in Atlanta to work half-time and raise her family. She was then made vice president and chief financial officer. Recently, she was offered the presidency again. She's not sure she will accept. That says something about how much she is valued by her company as well as how much she values family. To me, that's all fantastic, but that's not the heart of it.

I enjoy Nina. She reminds me so much of my mother that I sometimes find myself teasing her in similar ways: I like stirring things up. Both Nina and my mom spoke English with a foreign accent, both were extremely hard workers, both were relatively adamant in their views, and both were lionesses when it comes to their families.

I love interacting with Nina because she always tells the truth as she sees it—she's just incapable of doing anything else. One night, after wine and dinner and the kids in bed, she let me know in her serious Germanic way that I am not the man her father is. Her tone embodied the practical, self-evident certainty of her conviction. Please understand that she was not being malicious or attacking, it was only factual. She did not tell me this to wound me, just responded honestly when the conversation veered in this direction. Well, maybe "veered" isn't the right word; I think I found some way to bring it into play. I can't help it; I love stirring the pot and exploring peoples' beliefs.

In any event, I cannot debate her assertion. In her eyes, I cannot hold a candle to her dad. Indeed, her father is a good and fine man, and I've enjoyed his company the few times we've met, though we don't share a language. And, truth be told, she's right. I *am not* the man her father is. But I for one have no problem with that; after all, I rather like being me.

I think that one of the things Nina prizes in her dad is that when he visits he actively seeks a list of things that need doing around the house. In this way, he helps them out and keeps himself busy and productive. That said, doing repairs around the house is not my thing; only reluctantly do I repair my *own* house. Still, after several conversational forays on my part, Nina couldn't seem to think of a *single* way in which I might surpass her father. I was enjoying myself. My failings were seemingly writ large. All the while Chandler softly cautioned, "Be careful. My dad is very sensitive." I can see why he would say this—I can be—but I wasn't feeling so at that time. Indeed, I couldn't help but bait the moment, secretly delighting inside because I believed Nina's assertion that there was not a single way in which I might exceed her father could not possibly hold up in any world where reason and logic reigned. Consequently, I assumed the affectation of a little boy, and asked in a near whiny voice, "Reeaaaalllyy, there is noth-h-h-i-i-n-n-n-g that *I* am better at than *your* dad?"

In true Germanic fashion, Nina took this question very seriously and, after another sip of wine, pondered it for some time. While she was considering this question, I was imagining that she recognized that in the entire universe of possible human attributes that there must be at least one, or maybe even one half of one, that I might be a little better at than her dad. After her immersive reflection, but still with more than a hint of reticence, I imagine cued by a faint *souci* of disloyalty to her father, Nina said, "*Maybe*, you are a *little* easier to talk to," emphasizing the words "maybe" and "little." At that I laughed out loud. I loved it! Talk about damning with faint praise. Nonetheless, I knew that was not easy for her, and I also accepted that characterization as the highest praise of any on *my* scale of desirable attributes. Moreover, I love her loyalty to her dad, to her family, and to her honesty. I love having her in my life—so reminiscent of Mom.

Keeley married Jason, an African-American, who is another joy of my life. We became fast friends from the beginning. When Keeley brought him home for the first introduction, they were supposedly on their way somewhere. However, he and I became so involved in conversation that we were still talking six hours later, and Keeley, despite repeatedly imploring that it was time to leave, finally just threw up her hands—since then Keeley has always joked that Jason married her to get to me.

Jay routinely makes the trek out to the house to hang out with Janet and me when he needs a respite from being a husband and a father. Jay is fun, witty, opinionated, provocative, and loves—like me—to stir things up. I consider Jay the world's foremost authority in discovering *really bad* obscure action flicks that we love watching together. Jay is a good man, husband, and father.

Janet says, "He's the nicest person I know." He makes living and loving fun. Before young children curtailed his ability, he had a practice of starting each day reading the Bible. What a great meditative practice, the morning meditation of an everyday saint of the ordinary good.

Caitlin is about to marry Justin, the bald, tattooed Muslim. At this writing, she doesn't know that yet. He has just called to ask for her hand in marriage. He announced, "You're an old guy, so I'm doing an old-school thing of asking for your blessing to marry Caitlin," plainly letting me know he is his own man and that this was only a formality. I responded, "I'm pleased as punch." Given the ensuing silence, I suspected he was confused by this expression and explained: "That's an old school way of saying, yes."

Justin had already heard that when Jason came by to ask for my blessing to marry Keeley, I had insisted there be a trial by combat for him to prove his worthiness: he would have to beat me in a game of Wii Tennis. I soon regretted setting that bar so high because I thought that match would never end. I explained to Justin, "No worries, I'm past my Wii Tennis days." He later told Keeley that he was sure he could take me. Keeley told him, "I don't think my dad has a Wii anymore. Maybe you can compete in pushups." Justin responded, "I think I can take him in that too." He wasn't so haughty when I beat him and Jason in swimming the greatest distance underwater before needing to take a breath. Jason just shook his head, commenting, "I can't believe it, you're closer to seventy than I am to forty." Never one to miss an opportunity, I said, "I can't believe it either. I'm in terrible shape. You young guys should be totally ashamed"—I'm now secretly practicing for the rematch that I know will be demanded.

Justin is a computer geek and studying cyber-security. He is quiet but accessible, notably on a one-on-one basis. He also comes from a troubled family background and essentially raised himself. I've enjoyed our talks together and his authenticity; he never sugarcoats or bullshits. He is, however, newest to my acquaintance and I don't know him as well. But I've liked what I've seen. I like that he has an excellent work ethic, is strongly bonded with Caitlin's son Ryan, and unashamed*ly* loves and adores Caitlin: each of these attributes is critical for me, though no one is asking.

The amazing thing, and it made me burst out laughing, was that Cait and Justin started dating when Caitlin was pregnant with Ryan, another man's child from a previous relationship that had gone bad quickly. I couldn't believe it when she stood there in my kitchen, belly protruding, telling me she was in a new relationship. I struggled to imagine how that Match.com profile would read. "Short, full-figured young woman, with brown hair and hazel eyes, well along with child, seeking love, romance and a father to my soon-to-be-born baby." Can't you see it? I could just imagine guys falling all over one another to get in line. Then I asked myself, "What kind of man would respond to that ad? Someone with a pregnant lady fetish?" I couldn't imagine how anything good could come from this. Thankfully, Cait, eyes bemused as the panoply of emotions sped across my face, quickly solved the mystery. She had known Justin from work for several years, and they had always been attracted to one another, but never available for romantic relationship at the same time until now. What I didn't know then having yet to meet Justin was how clearly his love of Caitlin shines through—and now, of Ryan. I had no need to worry.

So as you can see, they don't write works of fiction as good as that. Life just gets ever more interesting, complicated and challenging to navigate as I grow older—more variables, not fewer, come into play. Talk about diversity; we have it in this family. And it's wonderful. At each family occasion, the chemistry stoked by all the different personalities and cultural influences, along with the ready acceptance of differences, invariably gives rise to feel good moments of love and laughter, and the joy of mutual respect and appreciation. The family tree just keeps going on going on, continuing to sprout new branches—one indicator of a healthy family.

In thinking about my kids and my relationships with them, I feel profoundly blessed. I could have done a better job as a dad, but I also could have done much, much worse. I tried to instill a work ethic, the importance of kindness and integrity, the will to persevere, a valuing of being able to think for yourself, and the importance of thinking all one's thoughts and feeling all one's feelings. I think I fostered in my kids a willingness to think outside the box, to experiment, to explore, to push their comfort zones, and to live life somewhat as a revolution, overthrowing dogma and the obsolete lessons of the past for new discoveries in the present.

Each of my kids has grown into a person whom I not only love, but, far more importantly, like and respect. Now, we relate human being to human being, peer to peer, and not through the idealized mythology of a child to a parent, or vice-versa.

Where once the kids' lives were in orbit around mine and Jane's in our roles as the Sun and the Moon, now we're in separate orbits that intersect from time to time. They each are at the center of their own lives, dealing with their partners, children, and jobs, balancing as best they can work, love and leisure in the finitude of one life. Of course, this is as it should be. I wouldn't want it to be any other way.

To me, it's absolutely amazing. Is it despite or because of all the trials and tribulations that we've been through together that we've grown such an extensive family of genuine and resilient relationships? I think it's the latter. We have an amazing family. Sure, we're full of flaws; we can be disappointed, act badly, or get angry, but we don't have a need to pretend otherwise. We talk, laugh, and cry together. We can think and feel our way through messy moments and disappointments, as well as take pleasure in the other's successes. How real is that? How does it get any better? I have scoured the horizon of all possible worlds for better outcomes. I haven't been able to find any.

Still, that doesn't inoculate me from sometimes wanting to stop time, from feeling nostalgic, acutely aware that as the moon waxes in their hemisphere, it wanes in mine, fully understanding that in this way and only in this way does life go on. Nonetheless, from time to time, this knowledge sparks moments of sadness, as these developing families repeatedly remind me of different moments in my life and with my parents, and that all things pass and, at times, I wish they didn't.

So, is it this—my own finitude—that is the wellspring of my anxiety? Perhaps, but is there any place else I can look? Ah! Those damned grandkids.

CHAPTER 33

GRANDFATHER HOOD—PLAYTIME

N ow that's another iconic role: Grandfather. In my mind's eye, I see a white-bearded, bespectacled, slightly stout man, wearing a plaid shirt and baggy blue jeans, who radiates beneficence and wisdom. His patience is endless, and his counsel is sought and to the point. He says things softly, once and the light dawns in the grandchild's loving eyes as the scene moves smoothly forward.

Unnnnhhh! That's not me, and that's not them. I know less about being a granddad than I did about being a dad. At least I had a history with parents upon which I could draw. I never had grandparents. One was dead before I was born. The others I met at best a handful of times. I had no experience of them, certainly no relationship upon which to draw. The only grandparents I knew were my parents in relation to my kids.

After the birth of my kids, I had a more extensive relationship with my parents. We visited during holidays and family get-togethers. During summers, we would spend a week with them at the lake. Those, for the most part, were good times. My dad pulling the kids on an inner tube with his boat and fishing from the shore. Now, here I am, a granddad, with grandchildren of my own, a house on the water and a boat.

I go to Atlanta two or three times per year to visit Chan, Nina, and their kids, and the Atlantans visit Baltimore two or three times. It's not ideal, but it works pretty well. Ideal would be everyone living in the same town—that's just not the way it is.

I don't know what to do as a granddad. I don't feel any particular pride that I have grandchildren, though I must admit that when I recently saw all the grandkids together, along with my kids, I was struck by the thought, *Gosh, if it weren't for Jane and me, none of these people would be here.* It was an impactful thought. Even more so when I thought about all the generations to come. That's an amazing thing, a form of immortality—assuming the human race doesn't destroy itself.

But I don't feel I deserve any credit for that, the making of my kids—having sex had been fun, not work. I also don't give much importance to the fact that my ancestral line is being continued. I don't think that's all that special; billions of people do that. For whatever reason, none of these things feeds my ego. So I'm stuck with just what comes up naturally when I'm with them. And, maybe that's where the importance is: in the moment.

And that's not much different than when I was with my kids. Except the disciplining part. I don't do much of that unless I think it's really needed. And then I don't do it in the way I did it when I was a father. Rather, I try to follow my kids' parenting values, even if it sometimes drives me nuts. My advice isn't sought, so I keep quiet. I had my turn and made my mistakes. This is my children's turn to live their successes and to make their mistakes. Thankfully, for the most part, I think they each do a very good job and that each is at least as good a parent as I was.

Leaving all that aside, let me say that I like not having parental responsibilities and I particularly like being a *Bad Boy*. And I love being a *Very Bad Boy* when it comes to my grandkids, drawing outside the lines, advocating rebellion and revolution. And, not surprisingly, my grandkids like being *Very Bad Kids* with me. We're all so very *Bad* we have the *Goodest of Times.*

I'm at my house in Aberdeen, Maryland. Mimi, aka Janet, helps Cormac, Keeley and Jason's kid, don his Spiderman outfit for the first time: a Christmas gift from Tom and Peggy Beauchamp. Dark ringlets of hair frame his handsome brown face as his two startling blue eyes peer out upon me, glittering mischievously: Unaccountably, I feel like prey. Now fully uniformed, this three-year-old turned Spiderman Superhero moves quickly forward, then freezes, striking a picture-perfect Superhero pose, which he holds for at least half a minute, seeming to derive some magical strength from it, then, without further ado, clocks me upside the head with his tiny fist. I play my part. I fall to the ground. He giggles delightedly. Then I pick myself up, growling, baring my teeth, and strike my own ninja pose—a little less impressive, given my gut—readying for trial by combat.

I signal an end to all this displaying by giving a battle cry. He turns and runs, his excited laughter threatening to rob him of breath as his face flashes between desperation and glee in his frantic effort to get away. The contest is on. Round and round we go, alternately chasing one another. Me hiding on the floor behind the dining room table or behind a door. I watch him as he cautiously looks for me. At just the right moment, I jump out with a blood-curdling scream, only matched by his terrified one, before he remembers we're only playing. Then the chase is on again. Time and time again. Until... I'm exhausted.

Cormac is now better known by his nickname: Macaroni-Cheese-Noodle. Some may scoff, but this is a name of historic proportions. Mimi bestowed the nickname Macaroni in honor of the ringlets of hair that crown his beautiful head. Later, Keeley laughingly calls to tell me that Macaroni has expanded his nickname. Now and forever more, he shall be known as Macaroni-Cheese-Noodle in honor of his love of the same.

I'm in awe and somewhat jealous. What a spectacular nickname. I mean how does it get any better than that? Picking him up from the rowhouse of his babysitter, Amanda, I test Macaroni's allegiance to this new moniker. I've tilted my rearview mirror so I can look at him strapped in his car seat. I ask, as if uncertain and confused, "Your new name is… Macaroni… Cheese… *Paaa…Staaa?!*" Despite the energy with which I have imbued this statement, he stares back at me dourly and doesn't deign a response. I mentally shrug my shoulders and look forward again, thinking *That didn't get anywhere.* Sixty seconds later, Mac's voice arises from the backseat. Slowly and emphatically, he says, "Macaroni… Cheese…*Noodle!*" I can almost hear the "you fool" in his reproachful tone. I apologize for getting it wrong and laugh to myself. Clearly, the boy knows who he is and does not brook fools. Unfortunately, for him, his granddad *loves* playing the fool.

Macaroni gave me one of my two nicknames as an OPA. Opa is grandfather in German and I started being called that several years earlier with the birth of Nina and Chandler's kids. Chan asked me, "Dad, what do you want to be called?" I responded, "Whatever they come up with." So in the beginning, Nina called me, "Opa Charlie." And that carried on for a while until one day, Stella, their second born, called me Opa Cha-Cha, being unable to get her mouth around the sound "Charlie." So I became forever more known as Opa Cha-Cha to the Atlantans. I love that name as it puts me in mind of the dance and has pizazz.

Now, what you need to understand is that one of the silly things I sometimes like to do is to speak to young children with Donald-Duck-like noises. I'm not gifted enough to articulate words in Donald-Duck-ese, but I can string a series of Donald-Duck-ese sounds together that impersonate sentences to the delight of young children. At an age when Mac could barely speak, Keeley showed him a picture of me and asked him, "Who is that?" Mac responded, "Duck." The nickname stuck and I am forever honored. Now, I have two names: Opa Cha-Cha and Opa Duck.

Macaroni Cheese Noodle is not my first grandchild; he's my third, but he is the first to live near me. Then there's Alexandra, who I call Alexi, who isn't technically speaking my grandchild at all, but I refuse to accept that. She is the offspring of Janet's son Kevin and his wife Lindsay and is blond as blond can be. Alexi is four months younger than Macaroni. I was at the hospital when she was born. She is a bit of a scaredy-cat but has gradually channeled Macaroni's fearlessness, now readily jumping from the height of the ottoman to the living room floor, once she ensures everyone is looking.

Where at one time she was timid with me, she has embraced my joyous welcomes and my heart thrills to see her. I love to hear her once-timid voice booming out from another room with total confidence, "OPA!" which invariably means that I am about to be tasked with something—It makes Janet and I laugh every time. If she decides I'm misbehaving, she will tell me one of three things in her little girl voice that has a hard time pronouncing the words: "Opa, be nice." Or, "Opa, go outside." Or, "Opa, go watch TV." The other thing that tickles me is that she manifests some of Janet's traits, especially the one for orderliness. She will follow behind me to push a drawer all the way closed, or to put a cup just right on the kitchen counter. I smirk, Janet laughs. All is good.

Then there is the gang of three in Atlanta: Just-One-More-Time-Benjamin, Bella-Stella, and Jonny-the-Hitman-McCormack. All blessed with light brown to blond hair and blue eyes— I feel like I'm with the family Lannister in the television series *Game of Thrones*. They are a tightknit group, despite each kid being a character unto him or herself. Benjamin, like his parents, is going to be tall and lean and is the first born of his generation. He's caring and in fact a great big brother—always helping his siblings out—and very, very bright. Independent for his six years of age, he has traveled by plane by himself to Baltimore to visit, then all the way home from Germany after visiting with Nina's family. He's not pressured to; he begs to. Accustomed to lots of flying with his parents, it's not as big a deal as some might imagine. Still, a big deal nonetheless. When he traveled to Baltimore, his first solo trip, I met him at the gate and asked, "Benjamin, were you afraid to be flying alone?" He responded factually, reminiscent of his mother, "No. I was sitting next to a soldier. And there were soldiers sitting in front of me and in back of me. So I was really protected." I laughed.

As we were walking to exit the airport, I call his dad as requested by Chan. I ask Ben, "You want to talk to your dad?" He doesn't, makes a face, but isn't rude about it. I insist and push the phone upon him. For the next few minutes, I watch as he listens to what seems to be an endless barrage of questions from Chandler; I assume a failed attempt to draw Ben into conversation. Ben responds politely and with infinite patience, but monosyllabically and then, at last, relief upon his face, returns the phone to me. I can imagine him rolling his eyes about the unnecessary anxieties that parents have. But at least his dad is feeling better, and with that obligation over, Benjamin and I can finally get on with his visit.

I harken back to my times as a dad with Chandler. I feel for Chan; I remember when he wouldn't allow his mother or me to walk with him in the mall even though he wanted us to buy him a skateboard. We worked out a plan. He would make a signal indicating the board desired and then, once he had left the area, his mother and I would see if we were okay with it. Now I know what only the old can know: there is more of the same to come for my boy Chandler. Karma!

Benjamin stays with Mimi and me for three days before moving to his Oma Jane's house. At his request, we play competitive board games. Like his dad, Benjamin is very competitive and loves to play chess, checkers, backgammon, Legos, and a game called Four Across. When he wins, he's like a complex wine: he looks at me with a combination of unbridled joy and superiority, a faint smirk, along with a hint of empathy for my loss upon his face. When he wins, he seems to have a need to go into excruciating and patronizing detail of every thought process that led to his wresting the victory from me. Of course, I push down the urge to strangle him and would have if it wasn't all so hilarious. In all these ways, he stimulates memories that take me back to another age with Chandler, channeling Chandler dead on.

Bella-Stella is age four going on sixteen. She has her mother's willowy physique and Keeley's fashion sense at the same age, being very particular about what she wears, and exuberant when she finds a colorful dress. Of all the kids, she drives me nuts the most. Nothing a good spanking couldn't cure I tell myself, but, again, that's not up to me. My kids like to rely on time-outs, some more readily than others. My problem with time-outs is what if the child won't take one? What if you're in a situation where you can't easily pick them up and put them in a room? (Airport, city park, car, you name it). There needs to be something always available, that signals clearly and decisively that that behavior won't be tolerated.

But, as I said, I'm not the parent. Once Bella Stella and I were on a soccer field at her school and I saw her drop trash on the ground. I scolded her and explained she couldn't do that and must pick it up. To my astonishment, she simply walked away while I was talking. None of my kids would have dared to do that; their little butts would have been on fire. But she's not my child; she's Chandler's and Nina's, and I respect their right to parent in their way. I'd completely had it with Stella. Having no tolerance for her disrespectful behavior I coldly withdrew, the only consequence I can readily effect. As the arctic wind of my disapproval blew about me, people started closing the windows of the buildings on this warm summer day. Stella, sensed the chill. A few minutes later, I looked around to make sure she was not getting into trouble. I spotted her walking the grounds picking up trash. She doesn't like it when her Opa Cha-Cha is unhappy with her, That's Bella-Stella, one of those people who resist what you're saying but follows through in the end. That is so like Chandler, too. Her mom says, "She's stubborn." *Uummmhhh?* That's one word for it. I guess each of us has to pick our own words to fit whatever stories we want to tell. I praised Bella-Stella for picking up the trash and soon she was jumping into my arms and wrapping herself around me once again—no argument from me.

Then there is Jonny-The-Hitman-McCormack, age two and a half. The youngest Atlantan and a force with which to be reckoned. Jonny is *big* for his age, not fat: Middle linebacker big. He's also very compacted. It's like a scientist went mad in his laboratories and developed a human being whose molecules are packed ten times more densely together than any other living entity. He is *heavy, strong,* and *athletic.*

As an infant, he was able to hold his head up, and as a baby, he moved around easily before he could crawl. He would rely solely on his arms and upper body strength to pull himself about, disturbingly reminiscent of a double amputee pulling himself along on a wheeled pallet, except in Jonny's case there was no pallet. Now, he chugs along on two legs like a choo choo train, targeting and tackling me without warning, insistent upon bringing me down, as if doing so is the only thing that can bring meaning to life. He is completely indifferent to the size discrepancy and just about manages it, too, the sneaky little guy. Whenever he's around, I'm in continuous scan mode. It's not a comfortable feeling until I get into the spirit of it, catch him and turn the tables. Then he laughs hysterically. Once I let him go, he's back at it again.

The gang of three always welcomes me. Sooner, rather than later, they approach warily, tackle me around the legs and bring me down. They jump all over me, pushing me here and there until I'm on all fours. They then mount their newly minted horsey, laughing happily as horsey rides them, sometimes bucking and twisting in the attempt to toss them off. They are all laughing. Finally, exhausted, I plead for mercy. Benjamin then lives up to his nickname, "Opa Cha-Cha, just one more time? *Pleeaaassse.*" Of course, it's always "just one more time."

Another time, instigated by their cruel father, Benjamin and Stella drop their pajamas and shake their bare butts at me. Only Chan would think to have them do this to their venerable grandfather as Chandler laughs in the background. And *he* thinks *I'm* over the top.

Back in Baltimore, there is Caitlin's son, Ryan, whom I've nicknamed Little Buddha. At six months of age, one characteristic has consistently stood out—his sweet, smiling, and calm spirit. He is often breaking out into a *knowing smile*. Like an incarnation of the Buddha, he appears to know something the rest of us do not. I can't wait until he's old enough to tell me what that is. But right now, at age one, we are working out our relationship. Where once he would have nothing to do with me, now he will acknowledge my presence with his signature hello, raising his arm straight over his head, cocking his wrist like the periscope on a submarine, and waving. I had always given him the distance he wanted, then the breakthrough occurred. One day, as soon as I arrived in his presence, he held his arms out for me to pick him up. Amazingly, this now occurs even when he is being held by his mother. Caitlin remarks on the growing independence of her son, "I want this, but I still feel a little sad," as she learns a little something about waxing and waning herself.

Back in Aberdeen, during another visit by the Atlantans, my entire family goes for a walk at dusk. Mimi, Justin, Jason, Keeley, Cait, Nina, Chandler, Benjamin, Macaroni, Jony, Ryan and Bella Stella. Chandler carries Jonny. I carry Bella-Stella on my shoulders. She is excited. I match her mood. I begin jogging ahead, causing her to bounce and giggle hysterically. I run full-out—in a manner of speaking. Stella laughs delightedly. The other adults wryly note to one another as I *rocket* past them "He'll be sorry." I think, *What do they know?* The cramps don't hit till later.

In April 2016, Quincy, Keeley and Jason's second child, was born. He had liquid in the lungs and was kept in intensive care for five days. This was very hard on Keeley, whose maternal need to hold her baby and take him home was obstructed. She stayed at the hospital day and night. It was also hard on Jason, who spelled Keeley when she'd allow it and took care of Macaroni. Neither of them got much sleep, yet each of them wanted to give the other more.

And so it goes, new lives, new loves, new worries, new joys, and new memories and it just keeps on keeping on and it also reminds me that my time is coming to an end, a fact further prompted as arthritis stiffens my knees, feet, and hands. My time is not necessarily soon but certainly on the way as life and death forever dance hand in hand.

All I know is that my grandkids have taught me that it is never too late to have a happy childhood or at least moments of one. They help me with a problem I've had most of my life, the one my mother used to talk about: thinking too much. When I'm with them, all the thinking stops; the moment is now. They re-teach me that lesson I learned so long ago. When surfing those big waves during that howling nor'easter, I had to stop thinking, cease to be self-conscious, occupy the moment and let the moment fill me, or risk falling off the board. When I'm with my grandkids, everything is as it should be in the timelessness of the right now: play time!

Still, as soon as they are gone, I start thinking again. Life is good. Actually, it's great. So why is it I feel like I'm getting ready for calamity, as if something bad this way comes.

God! I'm a pain in my ass. I've got everything. What's wrong with me?

CHAPTER 34

BORING AND I LOVE IT THAT WAY

At this time I'm in another love story. This one has a different quality to it; the atmospheric change one experiences in moving from the glare and heat of an unremitting sun to the shade of an oak tree under which stands two chairs, a table, and an ice-cold pitcher of tea.

One of Janet's nicknames among my friends is Jane Plus, a play on words, using the small "t" in her name, to distinguish her from my first wife and from Jane-2. Janet, as with most beloved people, has several nicknames. She is known as "Wanda Wipe" in honor of her cleaning abilities, "The General" in recognition of her always thinking up things for me to do, and "Mimi," her self-chosen name for the grandchildren. Unlike my previous romantic relationships, this story is not dramatic or eventful. Frankly, it can be boring, and I love it that way.

Characterized by steadiness rather than drama, security rather than gut-twisting angst, and contentment rather than harrowing conflict or disconnect, there is little in the way of theatrical tensions with which to enthrall or entertain the everyday reader.

Let me try my best to bore you. Janet and I met on a social website. What attracted me, besides her figure, was her plain-spoken profile: she had a good job, owned her home, raised two boys largely on her own, all while obtaining a master's degree. These characteristics suggested a strong work ethic, strength of character, courage, the capacity to persevere, independence, intelligence and a well-established personhood. I was to learn that she was the Chief Technologist of Outpatient Diagnostic Radiology at Johns Hopkins Hospital and to discover that she also took pride in doing her own home repairs, proudly showing me the hardwood floor she had laid in her house, along with her prized circular saw.

I emailed her. She suggested we talk on the phone (little did I know she was already directing). I gulped, not expecting to be tossed into the fire so soon. I gamely called. She proposed we meet in person. I was thrown back on my heels once again. *Damn this woman moves quickly.* It already being Friday night, I suggested the following weekend. She demurred, explaining she had plans. Little did I know that she had another date. Feeling slightly off balance, I suggested the weekend following. Again she balked, this time noting that that was a long time off. I wondered *What is going on? Wasn't she the one who suggested we get together? Why the pushback?* The only time remaining that I could think was the next night. Without hesitation, she chirped, "That works fine." I then realized she had been a step ahead all along, herding me toward what she wanted. You can see how she earned the nickname The General.

Janet had me pick her up at her home. I approached the split-level brick and aluminum sided house in a middle class neighborhood and knocked on the front door. The first thing I saw when the door opened was the back of Janet's head, as she bent over struggling to keep her cat from escaping. From that ungainly position and awkward dance, she lifted her head and, struck by the humor of the inept greeting, smiled a smile that threatened to give itself over to laughter. Along with the warmth of her humor was the warmth of her eyes. One eye brown and the other green, but what I immediately drank in was the deep welcome of their winter's fire.

We went out to an Italian restaurant of her choosing and closed the place down. Not dancing the fandango but sitting in animated conversation. Talking small talk didn't seem small with Janet and having a few drinks didn't hurt either. And throughout, I kept watching, looking for the snake: looking for pretense or manipulation, or a vain woman's use of her wiles. I saw none of that. What I saw was that with Janet, what you see is what you get. It's amazing how that description can seem so commonplace and yet apply to so few.

The thing I found reassuring was that though I was attracted to Janet, I wasn't at risk of losing my head. I did not feel dumbstruck or infatuated, which was always my criteria for previous relationships and of all the romantic stories I had ever heard. Rather, I felt the somewhat pedestrian feeling of being at home with her: relaxed, comfortable, secure, and fun as if I had known her for a long time. Given the mind-frying electric overloads of previous relationships, which I had no wish to experience again, I wondered, *am I maturing?* At fifty-seven years of age, I was hoping so.

We spent every subsequent weekend together, mostly at my house with its huge great room and kitchen combination, sometimes at hers. We talked, cooked dinner together, slowed danced to music, and made love in various rooms and in front of the fireplace. But the naked truth was, it wasn't the best sex I had ever had, nor perhaps was it for Janet. Sadly, I thought, it seems that to have really great sex one has to be partly out of one's mind. I had no wish to lose mine again. It had been a consistently costly experience that I had every wish not to replicate.

Of course, some might say that Janet sounds like the safe choice of someone who now finds passion too risky, and in some respects, they might be right, but I don't care. What I *know* is that with Janet I have an abiding contentment and happiness in a relationship that, despite its flaws, is well beyond any I've known before. While other relationships have had hard-earned spikes of ecstasy, with no ceiling in sight, none other has come close to providing the high floor of happiness and fulfillment that I have with Janet. I'll take that swap and gladly.

Years ago, I remember taking great umbrage at any idea of "settling" in a relationship, and I still do. But what I've learned is that settling is not the same as compromise. Settling implies serious discontent, resignation, and a certain contempt for the person you have settled for. Compromise, on the other hand, is necessary in any relationship and especially romantic ones. How could it be otherwise? Two different people come together, not to be one (even though that blather harkening to the time of the early mother-infant relationship is much ballyhooed), but to form a third, a relationship that both separates and connects the partners.

A relationship is like a vase rising on the potter's wheel, except that two potters are shaping it, not one. The problem with the idea of two becoming one is that it always leads to the question, "Whose one is it?" and the power struggles that follow. If the potters don't work together and take each other into account, the vase will grow asymmetrically, tilting lopsided to one side or the other, or collapse altogether. Successful potters understand that to shape an enduring relationship, each has to work the relationship and be worked by it. In this way the partners dance together, co-mingling as they work in concert, rather than co-mangling as each strives for power and control, eventually destroying the relationship itself.

Every relationship entails multiple axes of relatedness. Label them whatever you want, whatever is important to you. Each axis represents a different plane of relatedness that is valued by one or both partners. They will probably include sex, finances, home organization and cleanliness, division of labor, and how much the partners wish to do things together and how much apart. Whatever the axes of relationship, the two partners, each a unique individual with varying needs and different rhythms and cycles, will never be perfectly aligned all the time on any one axis, much less all of them. So, in a realistic relationship, each partner will suffer repeated disappointments, as well as satisfactions, in the conjoining of their respective desires. It can be no other way.

Now, if one axis of relatedness is significantly more important to one partner than the other, such as sex, then this lack of synchronicity of need may lead to repeated disappointments and dissatisfactions. Indeed, the more sex-driven partner may interpret the other's lesser interest as rejecting. And it may be. But it also may simply be the differences between two people. Is it any more valid to say "If you loved me you would want to have sex more often," than to say, "If you loved me you wouldn't pressure me to have sex so much"? I don't think so.

It can also be the case that one person is sexually thrilled by the other while the second person thinks the sex is fine, but not world-shaking. If this disparity is okay with both of them, no harm done, however if the level of dissatisfaction or disparity is acute they may conclude they are not a good fit. Yet, even here we can't necessarily jump to conclusions. Sometimes one spouse might use complaints in one axis of relationship, such as sex, as a lightning rod for other more widespread feelings of loneliness and disconnect. One spouse may interpersonalize his individual deficits, such as a near constant need of soothing, and attribute this deficit to the lack of care being provided by the other. This was the case with one couple I worked with in which the woman demanded sex five times per day and with another couple where the husband insisted on being held for hours.

When you add the mere fact that two individuals, perfectly matched in terms of intensity of needs may not have the same need at the same time, you can see that any couple must navigate the disappointments of desire (along whatever axis), without catastrophizing these as tends to occur when people are not secure in themselves. Here, the insecure partner may place demands on the other, insisting that the other meet their need to maintain their personal psychic equilibrium which in adulthood is usually an individual task, not an interpersonal one.

What I have found is that great sex is mainly psychological. After all, it is true that beauty is often in the eyes of the beholder. The best sex occurs when the psyche is stimulated. Who hasn't enjoyed makeup sex or sex when you're angry? Or sex following the agony of titillation and deprivation, or stabbing jealousy? Hell, even breakup sex can be great. Personally, I've loved and hated it all. All of them were good but often purchased at the price of wrenching insecurity and angst, not typically traits held to be the hallmark of secure attachment.

Is it any accident that some of the best sex I had was with people I barely knew? When you first start dating, the unknown, the freshness, the thrill and the ecstasy of the courtship dance are all absolutely captivating. It's not any accident that this is called the honeymoon phase, a term which itself declares that it's a temporary state. When I was a teenager and into my early twenties I was promiscuous—isn't it funny how that term is rarely applied to males—whenever I could be. Although I was never unfaithful in a relationship, I was always in hot pursuit when outside of one. Driven by lust, I sometimes objectified women who were strangers to me. My life was a series of feasts and famines; the feasts made all the more glorious by the ravenous hunger. I had the philosophy that one way to stay centered was to do everything to the extreme. Unfortunately, it doesn't work that way. Anyway,

those were the days, and I'm glad they're over. When you're growing up, you've got a lot to learn, and there is room for all of it. I'm
glad I had it all. But, as I learned and re-learned over the years,
too much of anything becomes routine, if not outright tiresome.

One of the great ironies of most human beings is that if you
get all you want of anything, whenever you want it, your desire
for it and happiness with it declines. This is one of the challenges of a stable and secure relationship, the very kind of relationship to which most people aspire. It's no different than
anything else. Take food. Keep going to the same restaurant,
even a great one, and we human beings will tire of it—at some
point, we'll be dying for a hamburger. Keep eating your favorite
meal, and you'll grow to hate it. Have anything readily available,
and you begin to take it for granted. Damn, I got tired of looking at the Grand Canyon after a couple of hours and of visiting
churches in Italy. Old? Check. Beautiful? Check. Gold adorned?
Check. Stunning tile murals on the floor? Check. Lots of history? Check. Architectural feat? Check. After twenty or so. Yawn.
Check. So you can keep changing partners, enter swinging relationships, have affairs, snort cocaine, have sex under the influence of LSD, flirt outrageously with others, pop amyl nitrate
just as you're about to orgasm, drink prodigious amounts of alcohol, smoke pot, instigate fights, create repeated instances of
warmth through friction, and have a partner do the same to you
to achieve those addictive passions, only inevitably to get a declining return on your costly investments, as well as a hell of an
emotional and physical hangover. At some point, you've just got
to say "Stop!" or you incinerate.

Of course, I can imagine other people who are so comfortable with their sexuality that they are free to push taboos and
ignite excitements in that way. Still, in any monogamous relationship, the passion will decline. Sex still occurs and can be good,
but it typically won't have the exhilaration of that roller-coaster

ride characteristic of the early days. You know, the slow anticipatory click-clacking ascents and the exhilarating, breathtaking
drops and twisting turns. Hell, go ahead, ride the biggest roller
coaster in the world, its every rise and heart-dropping fall, then
do it over and over again. Even that will eventually become well
known and predictable, thus losing the thrill of the unexpected,
and fail to provide the exhilaration of old.

Certainly, this loss must be grieved, but what else is new?
Every step of the developmental way entails leaving behind something highly prized from the previous era. Hey, the kid giving
up his reliance on the breast or pacifier is rarely happy about
it. But such losses are necessary to the child's relinquishing his
dependence on these objects of desire to move toward greater
independence and freedom to explore the world.

If you're young and this disappoints you, I get it. Trust me;
I get it. Hell, I'm old, and it disappoints me. But one of the re-
quirements of a happy and meaningful life is the ability to accept
necessary losses when the time arrives. It reminds me of a beautiful woman I knew who kept pursuing plastic surgery. She would
see wrinkles where I would not. The poignancy of her situation
struck me. Desolately, she described her efforts as akin to bailing
out a sinking boat with a teaspoon. The point is you can either
fight reality, or you can learn to accept it gracefully, opening
yourself to the gains to be found in the next phase of life.

So, you choose. If you want repeated experiences of great sex
and intense emotions live a tumultuous life. Have at it. I did. I
came to hate it.

But do not despair; all is not loss. What you come to realize
is that while passion may decline, there is a joy in making love to
this other person, not just another body, but this soul that you've
traveled with and come to know (if you haven't been too conflict avoidant) through the years. It is like moving from the highs
and lows that can be graphed along a two-dimensional plane to

the breadth and depth and personal meaning of a three or even four-dimensional one. Here intercourse is not only found in the physical act but in the ongoing tensions and resolutions taking place within and among all the different axes of the relational field. Orgasm isn't the only goal. In some ways, it's the least of them.

All I know is that I'm happier than I've ever been on a prolonged basis, though sometimes I do find myself thinking nostalgically back upon the ecstasy and agony of some of those great roller-coaster rides—that is until I snap out of it by reminding myself of the inevitable hangovers that followed.

These are the concerns of youth through mid-life. But there are also the concerns of the aging and the aged. One of the fears of youth is growing old. That is until you get there and realize how absurd that fear was, given the alternative. As we all know, in some ways the Golden Years aren't so golden. Decreased sexual drive and the ravages of menopause, increased risk of cancer with hormonal therapies (perhaps overblown but on an individual basis maybe not), erectile dysfunction and the loss of lubrication and elasticity all serve to create a warren of challenges that need to be dealt with in one way or another. And this list doesn't even include other physical challenges as we age that may get in the way or make sex more difficult like degenerative disk disease or arthritis.

Understandably, many people take the path of least resistance and resign themselves to a platonic relationship. In my view, that's a mistake. Sensory experience forms the platform upon which all other senses of self rest. If you doubt this, just remember the last hangover you had. How good did the rest of you feel until it receded? Or ask older people suffering from hip, neck, or foot problems or some other malady. They'll tell you, pain is fatiguing, reduces what you can do and makes you feel old before your time. Similarly, the sensory relationship between two people provided in lovemaking forms the foundation upon which all other senses of coupledom reside. At the end of the day, it doesn't matter how blindly passionate the experience is, although passion is much desired. The main thing is to get naked and to have as much skin-to-skin contact as you can. Orgasm would be great but is only a secondary consideration in the larger realm of things. Once a couple engages in sensual contact, hugging, kissing, touching, whether or not orgasm is achieved, they often go about the rest of their day feeling more relaxed and joined. Why? Because this act, the nakedness, the skin-to-skin contact, the sensual experience, served to reaffirm their coupledom on a bodily level, not only a cognitive one. Furthermore, the physicality serves to differentiate this relationship from all the other relationships in their lives: the essence of couple. Remember, the head doesn't only speak to the body, but the body also speaks to the head. Indeed, the body often knows what the head does not.

The thing to appreciate is that aging offers no quarter and takes no captives. Sooner or later, sex becomes relatively impossible. But it's quite one thing to have sex taken away because of illness or the aging process, and quite another to choose to give it up. The latter to me is another version of becoming a finished product and limits the depth of the couple's connection.

What I love about Janet goes well beyond the sexual relationship. What I found was that though I missed intoxicating levels of passion I also loved connecting with Janet in so many other ways that had eluded me in previous relationships.

This reminds me of a study I read on the topic of relationship attraction. The researchers divided ten males and ten females into two separate groups. Each member of the group was then asked to rank the members of the other group in terms of attractiveness without talking to them—that is solely based on visual attraction. They then blindfolded the participants and had them talk to each member of the other group for a few minutes and then again rank them in terms of attractiveness, of who they would like to have a relationship with. Unsurprisingly, the two choices did not coincide. The question for the long haul is which is more important to you.

Unapologetically, I can say Janet's not the most physically beautiful woman I've ever known in the biblical sense. But her femininity, her sense of humor, her unwillingness to give up her point of view even if she cannot always readily articulate it, her straightforwardness, her lack of manipulativeness, her enjoyment of ordinary things, and her unwavering love and regard for me through good times and bad I find enchanting. I love the warmth of her touch and of her look, the spontaneous hugs, and kisses that we regualarly give one another. I love looking over at her as she sits apart from me doing her own thing, and her coming over to sit next to me, hip to hip or feet on my lap to watch television together. I love that goodnight kiss as we're about to part to enter our separate dream state journeys, and the farewell goodbye as we part ways for the day, each respecting that there is always a last of things and that no one can predict with absolute confidence when that might be. I love the planning of trips, the discussing what to get the grandkids, the thinking together about what to do when our kids might need help. I love losing and winning at cards with her, her passive aggressive withholding of her score when she wins a hand or teasingly provides supportive, not at all felt, words of encouragement. I love the fact that sex, of whatever kind, is something she also feels is important. Finally, I love the experience of being happier in an ongoing and more rounded way, involving far more axes of relationship, than I have ever known.

Everyone likes Janet. This is surprising because no one would accuse her of being a people pleaser. She speaks her mind and holds her ground but never nastily. What people recognize is that she possesses a generosity of spirit combined with personal integrity. She never talks the talk; she simply, without apology, fanfare, or self-promotion, walks the walk. She is just who she is and comfortable with it.

The final stamp of approval came from my family and friends. They all liked her—except Cait, who was territorial—better than me actually, and she liked them. Now, it's like we've all been together forever. Keeley and Peggy Beauchamp are more likely to call her than me. Ron-Z will call her, as will Tom Beauchamp, from time to time just to say hi. And, over the years, even Cait has come around. Janet earned her trust and respect without effort, just by being Janet, consistently, predictably, safely without criticism or drama over an extended period of time, regardless of Cait's holding back behavior.

Lord help me, but the neighbors like her too. Where in previous renditions of my life my sole focus when arriving home from work was to scurry inside the house to avoid small talk with the neighbors, with Janet that's no longer possible. Horror of horrors, she even invites them over. I have no place to hide. She's always enjoyed her neighbors. As a single mother with two children, neighbors had been an important support group to her. Consequently, she has brought them into my life as well and helped me discover how important an addition they can be. They've become part of the fabric of my life, sharing their journeys with me, as I share mine with them. We help each other out as is often required in this riverside community. When Janet and I sold our respective homes and moved to this new house together, these new neighbors threw a welcoming party. I told them truthfully, "I'm impressed. Usually, the neighbors throw a party when I'm leaving." They all laughed. I liked them right away.

As if all these things are not enough, Janet enjoys cooking and making a welcoming home. Good food and, now with my influence, good wine, are her idea of a good evening. Cooking is her hobby. Typically, when she's relaxing, I can find her reading one of her many food magazines. Even if I'm in another room, she'll call out, "Charlie, listen to this recipe," then exclaim, "Doesn't that sound yummy?!" In the middle of the evening, while I'm watching TV, she'll get up and go to the kitchen, feeling a sudden desire to bake a cake. She's absolutely out of her mind, and I love her for it. I love her willingness to follow her heart without apology. Good smells fill the house.

Janet's biggest complaint about me is that I'm oblivious. She loves to keep a beautiful, neat and orderly home and to decorate seasonally. Where I see nothing askew, she is regularly on the job maintaining the house. She asks, "Charlie, do you need five pairs of shoes scattered around the living room?" Or, she'll say, "Are the socks on the kitchen counter dirty or clean? Are they to be part of our meal tonight?" She is stunned by my distractedness. I won't notice a hamper full of clean clothes strategically placed for me to take up the stairs. Sometimes, I'll become aware of a change in décor and proudly give voice to my discovery, momentarily feeling smug that on this occasion Janet does not, in fact, have me pegged. That is until Janet shakes her head in disbelieving fashion and informs me, "Charlie, I did that two weeks ago."

Janet is honestly confounded by me. She remarks, "I keep trying to imagine what you are seeing, and I just can't." Thankfully, what she has come to understand and accept is that I am not shirking duties; I simply don't notice these things; they don't register in my consciousness. She also knows that if she points them out, ninety-five percent of the time I'll do what she asks without complaint.

I'm not sure why I'm so oblivious. Maybe it's gender differences, at least in part. After all, in my practice, stories of the males not being able to find an item in the refrigerator, where the woman finds it right away, abound. But I suspect it may be that I'm simply too caught up in the workings of my mind. In defense, I show Janet a cartoon given to me by one of my female patients. It is a drawing of a guy lying on a couch. The caption reads, "Ladies, if your man says he is going to do something he will. There is no need to keep reminding him of it every six months."

Food, wine, gardening, home, seasonal decorations, rides on our boat during the dog days of summer and walks among the copper and gold gilded trees during the waning days of fall. These are the things she loves and enjoys. I love that in her and appreciate her sharing her wonder with me.

However, there is one other thing I value about Janet that stands outside the ordinary: her willingness to go along on my occasional *adventures*. These are important to me because they provide a time in my life where the novelty of the new experience gets me out of my head. These are times I am neither oblivious or distracted. Before we were married, she went with me, along with my daughters and son-in-law Jason, for a ten-day sailing vacation around the Greek Isles. I had hired a boat and captain so on the cheap (that was the only way I could afford it) that I had concerns. Primarily, I wondered if the vessel and the captain were seaworthy. The trip turned out great, adventures everyone shared together and remembers with gladness to this day. Memories such as of our Captain George who would loudly announce each morning around 9 am that it was, "Beer-O'clock!" and crack his first beer of the day. And when he would laugh uproariously in the evening while telling the tale of an English gentlemen who, when the cocktail hour arrived, would announce "It's time for a stiffy." We all enjoyed the sights and laughed together at Jason's newly discovered love of goat meat; he earned the nickname: The Goat Hunter. We all also felt for Cait when at a shack of a restaurant we so entertained the owner that he went outside to get us what he promised was a special treat. He returned minutes later with a liver just cut from a baby goat, still dripping in its jellies. Cait burst into tears.

We built wonderful memories during that ten-day trip, but the most notable of these was on the flight over. Janet and I had a seven-hour layover in Athens, and I researched and formed a plan. I told Janet that there was a renowned restaurant I wanted to try. The cab dropped us off in a narrow and crowded alley-way, colorful garments hanging from poles and gifts adorning makeshift shelves set up outside of storefronts. To my pretended dismay, there was no restaurant at the address, only a jewelry store. Janet asked, "Where's the restaurant?" I replied, "It must be around here somewhere." All the while, Janet, as is her way, became captivated by objects in the jewelry store window. After watching her for a few minutes, her eyes alight with the joy of looking at the sparkling objects, I leaned over and whispered in her ear, "While you're looking, why don't you pick out a wedding ring?" Her surprise gave way to an incandescent smile that was all for me, causing my heart to brim with love.

On another occasion, Janet overcame her doubts to go along with my desire to rent a trawler in Sarasota, Florida, to cruise the intercoastal waterway. My aim was to see if we enjoyed it enough to sell our house, buy a boat and cruise the Great Loop. Unfortunately, we encountered a squall, which brought rain and wind so hard that visibility was reduced to near zero. The storm was so violent that it whipped our 25,000-pound trawler around like a miniature toy and then ran us aground. During those blinded and terrifying moments, life sprung on us one of its little surprises. The windlass (the automatic anchor release mechanism) failed and would not stop unspooling; we watched helplessly as the anchor and 1500 feet of chain were lost overboard. This was how we had become so completely vulnerable to the whims of nature. The anchor had not been tethered to the boat. We had both been shaken by those terrifying moments as the rain blinded us and I fought to steer in the violent wind as Janet struggled with the windlass on the heaving deck below, causing me to fear her falling overboard. Then, when the squall passed, we realized we were aground, facing 180 degrees the opposite direction from when it had begun, and were starting to tilt over, not knowing when or if the boat would stop its roll. Finally, it settled on a twenty-degree angle leading to many gallons of diesel fuel spilling from the tanks into the cabin. Driven out by fumes and worried about fire, we spent the night on deck, feet propped against railings to hold us upright, as we looked upon the moon and stars awaiting rescue.

That was enough for Janet to nix any idea of her traveling the Great Loop.

In Janet, I found a whole person. She does not avoid conflict and speaks her mind. Along with me, she uses conflict as a means of deepening our understanding of one another. This doesn't always occur at the first go around, but eventually, we get there. Indeed, this is one of my contributions to the relationship; I insist on it. I never again want to be in another relationship in which I am a cipher to the other or she to me. I want to love and be loved for who we are in reality. So, Janet and I accept each other with our respective foibles and try not to change the other, all the while considering how we might want to change ourselves, not because we must, but because we want to.

I tell my patients that intimacy is a process of sharing the thoughts and feelings that arise in relationship with another, without blame, shame, attack or demand for change. In that it does not rely on power and doesn't make demands, it requires courage: a willingness to be vulnerable, somewhat akin to a dog exposing its neck to a potential foe to show that it means no harm.

If one person is intimate (unilateral intimacy), it doesn't guarantee that the other will respond in kind (bilateral intimacy). Intimacy is simply a way for two people to deal accurately with themselves and with each other. Because of these characteristics, intimacy goes against the survival instinct and is very hard to do. I always tell couples it takes a *will toward vulnerability*. I also caution the couples that intimacy is the Royal Road. It can lead to a deepening of relationship where it meets with good results, or to separation or divorce where it does not.

In my relationship with Janet, now ten years and seven grandchildren long, with another on the way, intimacy has consistently, although not always easily, met with good results. Thus far—I never take relationships for granted anymore—our satisfaction in our lives and relationship continues to rise. Not as in relationships between younger folks, that can be built on sand, albeit with all the fire of Halley's comet, but slow and steady as people who have learned both the importance of the long haul and the terrible temporariness of all things.

Several days a week, Janet and I play a hand of cards while drinking a glass of wine before dinner and use that time to talk about whatever's on our minds. Every day we laugh together and think together. Sometimes, we cry together, mostly in joy, sometimes in sorrow.

Recently, Janet looked over at me and said, eyes welling with tears, "Charlie, I'm so happy with my life and that mainly has to do with you. Thank you. I love you." At that, she was not the only person with tears in her eyes.

Now, I show Janet, my third wife, who is not doe eyed, petite, or timid at all and has a definite voice of her own, while somehow remaining very feminine, sweet and loving, the lyrics of a song I've been working on:

Loving you ain't always easy
Loving me, you say, is harder yet
It's not how I imagined it…
So why am I so happy?

She laughs her wonderful laugh, brimming my heart with love.

CHAPTER 35

AS HAPPY AS I CAN STAND

I have room for few complaints in my life. I've achieved my fair share of professional and personal success. There are people who care about me and people for whom I care. There are the adult children getting along well in their lives, and grandchildren galore to bite my ankles. There is Janet, who brings me connection and contentment. There is tasty food on the table and wine to match. Given all that, what troubles me?

When I started writing this book, I recognized a recurring theme in my life: I have been my happiest and my unhappiest in the midst of romantic relationships. However, as I get closer to the end, I came to understand that this was only a partial truth: I was using the idea of romantic relationships to represent a broader group of experiences of the best and worst of times in my life. These included the wonder of a romantic moment, but also the times of ecstasy charging through my body such as when learning that the sparkling red bicycle under the Christmas tree was for me or a moment of profound connection such as when receiving that letter from Cait. Now, I was growing to appreciate that it wasn't only the loss of a partner or the recurrent disappointment of a romantic desire that rendered me low, but something more at the core and resident within me.

Something was hindering my ability to feel securely optimistic and positive no matter how good the circumstances. I was looking through a glass darkly. However positive things were, my feelings would soon dampen as I returned to the fear-filled basement of my psyche. I had this revelation while watching a raindrop descend a windowpane one stormy summer night. I wrote the words in my mind as I struggled to describe its descent, and to understand the feeling of fatedness it was inspiring within me.

The rain, dancing in the jerky ebb and flow of gusting wind, splashed, thumped, and caressed the windowpane. Lightning flashed, and the glass washed white; lightning faded, and the window went gray, creating chaotic cycles of night and day.

During a lull, my eyes settled upon a single raindrop wending its drunken way down the beaded landscape. Like a toddler, its meanderings as unpredictable as its pace, it veered suddenly right, then slowed and rotated left, but its general direction remained inevitably downward. Slower, then faster, starting then stopping, to sooner or later renew its journey, variable in its methods but as unrelenting as the passage of time and, just like time, with no destination in mind.

I questioned, "What resisted its passage? What troubled its pace? No visible obstacles stood clear." Nevertheless, now and then something held Raindrop back as if it was coveted or coveting. Were parts of the windowpane dryer than others, sucking upon Raindrop like the desiccated lips of a rejected lover, or was the descent into the void too heart-stopping, justifying moments of stasis? It appeared to me that Raindrop was as content to wait as it was to move along. It didn't seem the least bit curious and certainly not haunted by such wonderings as mine. It just jigged and juked and tap-danced its way across the stage, then waited with mindless patience for the next tune to begin.

Lightning flashed, thunder boomed, sound drummed against windowpane, Gene Krupa style.

I wondered, "If Raindrop didn't care, why should I?" But I did.

I noticed that every move left some of it behind, a trail of tear belying the adage that what does not kill us makes us stronger.

Raindrop, transformed to mercury in a flash of light, slipped down its silvery slide, veering unexpectedly into the rivulet wake of another. Passage eased, accelerating, hot on the trail, until the two became one, without ceremony. Combined, their substance, illusions, hopes and dreams revitalized, they moved more easily along the plane of their existence, all the while leaving a wider track of tear in their wake.

Eventually, another one of those unforeseen, if not unforeseeable, obstacles halted their movement. But this one was different. The couple seems unable to go around, through, or over. Suspended in perfect balance, they hang and hang.

They feign lack of concern but tremble in place as another cannon volley arced electric through the night sky. How long could they stay in this state of suspended animation? Was it an end or a pause? And, as time passed, as lightning flashed neon, as thunder rolled, Raindrop trembled, then slowly, so slowly, the weight of the deadlocked couple pressed upon the divide. And slowly, so slowly, the gravity of their impasse rent them, until suddenly, one again became two.

A flurry of wind, a fresh patter of rain, tears too numerous to count chorused Raindrop's abiding sadness. Raindrop had forever changed, leaving a part of itself with the other and carrying a part of the other with itself. Heartbroken and wizened, Raindrop renewed its singular journey, arrhythmically continuing its heart-stopping descent along the now blackened stone of the plane of its existence, resolute in its aloneness.

Wandering course? Fate or destiny? Revolving or evolving? Raindrop did not ask, and I could not tell.

But as I watched Raindrop on that stormy summer evening I knew I lied. I could tell, no matter how much I did not want to. What halted my passage was often unknown to me, out of sight and out of mind, and just like Raindrop, I kept dancing until the music stopped, and I found a way to start it again. But nothing was new. It was the same old steps to the same old song with no destination in mind except a self-delusional one: A perfect relationship or the perfect moment that lasted forever—how could you possibly tell them apart. This feeling of being fated, of unchangeable destiny, of inevitable loss, was at the core of me, rattling like a skeleton. I could imagine a different outcome, but I couldn't envision being in it.

I now recognized that underneath I was always on the look-out for the good thing ending. I understood in mind and body that the good thing was a temporary state and that my default fear and expectation in life was one of abandonment and alone-ness. This feeling was a carryover from my childhood and ado-lescence. Who would not have a hard time feeling content and fulfilled if they believed or, more accurately, *knew* that the bad thing happening was what was in store for them no matter how good things got?

This story line was only buttressed by my paying unwise hom-age to the experience of constant uprooting and upset in child-hood and beyond, thus feeding *The Evil Wolf.* Any disappointment could rattle that skeleton as if the past and the present were the same. But I could not exorcise these haunting memories, brand-ed upon my soul: I *knew* such moments were coming again, the only question was when?

Indeed, I carried them close to my heart in the emotional amber of my memories to ensure that I would stay on guard against them. In doing so, I maintained the apprehension of reaching for my mother's skirt. I returned to the horror of my father's beating of my brother Cris propelled by the ugliness of my mother's murderous rage. I re-visited the implicit violence of racism and the fear of drinking from the Negro fountain. I re-lived the grief of leaving Montgomery, Alabama, saying goodbye to my best buddy Greg Cook, and the ending of those idyllic and secure evenings playing red light, green light in the failing daylight of a summer night. I revived the memory of confusion moving from Hanau to Heidelberg, sleeping on a cot in the BOQ unknowingly having been assigned to keep watch over my father. I recalled the anxiety inspired by the teachers shouting their spittle-strewn babble at the Spire school for military dependents, and I recreated the shame of my telling on the little girl who soiled her pants in the pathetically desperate grab to feel some power of my own. I plummeted down the gaping maw of Collège St. Etienne, like Jonah swallowed by the whale, the dark abyss becoming my surround while I'm partially digested in the gastric juices of near total abandonment. I recollected the terror and surprise of being kicked about without warning in the dining room at Collège St. Etienne and The Priest's coming to mock me in the infirmary in the middle of the night. I recall the beating I took outside Heidelberg's teen club because I won a game of pool. I remembered the unsettling confusion of being moved back and forth between grades and age groups without forewarning or apparent reason. I felt the shame of being ejected from Lynchburg College, of only seeming to find more ways to fail, all the while internally yelling "Fuck you!" at the world. I live once again the humiliating rejection by that young woman with the red painted lips and luminous smile. I could go on and on, but what's the point? The lesson was clear: Good things always end, and in the end, bad things prevail: I am doomed. Hell, let's be honest. We all are.

In the confluence of these events, The Generals in the War Room of my mind were birthed. They had and have my best interests in mind: to protect me from pain. But their thinking, as any child's, is myopically focused and short-term. They are always prepared, ceaselessly scanning the deep background and the future, readying for the next surprise attack. The Generals *know* what's on the way—not the specifics, but some yet-to-be-named form of terror, shock or dismay whose arrival is only a matter of time. The assault, if not today, *will* come tomorrow, and if not tomorrow the next day or year. It doesn't matter when; the when usually cannot be foretold. But it *is* coming, and I brace myself.

The Generals, forged in the miseries of the years, have a perfect memory. They warehouse all the feelings of loss, abandonment, and aloneness, of being bereft of love or comfort, and keep them hermetically sealed, untainted by any memory of the seductively weakening influences of any good that has occurred along the way. The Generals are not going to allow me to be duped and injured again. They are going to protect me from loss just as they tried to do during those picnics in Strasbourg all those years ago, smothering joy before it could be ripped from me.

The Generals understand love and happiness as Trojan Horses threatening the fall of the psyche. In their mission-focused way, they rule at a terrible cost: a mind under siege, protected within the battlements of its fortress, safely walled off from the outside world, drawbridges raised, The Generals implacably look out upon the countryside beyond the walls. There, people seem to be engaged in human interaction and commerce, sometimes happily, sometimes sadly, sometimes angrily, going on about their lives but more or less—the Generals note smugly—unprotected from hurt and dismay. Within the gray walls, eerily reminiscent of Collège St. Etienne, The Generals are determined to keep me safe.

What they do not seem to recognize is that as I grew ever pallid in their keeping, the people outside the walls had color and upon occasion smiled and, to give the Generals their due, also cried. But I began to notice. The Generals' overwrought defenses brought about exactly that against which they defended. They kept me alone, lost, abandoned and fear-ridden in a world of plenty. No one could see this looking from the outside, but these feelings percolated within, fetid as swamp mud. But I'm not alone in that. To one degree or another, I think many of us suffer this fate. What I was learning—and am still learning—was that The Generals don't know how to handle peace or happiness. Indeed, the more peaceful things are, the more paranoid they become. Consequently, I could only be as happy as *they* could stand.

I knew I couldn't allow them to continue to make me stupid. I had to move beyond the all-or-nothing thinking and omnipotent forms of self-protection characteristic of childhood. I had to find a way to be happier than I could stand.

CHAPTER 36

WHY CHANGE IS DIFFICULT

The human brain is friend and foe. It develops habituated ways of thinking and feeling that we use to connect both to the external world and, quite literally, to our *sense* of self. Habit is how the familial becomes the familiar. In childhood, it is not only dramatic events that shape us but the abiding emotional ambiance, the feelings that link us to our parents and siblings and ultimately to the world, become part of us, and yet are falsely equated with who we are. Thus, when we come up against feelings with which we're unaccustomed, they threaten to overthrow our most implicit beliefs, they threaten us with disorganization; we begin to feel "not myself" or "not me." This can be disconcerting.

I once heard that more people would rather sit with someone they didn't like than with someone they didn't know. The familiar, the known, the predictable, the manageable, seems more tolerable, even if unpleasant, to the uncertainty and anxiety of the unknown. In similar fashion, people unused to feeling happy or contented can feel intimidated by such feelings, not only because they trigger The Generals but because they can't identify with what they are feeling and thereby don't understand what is happening to them.

One patient thought he was having a panic attack when driving to a birthday party in his honor. He pulled to the side of the road to call me but then decided to try to sort himself out first. He later told me that sitting there on the edge of the highway, he realized he felt the exuberance of freedom for the first time in his life after a wretched childhood and equally difficult marriage. He was looking forward to joining his friends and realized that "What I was feeling was called happy."

All this is to say that none of us know ourselves as well as we think we do. We tend to fall into the trap of equating our thoughts and feelings with ourselves, assume that everybody thinks the way we do—or should—and that whatever we're thinking or feeling is what is. We egocentrically think we are the arbiters of reality, freely functioning individuals ready to take on everything and anything in open, new, objective and exciting ways.

This is far from the case. The brain is a highly habituated organ and extremely close-minded. Once it learns to do something, it tends to keep doing it, largely in the same way, outside of conscious awareness. We keep having the same thoughts and feelings, and we keep forcing our thinking down the same old story lines. Of course, this saves us from having to relearn things over and over again and allows us to accomplish complex tasks from throwing a ball to driving a car with little thought. The trouble sets in when those thoughts and feelings, born in childhood, no longer make sense. Then the familial and the familiar becomes the quicksand of adulthood. The problem is this thinking occurs in the deep background. So deep that though it governs much of our lives and greatly influences our ability to be happy or fulfilled, its tyrannical touch largely passes unnoticed.

As a younger man, I always thought, *What I feel is what I feel*, or *My thoughts are my thoughts*—as if such mental contents were straightforward, semi-solid, and readily understood. Now I know that not only is this often not the case but that it is usually not the case. The vast majority of what we're feeling and what motivates us goes on outside of our awareness. CT scans of brain functioning confirm this, identifying that parts of the brain not associated with consciousness often activate before those parts that are, and a subsequent course of action is initiated.

But this is not the only obstacle to self-awareness and self-governance. One of the things that differentiate the human species from other life forms is our considerable capacity for self-delusion. A story vividly illustrates this point. Sigmund Freud, the founder of psychoanalysis, early in his career, was interested in post-hypnotic suggestion. Post-hypnotic suggestion is when the subject is put into a trance and given an instruction (the suggestion) to do something after she awakens from the trance. Freud visited a nearby clinic researching this phenomenon. He observed the subjects being put into a trance during which they are told that two minutes after waking they are to walk to the umbrella located in the corner of the room, open it and hold it over their head. They are also instructed to forget they had been given this instruction.

Sure enough, each subject performed as instructed. What was interesting was that when each subject was asked why she was doing that peculiar behavior, each immediately came up with an answer to justify her actions. One might say, "I wanted to see the design." Another might claim, "I wanted to see what mechanism operated the umbrella." The point is, each subject came up with an answer right away, but none of the answers referenced the given instruction.

Also, when these justifications were challenged on their own merits, each subject fought to defend her rationale. Nonetheless, under the questioning of the researcher, each finally acknowledged to themselves and the researcher that she did not know why she had held the umbrella over her head. For example, if one subject claimed a desire to see the design, this was not compelling for the umbrella was black. Even if there had been a design, this purported motivation would not have accounted for the subject's picking the umbrella up when it did not belong to her nor for standing with the umbrella opened over her head inside the building.

The next thing that happened was that when each subject's "*I don't know* why I held the umbrella over my head" was not accepted as an answer, each was eventually able to remember the post-hypnotic suggestion.

This story illustrates something incredibly important that insight-oriented therapists witness all the time. More often than we know or might like to think we are not conscious of the reasons why we do what we do. And far from being open-minded and objective, when our actions are challenged, we instinctively come up with an answer to make sense of ourselves in a personally acceptable way, but not necessarily one that is true.

The important thing to recognize is that we are all guilty of this, and none of us are lying. We don't even know we're doing it. What we are doing is trying our best to make sense of ourselves in the most acceptable way possible when our underlying motivations are not readily understood. This is the captivating power of human self-delusion.

Change *is* difficult. The human brain poses many obstacles to it, and I have yet to talk of psychological defenses. These are also unconscious in their operation. Their job is to protect the person from psychological distress. They function with all the precision of a Star Wars multi-targeting laser defense system, shooting down or minimizing all thoughts, feelings, or desires that might threaten us before they can reach consciousness.

Psychological defenses are functioning all the time. I'm reminded of it each time I go for a surgical procedure. Invariably, I believe I feel fine and relatively unworried. Yet, when my blood pressure is taken, it's forty points higher than normal. The nurses laugh and pronounce what psychotherapists know: "Your body knows what your mind refuses to accept." In just this way, I've read that Palestinian kids who virtually live in a war zone, can not be differentiated from other children in an interview. What differentiates them is their heart rates, which are significantly higher. These are examples of our psychological defenses functioning to protect us from anxiety; they work on the mind, but they can't fool the body.

Psychoanalysis recognizes the nature of psychological defenses and tries to sidestep them through the injunction to the patient to say whatever thoughts and feelings come to mind, without pre-judgment or censorship. Thus, the patient is encouraged to share thoughts not only that stand out as dramatic, difficult or embarrassing, but also thoughts that seem unimportant or unrelated. Through this free-associative process, psychological defenses can be circumvented, allowing an opening to a pathway that leads to self-understanding or I should say greater self-understanding—there is no endpoint.

This process can also be used in everyday ways, outside of therapy. For instance, if I'm feeling anxious but can't identify the cause, I'll take a walk and think about what is going on in my life and what has been on my mind. During one such walk, I noted that I had been thinking about a drip below the kitchen sink that was rotting out the floor board, mortar coming loose between bricks on the house, a shrub that was not faring well in the yard, and so on. I don't know what others would have thought about these topics, but to me, none of them constituted a reason for the pervasive anxiety I was feeling.

Where did this leave me? Seemingly nowhere. I kept walking. I thought, "Well, the individual thoughts don't seem to warrant my anxiety so let me think about the themes." And here I hit upon something: decay, things dying, breaking down or falling apart. Then I got it. My fiftieth birthday was approaching, and this milestone was working me over far more than I had known.

In such ways, we can discover what is really on our minds: We can come to discover ourselves. Of course, all this goes against the wishes of The Generals. They do not like exposure to anything that threatens their security and certainly nothing that catches them by surprise. The good news here is that I'm not The Generals; they are a part of me, but only one part, and I grow tired of tyranny, even when it's of my making.

Unfortunately, this also is not a one and done process. The defenses never rest, and The Generals are hardest at work during times of peace. But more telling is the fact that we are living organisms and like any other part of nature are complex and ever changing. Across time and circumstance, we face the ebbs and flows of life, the river of necessary and unnecessary losses, and the different phases of body and mind through the life cycle, from which no one is immune.

We're all going to die. You're going to die. I'm going to die.

All this self-awareness business can sound overwhelming. Shit, sometimes it is. The question is: what's the alternative? We can put off the work, avoid the problems in our lives until declining capacities, physical decay, and mortality like storm troopers come kicking down the door of our denial. At the end of the day, each of us is left alone with ourselves. We each take that last breath by ourselves and in our own way. It is like the old Fram oil filter commercial use to say: "You can pay me now (the actor points to the five-dollar oil filter), or you can pay me later (the actor points to the two-thousand-dollar engine that has broken down)." Just like the detritus of wear and tear needs to be removed from the engine by the filter to give the engine a longer and healthier life, so we human beings have to deal with the wear and tear on our psyches, or we'll get into all kinds of trouble as the miles continue to mount.

In like fashion, when we don't confront our fears of living, losing, and dying along the way, we don't miraculously develop the capacity to deal with them late in life, as we fearfully watch their approach, any more than we grow new muscle without exercise. Avoidance and denial lead not only to a superficial, pallid and unfulfilling life, full of fear and anxiety (no matter how well hidden from others) but to an equally miserable death. Here is why some people facing death claw desperately to hold onto life at all costs while others pass gracefully into that long night.

The first group of people's dying is not a pretty sight. Witness my dad's. This is why he needed a child with him when he was transferred to Heidelberg, Germany. This was why he couldn't stand to do many things alone and co-opted his children to be with him. This is why he could never acknowledge his fears or vulnerabilities. This is why when he lived alone for a while in Charlottesville, VA, he carried a gun because he was so frightened of his neighbors, African-Americans who played loud music but had done him no harm. He had never been able to pay attention to his feelings as communications from himself to himself and consequently, absent that internal discussion, was unable to learn and grow and reconcile himself with his feelings. He was never able to become the man he might have been.

In contrast, my mother, from her middle years on, continually worked on herself. She had her meditations that included prayer, going to church regularly, and taking long walks in the evening during which, in her growing spirituality, she spoke in first person terms with her God. By this time, she had grown beyond prayer as a form of asking for things and entered active dialogue in which she put her fears and worries into words: her worries for her kids, her husband, her friends and what would happen to them all after she died. She wasn't worried about death itself. She fully believed in life after death and that she would meet everyone once again. Of course, that might or might not be self-delusion but if so, what a great and comforting delusion to have. In any event, as she lived her life, she lived her dying, and she showed me how truly beautiful and inspired that could be: the gift of gifts.

No question, change is difficult but very doable. You may ask "How?" and my answer would be to tell another story.

A man is walking down a sidewalk, takes a right turn at the next block, and continues until he suddenly falls into a sinkhole he did not see. The man cries out for help. Someone comes along, gives him an assist, and the man is on his way. The next day, the man repeats his journey, more or less on auto-pilot, and once again falls into the hole he did not see. He again calls for help, someone responds, and again he is soon on his way. Day after day, week after week, the man continues to take that right turn and fall into that hole to which he is blind. At first, he forgets about what happens each day, but then, as the number of falls increases and his discomfort grows, he begins to remember that there is a hole. This remembering helps him to stay on the lookout for it.

Thus, he strives hard to be alert, and one day sees the hole, but then, to his dismay, falls in nonetheless. He could not stop himself; it was as if his feet had a mind of their own. This process of seeing the hole but nevertheless falling in repeats itself time and again until one day the man is so upset and made miserable by this recurring experience that when he sees the hole, he aggressively forces himself to stop. There he teeters on the edge, arms windmilling frantically, and regains his balance, finally stopping in time. He considers his situation and despite being ill at ease with doing anything different, anything unknown, forces himself to walk around the hole. Again, this pattern repeats itself, seeing the hole and walking around, until the new route becomes routine, ordinary, familiar. In some ways, it doesn't have the appeal of the hole. That heart-stopping fall, followed by the thrill of being saved had an allure of its own, but the longer-lasting pain and misery put the appeal in perspective, and the man opts to continue walking around the hole.

Then one day the man begins his walk, but when he reaches the point of the right-hand turn, he pauses. He's tired of the new—now old—route; he wants to break free of deadening habit, and he wants to seek new experiences. Since he stopped doing the same old thing in the same old way, he's come to feel a new-found sense of possibilities. He decides to explore. He is both fearful and excited in that he does not know where this urge for discovery will lead, but feels confident that he can manage whatever new successes and failures might come his way: For the first time in a long time, he feels truly alive. He has discovered that life is best lived on the edge of his comfort zone and not with a moronic devotion to repeating the same old thing. He had learned from remembering, not denying the pain, and from reflecting long and hard on his experience. He doesn't make that right-hand turn.

In just such ways, I was working hard to become aware of my deeply embedded ways of being and relating in the world. I was growing increasingly aware of the sinkhole of unease in my life. I needed to find a way to stop falling in and then, eventually, to stop walking down that damn block.

PART VII

FULL FILLMENT – SORTA, KINDA

Fulfillment. What a word. I think it has something to do with feeling full. I don't like feeling full all the time. I like to get hungry, as hunger is its own ingredient, making everything taste better. I don't think fulfillment is a chronic state or that it can continuously be maintained given the human trait of quickly becoming desensitized to experience, good or bad.

So, as strange as it seems, I think it's best not to feel full-filled all the time. I mean, my God, I think I would walk around like a rooster, strutting about with my head jerking back and forth with the incredible wonderfulness of myself. I'd rather not do that. I'd want to miss the feeling from time to time, so I could enjoy it more and not get too filled-full of myself.

Here the wisdom of a borderline psychotic patient whose husband had been away a night for the first time in years is worth mentioning: She said, "I was worried about his going away. But it was okay. I missed him." Then she turned to me and asked in a voice full of wonder, "How does it get any better than that?"

CHAPTER 37

THE CLIFF

I think I am about to disappoint many of you. Especially those of you, like me, who love the idea of wondrous, life-changing epiphanies and spiritual awakenings that possess all the glamor of miracle and magic. But, regretfully, just as I had discovered there is no enchanted woman out there to rescue me from myself, I have not been able to find a magic way to happiness. What I have discovered for many, if not most, is a terrible truth: we *have* to actually live our lives; there are no short-cuts.

Also, I don't think a state of permanent happiness exists. Even Jesus sweated blood when he anticipated his crucifixion, and the Dalai Lama acknowledges not being at peace with himself all the time. Rather, I believe it is a state gained, lost and gained again, and that we can get better at it over time and gradually raise the floor of our default feeling state, leading to a well-earned and hence well-founded feeling of relative contentment and fulfillment. The key? Learning to look at ourselves honestly and get out of our own way in the practice of following our hearts rather than our fears.

For me, a personally meaningful life entails my acceptance of myself as the architect of my existence and the interpreter of my meaning. This means accepting that I'm responsible for my life: How I live it and how I feel. I am responsible for my sense of self, nothing and no one else. Please don't misunderstand me. I care about what other people think and think of me. I'm typically very respectful of the feelings of others toward me. But, at the same time, it is up to me to evaluate my life. For instance, some people might take issue with something I've said because they have a different sensibility or different beliefs than I do. Because they feel hurt, they may assume I was attacking them, not realizing that I don't think the way they do and would not find the same thing said to me to be hurtful at all. So sometimes it doesn't occur to me it would be hurtful to them, perhaps even occasionally when it should. After all, I live much of my life, my work life, at the far edge of the bell-shaped curve of what is socially acceptable. Still, I have no desire to worry continually about how everyone else might take what I have to say. For the most part, what I have to say meets with good results, and this is what I rely on. This isn't to say that I don't make mistakes; I do. And it's not to say that sometimes I can't be an ass; I can. It is to say that I would rather err in the direction of spontaneity and candor than a caution that would render me mute and less playful.

I had to release the past and open myself to the present, accepting that it is inherently perfect in its form even if not what I had hoped or imagined. I had been learning how to do this all along the way, all throughout my life, getting incrementally better at it. I've come to understand that because something disappoints me or worries me doesn't make it wrong. I continue my struggle to mature and to overcome any idealized notions of how things *should be*. I'm continuing to learn that disappointment in life is inevitable and that there is no need nor legitimacy in using such moments to resurrect time-treasured and time-failed story lines and the dark musings that travel with them. But I have to keep working at it.

In the effort to overcome habituated ways of thinking and feeling, I try to think of three specific things that have occurred each day for which I'm grateful. This practice helps offset any tendency toward depressive habituated feeling states. Just yesterday, I was taking an afternoon walk, the sun shining behind me, casting my shadow long when unexpectedly a butterfly shadow appeared dancing over my right shoulder. Together, our shadows walked for quite a while my heart soaring with the joy of it before the butterfly shadow flitted away.

Over the last several weeks, I've noticed that a praying mantis has taken up residence on the side of my hummingbird feeder. I get such a kick out of it. He just sits there. Recently, I reached out and touched him, and he didn't jump away. I found that unbelievable.

Then there was the huge Grasshopper, clearly a grandfather to his kind. I was on a ladder, drilling holes in the brick and mortar wall of my house to put up a shutter when he climbed the wall to join me. I was incredulous as I watched him slowly but determinedly cross that great distance a millimeter at a time, to eventually arrive mere inches from my face, completely ignoring the clamor of the drill and the dust and bits of brick erupting volcanically from the hole. Nothing deterred him; he just kept on coming one slow and steady step at a time. In homage, I turned off the drill and removed the bit from the hole. He just kept coming, seemingly totally assured that this the only possible action that could have been made. Now, he sidles up to the hole and places his body upon it as if in protection. Perched on my ladder, just inches away, I can only marvel at him. What ever happened to this Granddaddy Grasshopper's survival instinct? Why had it dared to approach all the sound and fury in its unconcerned fashion? I watched for a while and then reached out with my finger and played with his whiskers. Unperturbed, he continued to sit, like a grasshopper Buddha. So, while I remained perched in front of the hole, he continued to sit upon it, mere inches away, and there we were for several minutes, two grandfathers joined in the moment and the warmth of the sun, communing. I didn't know how long he planned to stay there. But, that didn't matter, I would wait as long as necessary or come back another time to complete my task. Eventually, for reasons not clear to me, Grasshopper decided it was time to move on. He lifted himself up and in his signature slow and steady movement gradually made his way across the brick and out of my life.

Earlier this summer there was a once in a lifetime event. I had never seen anything like it, nor had Janet. Driving home from dinner, the light leaching from the sky, we passed a farmer's field. Emerging from the tall grass were hundreds of thousands of fireflies, twinkling into the night like sparks from a bonfire. Janet and I were so in awe we pulled over to the side of the road, turned the car off and sat there silently watching the spectacle, taking it in. Another car pulled over in the distance, obviously witnessing the same thing and as drawn to it as we.

All these events remind me that all the drama that men create stand as nothing against the timeless beauty of nature and, if spiritual, God's touch. All these experiences fill me with joy, and I am grateful for the wonder of them all.

Another thing that brings me joy is my cat Emma rushing to the top of the steps each morning as I begin to descend, placing her head between the balusters where I give her a gentle caress, and we rub our heads together for a moment before going on with our day. The same is true in getting together with family and friends, and those superheroes called my grandchildren. Such moments are often divine and lead to moments of feeling my life to be a spring-fed pond.

And, every day, if something disappoints or pulls on a thread of depressive thought, I pause to consider if I am re-writing old narratives or developing new ones. I ask myself, "Am I lazy, running on auto-pilot and in a trance? Am I letting fear of the unknown—of a real future—govern me in the form of re-creating the past? Am I ruminating, falling back into timeworn internal narratives in defense against a future of unknowns." When I find that to be the case, I gently chastise myself, "How boring and unoriginal can I be? Must I continue to write that ever-repeating one-act play?" and, in answer, press the stop button on that endless muck-digging loop before it can take tyrannical hold to return to the moment and remain receptive and curious to whatever is going on within and around me right now.

At the same time, I don't dispel my negative feelings without evaluation. Where I find cause for concern, I address it, whether the issue arises from within me as an individual or in relationship to another. This takes time because the two can be confusingly intertwined. Addressing relationship issues entails going against my survival instinct, defying the Generals, sharing my thoughts and feelings with another even though this makes me feel uncomfortable, vulnerable and exposed. I hold myself to the standard of sitting with my thoughts and feelings until I can share them with the other in a way that is without blame, shame, attack, or a demand for change. I struggle to walk the walk of my talk. And with the years of practice, this has gotten increasingly easier.

Unfortunately, a sustained sense of fulfillment is not a gift with which most of us are blessed. Many people tell themselves or others they are happy and that their lives are wonderful, but I'm dubious. Some of the "happiest" people I know are obstinately focused on having a good time. I don't think what they are talking about is the kind of deep-rooted happiness or fulfillment I mean. I am not talking about an experience derived from psychological defenses that avoid, deny or minimize one's concerns or reject looking at oneself. Nor am I talking about a feeling of supposed fulfillment derived from constant fine dining or five-star travel, a devotion to rose-colored glasses, the plastering of a fixed smile on one's face, or the idea that if everything looks good, it is good. I'm also not talking about people-pleasing or the maintaining of the illusion of harmony via the avoidance of conflict, or about those people who consider themselves happy only becaus*e* they have never entertained a suicidal thought. You know, people who regularly say when asked how they're doing, "O*kay*. Can't complain" —which leads me to conclude they must have a lack of imagination—but never say, "The most astonishing thing happened yesterday..."

I know some people who are very successful and happy almost all the time, but are unable to engage in any personally meaningful emotional conversation; they just don't let anybody in nor themselves out. At the same time, they may often feel victimized. Isn't that a curious stew?

What *I am* talking about is that sense of fulfillment that derives from striving to live a personally meaningful life, which by definition involves the valuing of all our thoughts and feelings, both the painful and the happy, the good and the bad. In turn, this leads to the *need* to address the conflicts that arise in life rather than to sweep them under the rug. I am talking about a kind of happiness or contentment that derives exactly from having confronted directly that which most ails us, that which has kept us up in the middle of the night, that which has led to a feeling of disconnect from our others. The happiness or contentment I'm talking about is a result of embracing all of our experiences (thoughts, feelings, and sensations) and acknowledges the finiteness of all things, most especially ourselves.

I'm talking about a contentment that includes the awareness of *the last of things*. Understanding that there will inevitably be that last kiss, that final hug, that permanent leaving of a place called home. I'm talking about a sense of fulfillment that springs from the watercolors of the sunset which are vivified exactly because of the awareness that this may be the last sunset shared with another or the ultimate sunset beheld by oneself. I'm talking about knowing that often we will not know when that last of things moment is upon us until it is gone.

Ironically, it is embracing this awareness of the last of things, the finiteness that rules all things and everyone's life, the sadness that it will one day come to an end, that gives life and all that occurs within its meaning and value.

This ongoing process of striving to be a sentient being is life itself. By its nature, it is replete with gains and losses, joys and sadness, moments of falling off track and getting back on again. What is important is to embrace the experience, to string as many such moments together as possible and, when the string breaks, begin anew.

The not-so-funny thing is that what gives each of us purpose and meaning also changes over time. Early on in the happiness quest, I loved sports, adventure, and romantic relationships. Later I found it in my friends, my marriage, my kids, and my career. But after the kids, after the job, after the relationships, that's when I get down to the nub of it, that's when at the end of days, I am rendered alone, once again, with myself, right where I started—I guess that's what's called a pisser. We all end up there; we all do our dying alone. The question is, "Will I be okay with myself? Will I be able to embrace my dying?" I strongly suspect that the answer lies in how well I have embraced my living.

I ask, "What is my purpose now? Who am I now? What do I want now? What is meaningful to me now?" I don't think the answers to these questions are givens; most of us have to search for them. Indeed, that's part of living one's life. The one thing I do know is that happiness is not a hedonistic state. It includes a generosity of spirit, of helping others, sacrificing, or going the extra mile for someone in need. For me, it also includes time to think and to feel, and to experience the unfolding mystery that I am to myself—sometimes not a pleasant process at all.

The pursuit of happiness or fulfillment or whatever else you might want to call *it* is the impetus for continuing growth as a human being throughout life. How well I have or haven't succeeded in it will ultimately be unveiled during the so-called Golden Years, which I am living now, and I must say I'm not doing badly at all. I'm enjoying myself and my life. But I think if there is any final test of how well we've lived our lives it will be in the way we live our dying. You know, that time after the Golden Years, when the real process of decay goes into high gear.

For me, happiness and fulfillment entail making repeated trips to the edge of my comfort zone. When there, I feel most present, like I'm occupying my life and my life is occupying me. I feel vulnerable and alive. Conversely, unhappiness, a lack of fulfillment, I associate with the fear-ridden need of excessive security which can lead to stasis, apathy, and atrophy, an implicit declaration that I'm done, I'm finished; I'm resigned to my tomorrows being just like my yesterdays.

We all have a choice to make: To embrace your living and your dying, or to reject all the risks and uncertainties that are life, to live within the castle walls constructed by the generals in the war room of your mind, and run in terror from your dying. Just don't make it too late. You have to jump while you still have the strength.

CHAPTER 38

AU REVOIR

Now, all these years later, I'm on another cliff face. As I look around the room, I imagine all of you in my mind's eye, many of you are grown, having left home and created lives and families of your own. Others of you are new to the fold, your lives just beginning. I also see my patients who have honored me by allowing me into your lives thereby adding to my own. And I see others yet, you strangers who are not really strangers at all, who have stumbled upon this work and recognize yourselves in me and me in yourselves in our joint humanity.

For my part, I live much of my life in solitude, or at least I try. That may sound as if I'm going against everything I have just said, but don't be fooled. I like it. I enjoy the oscillating interplay of being with others and then the luxury of being with myself.

Certainly, Janet is around, but we each largely do our own thing during the day, coming together for cards, TV, and dinner in the evening, or for a boat ride or the occasional trip. We have our dustups, but most of the time we enjoy each other's company and take each other seriously in love and play. I've pared the "to do" list of daily life and obligations to essentials, trying to limit my brain's creation of false concerns and obligations. For the last few years, partially retired, I have had larger periods of time to myself while Janet, now fully retired, has moved smoothly into filling her day with projects pleasing to her; that is her gift.

I'm in the wonderful position of being able to do what I want when I want, an experience I found oddly discombobulating early on after years of maintaining stimulating identities as friend, father, therapist, author, lecturer and mate. Somewhat inanely, I ask myself, "Who am I now? Who am I becoming? Who do I want to become?"

I have discovered that one of my two main challenges is to quiet the frightened jabber of my mind when it arises, which happens with increasing rarity as I've learned not to feed the Evil Wolf. When fear does snake in, undermining my serenity, demanding that I "do something," echoing that feeling on B-2 from all those years ago, I resist. I've learned to find such moments interesting. I watch my mind do its hackneyed thing while I insist that whatever need I have must arise from within. I do not want to *kill time* by going through the motions or by staying busy for busy's sake. And eventually, fears not fed, I return to the moment, calling on myself to be patient, to take one step at a time, to be with myself then to go on being with myself until I figure out where my being is going. In this way, I continue on until I can answer the question *What is emerging from within?* That is my second challenge.

It is just this process of questioning myself that led to the writing of this book. The drive and the need arose from within me, and my making room to hear and to listen to it has only met with good results. It has been incredibly therapeutic. It has helped me make sense of things I didn't know I didn't understand. But soon I will be finished writing, and then the question will arise again, *What now?* I will sit with that question, giving time for whatever is going to emerge to make itself known.

Through the course of a day, I move from seeing a few patients, to reading, to picking a guitar, to writing, to swimming or going boating with Janet, finding joy in the seagulls in shallow flight following in our wake. I sit in the sunroom listening to the river lapping against the beach as the leaves of the ancient oaks whisper their secrets, as squirrels chatter and scramble up tree trunks, and as birds chirp and squawk. I watch geese moving to the sandy beach below my house, smiling in memory at the shenanigans of Mom and Dad and fully appreciating the problem of poop. I listen to the wind and, on those rainy days, the thrumming of the drops on the window pane, noticing now that only some make that slippery slide, while others stay seated in place, content to enjoy the moment. All these sounds intone in the deep background of my consciousness, speaking to the ghosts of decades past in a language before and beyond words, soothing them like the rhythmic sound of ocean waves or a mother's heartbeat comforts a child.

I go on long walks, the repetitive movement of my feet lending its rhythmic comfort. I find all this interesting.

I learn from my kids. Recently, I received a text from Cait encouraging me to remain in contact; she misses me. I make a vow to myself to overcome yet another block to my happiness: my hesitancy to call and intrude on the lives of my kids. I'm worried that I might intrude on their lives like my dad did on mine. I struggle, making a point of being in more regular and casual contact, to engage in that most difficult of all things: *small talk*. Talk about the wrong adjective. There is nothing *small* about small talk. Sometimes, I force myself to call even when I don't have anything *important* to say. Admittedly, still not very often, but I'm working at it. All the while I watch with admiration and envy as Chandler and Keeley engage in such talk with ease and enjoyment, while I see myself in Cait's discomfort.

I look forward to visiting with my grandkids, watching the joy that lights their faces when they see me, only equaled, if not surpassed, by my joy in seeing and playing with them. I also enjoy their eventual parting when, body aching and mind exhausted, I am glad to get back to my pursuits.

I do question myself from time to time: *Am I in the most secure position, but one from which I am guaranteed to fall? Or am I in mid-leap, letting go of over-used and increasingly obsolete senses of self in search of more internally emerging ones?* Sometimes I know the answer; sometimes I don't. I catch myself smiling ruefully.

There are always reasons to be happy, just as there are always reasons to worry or be sad. I ask myself, why am I paying attention to one more than the other? Don't life and death dance hand in hand all the time?

I used to ask this one question at each psychoanalytic conference I attended. "What makes the difference between those who fall and can't get up and those who fall and do get up and go on to live meaningful lives?" Never, from all those world-class thinkers, did I receive an answer. Then one night, while paging through a book of art in in the Z-Man's apartment, I happened upon a picture of a seventeenth-century American Indian shaman with the following caption.

> What I am trying to say is hard to tell and hard to understand...
> unless, unless...
> you have been yourself at the edge of the Deep Canyon and have come back unharmed.
> Maybe it all depends on something within yourself—
> whether you are trying to see the Watersnake or the sacred Cornflower,
> whether you go out to meet death or to Seek Life.
> *Shaman: The Paintings of Susan Seddon Boulet (1989)*

You see? It depends on what *you* are looking for. Are you looking for life or death? A continual re-working of the unworkable past or a fresh day and future? Are you looking to play the music of your life like yourself, to compose new melodies, or like that of your childhood, your parents and their parents and the generations before them? The Indian shaman and the Bible agree, "Seek, and ye shall find."

Now, it is time for me to embark on my solo trip to Norfolk, 180 nautical miles away, on my 25' deck boat. It is once again time to push my comfort zone. I have never done anything like this before but I need to clear the cobwebs and, as you know, there is nothing like a Great Adventure to do that.

I could not find anyone both crazy enough and available to go along with me, so I am going alone. I just have to go. I feel the need to meet myself again. My main worry is that there are parts of the journey where land is not visible and where cell phone reception is not available. What happens if the engine throws a belt or if one of the Chesapeake Bay's infamous thunderstorms catches me in a squall? I know what a squall can do to a twenty-five-thousand-pound trawler, what could it do to my thirty-five-hundred-pound deck boat? It's not pleasant to imagine, but it is exciting.

Ah! These worries, these risks, are the point. I prepare for the journey with them in mind. Depending upon sea and weather conditions, the trip could take anywhere from eight hours to eighteen hours, or might not be completed at all. I buy a good spotlight in case I am caught out after dark. I double check on all the safety equipment. I scour marine weather forecasts, wave heights and frequency, currents, wind speed and direction predictions for mine is not a suicidal wish, but the need for adventure. What better way to clear a mind than dancing with Mother Nature? It all looks good, but I know marine forecasts can be as deceiving as any other kind of weather forecast and given to sudden change.

The night before my trip a quarter moon graces the black ink sky, framed by five stars rendering elegance in the far distance. The skyline Rosetta colored, the sun having set long ago, its rays now traveling so far around the world they barely blush the edge of the night. Pilings standing tall casting darker shadows upon the already shadowed water, still as if waiting to take a breath. Canadian Geese caw unseen in the distance as they prepare for their winter migration. The black profile of a blue heron cuts the night right in front of my eyes without making a sound. I'm filled with gratitude for this moment and to be a living part of this planet for however long that is allowed.

At 6:15 the next morning, as I say goodbye to Janet, tears in our eyes, and my heart in my throat, I start the engine, put the boat into gear, and begin cruising away from Janet, from home, wondering if this will be a *last of things* as I travel toward the dawning sun.

I feel so alive!

I hear my mother calling.

"Have a *good life!* Have a *good life!*"

And I hear Aunt Dot's honeyed voice echoing down through the years—

"Bon Voyage!"

Here, Charles C. McCormack, MA, MSW, LCSW-C, is pictured with his grandson Benjamin, a first grader and a winner of the MLK Jr. World Peace Rose Garden contest in Atlanta, GA for the following poem which is commemorated with a plaque at the MLK National Historic site.

Peace is love
Peace is calm and kind
Peace is not grumpy or sad
Or anger or yelling
It's nice and happy
And helpful too
Peace is caring
Peace is all around you

Among other writings, Mr. McCormack is the author of the 1989 article "The Borderline/Schizoid Marriage: The Holding

Environment as an Essential Treatment Construct" and the book *Treating Borderline States in Marriage: Dealing with Oppositionalism, Ruthless Aggression, and Severe Resistance* (2000).

McCormack was guest faculty of the Washington School of Psychiatry, the Senior Social Worker of Adult Long-Term Inpatient Services and member of the Teaching and Supervisory Faculty of Sheppard-Pratt Hospital. He was named Clinician of the Year in 1994 by the Maryland Society of Clinical Social Workers. He is married with three children and seven grandchildren, with at least one more on the way. He lives in Aberdeen, Maryland.

Made in the USA
Middletown, DE
16 April 2017